Mother India

KATHERINE MAYO

Edited and with an Introduction by Mrinalini Sinha

Ann Arbor

THE UNIVERSITY OF MICHIGAN PRESS

Mother India by Katherine Mayo was published
simultaneously in 1927 by Jonathan Cape Ltd. in Britain and
by Harcourt, Brace and Company in the United States.

Selections from Mother India edited by Mrinalini Sinha
was originally published in 1998 by Kali for Women Press, New Delhi.
Introduction copyright © Mrinalini Sinha 1998.

First published by the University of Michigan Press 2000
Introduction copyright © Mrinalini Sinha 2000
All rights reserved
Published in the United States of America by
The University of Michigan Press
Manufactured in the United States of America
♾ Printed on acid-free paper

2003   2002   2001   2000   4   3   2   1

A CIP catalog record for this book is available from the British Library.

Library of Congress Cataloging-in-Publication Data

Mayo, Katherine, 1868?–1940.
   [Mother India. Selections]
   Selections from Mother India / Katherine Mayo ; edited and with an
introduction by Mrinalini Sinha.
      p.   cm.
   Includes bibliographical references.
   ISBN 0-472-09715-6 (cloth : alk. paper) — ISBN 0-472-06715-X
(pbk. : alk. paper)
      1. India—Civilization—1765–1947.   2. India—Social conditions.   3.
Women—India—Social conditions.   4. Mayo, Katherine, 1868? 1940.
Mother India.   I. Title: Mother India.   II. Sinha, Mrinalini, 1960–.
III. Title.
DS428.M382 2000
954.03—dc21   99-058162

CONTENTS

INTRODUCTION

Mrinalini Sinha

Mother India, a polemical attack against Indian self-rule written by U.S. author Katherine Mayo, has acquired something
of a legendary status among students of colonial India and, in
particular, of Indian women. When *Mother India* was published jointly in the United States (Harcourt, Brace and Company) and in Britain (Jonathan Cape) in the summer of 1927, it
was celebrated and reviled by die-hard imperialists and outraged nationalists. The imperialist/nationalist controversy that
it generated reverberates even today and thus is still worth
revisiting now, some fifty years after Indian independence.
One reason, of course, is that the echoes of the controversy
still haunt contemporary discussions of the nature of Mayo's
intervention in *Mother India*. Another reason, however, is that
the massive controversy over *Mother India* was itself an important event with long-term implications for the future development of modern nationalism as well as of middle-class feminism
in India. For, in responding to Mayo's polemical argument in
Mother India, the leaders of the nationalist movement and of
the independent all-India women's movement laid the foundations of an alliance that gave modern Indian nationalism its
distinctive character, captured in the popular nationalist slo-
gan: "India cannot be free until its women are free and
women cannot be free until India is free."[1] The controversy

[1]Although the significance of the "woman question" in Indian nationalism predated the *Mother India* controversy, I argue that the alliance
between a nascent all-India women's movement and Indian nationalism
was forged in the wake of the controversy. See Mrinalini Sinha, "Refashioning Mother India: The Advent of a Nationalist "Indian" Modernity in
Late Colonial India," MS.

surrounding *Mother India* thus marked a crucial turning point in the history of modern nationalism and feminism in late colonial India.

When Mayo's book was first published, it created a sensation on three continents. Even today few books—apart, perhaps, from Salman Rushdie's *Satanic Verses* (1989)—can match the scale of the international controversy generated by *Mother India*.[2] The book quickly became something of a cause célèbre in the United States, Britain, and India. It was hotly debated on public platforms and journal and newspaper columns in all three countries. It was protested on the streets of New York, San Francisco, London, and Calcutta and was burned outside the Town Hall in New York City.[3] Questions about the British government's involvement in the book were raised in the Central Legislative Assembly in India as well as in Parliament in Britain. Some Indian members of the Legislative Assembly even called for banning the book in India. Far from being banned, however, the book was made available to a larger reading public both abroad and in India through translations of the entire book (or of selected extracts) into various European and vernacular Indian languages, including Hindi, Urdu, Bengali, Tamil, Telugu, and Marathi.[4] *Mother India*, in fact, spawned something of a mini-industry, with more than fifty books and pamphlets published in response to it. Mayo's book also inspired a Broadway musical, Madame Nazimova's *India*, about a twelve-year-old Hindu child-bride married to an old and sickly man. Even Hollywood was drawn into the hype surrounding the book and made an abortive bid to secure the rights to immortalize *Mother India* on the big screen.[5] *Mother India*, moreover, also featured in

[2]Salman Rushdie, *The Satanic Verses* (London: Viking Penguin, 1989).
[3]22 Jan. 1928, *New York Times*, p. 3.
[4]I examine the various responses to *Mother India* in *Refashioning Mother India*.
[5]The Broadway musical opened at the Palace Theatre in 1928; see Notice, in Folder no. 41, Ser. 1, Box 6, *Katherine Mayo Papers*, Manuscript Group No. 35 at the Manuscript Archives Division, Sterling Memorial Library, Yale University (henceforth: *K.M. Papers*). For Hollywood's abortive bid to the film *Mother India*, see Raymond Crossell of

the discussions around several contemporary legislative initiatives: the fate of the Hindu (a term used loosely for all the inhabitants of India) Citizenship Bill in the U.S. Senate; the composition of the Indian Statutory Commission appointed by the British Parliament; the passage of the Child-Marriage Restraint Act for India in the Legislative Assembly; and the passage of the Age of Marriage Act in the British Parliament. Finally, Mayo's *Mother India* attracted the attention of such famous contemporaries as M.K. Gandhi, Sarojini Naidu, Rabindranath Tagore, E.V. Ramaswami Periyar, Muthulakshmi Reddi, Winston Churchill, Rudyard Kipling, Edward Thompson, Eleanor Rathbone, Annie Besant, Romaine Rolland, Wyndham Lewis, Norman Brown, and Agnes Smedley.

Mother India was written after Mayo and her friend and collaborator, Moyca Newell, made a three-month tour of India in the winter of 1925–26. The four hundred–odd pages of the book, backed by copious references to several official and non-official sources on India, contained a strong indictment of the demands for Indian self-rule and an argument in favor of continued British rule over India. *Mother India* offered a wide ranging discussion of the various ills that Mayo felt beset Indian society: the deplorable treatment of women, of "untouchables,"[6] and of animals; the unsanitary conditions of Indian life; and the hypocrisy and hollowness of the educated Indians, especially of the new breed of nationalist Indian politicians in the 1920s. The main thesis of *Mother India*, however, was contained in Parts 1 and 2 of the book. Here Mayo laid out her central argument that the root of all of India's problems lay in the sexual organization of Hindu society. "The whole pyramid of the Indian's woes," she wrote, was the result not of any political or economic causes, but of the Indian male's "manner of getting into this world and his sex-life thereafter" (p. 83). The book thus painted a highly sensationalized picture of

---

Curtis Brown Ltd. to Mayo, 19 Oct. 1932, in Folder no. 62, Ser. 1, Box 7, *K.M. Papers.*

[6]The term that was used to describe persons whose very touch was considered polluting by caste Hindus.

rampant sexuality and its consequences in India: masturba-
tion, rape, homosexuality, prostitution, venereal diseases,
and, most important of all, early sexual intercourse and premature maternity. It was the sexual excess of the Indian male,
Mayo concluded, that had left him with hands, "too weak, too
fluttering . . . to hold the reins of Government" (p. 92).
Mayo's further point was that the ills of Indian society, unlike
anything to be found in the West, were not merely problems
that were regrettable and thus subject to correction. Rather,
the ills of Indian society belonged to the very essence of Hinduism and, as such, were actually condoned by Hindu religion
and culture. Her argument that the backwardness of India
stemmed not from political or economic causes but from religious and cultural ones served two important purposes: it
countered nationalist Indian claims of Indian superiority in the
realm of culture and spirituality over the materialistic West;[7]
and it exempted colonial rule from any responsibility for the
backwardness of India, eliciting instead sympathy for the reform work of the countless British men and women who la-
bored selflessly against such odds.

For such a crudely propagandistic work, however, Mother
India has enjoyed a curiously long life. The popularity of Mother
India has long outlived the immediate circumstances of its intervention. This is reflected, for example, in the publishing history
of Mother India. By the 1950s Harcourt, Brace and Company
alone reported a sales of 395,678 copies for its various editions of
Mother India.[8] The book was reprinted several times, including a
cheaper edition published by Jonathan Cape in 1930 and a separate Indian edition published by Allied Publishers of Bombay in
1945. Even more recent reprints of Mother India—including a
1970 reprint in Britain, a 1984 reprint in the United States, and a

[7]The discourse of "official" Indian nationalism, as Partha Chatterjee
has argued, acknowledged its surrender to the West in the "material"
realm and claimed superiority for itself in the "spiritual" realm; see P.
Chatterjee, Nationalist Thought and the Colonial World: A Derivative Discourse? (London: Zed Publications, 1986).

[8]Letter from Harcourt, Brace, and Co. to Moyca Newell, 23 June 1955,
in Folder no. 96, Ser. 1, Box 11, K.M. Papers.

1986 reprint in India—have done little to question the myths surrounding *Mother India*.[9]

Although in the 1920s and 1930s leaders of both the nationalist and the women's movements in India had strongly condemned *Mother India*, the book continued to have an enormous influence in shaping perceptions about India and Indian women, especially in Mayo's home country. A survey of some 350 adults in the United States in the 1950s revealed that *Mother India* was second only to the works of Rudyard Kipling as the most popular source of information in the United States on India.[10] Anecdotal evidence further suggests that *Mother India* was still being recommended to Peace Corps volunteers as an introduction to India up until the 1970s. The latest chapter in the legend of *Mother India*, however, has been the product of some feminist- and women's studies–inspired scholarship in the United States. Mary Daly's *Gyn/Ecology: The Metaethics of Radical Feminism* (1978) marked this latest revival in *Mother India*'s reputation. Daly's theory of "planetary patriarchy" relied on, and celebrated, Mayo's contribution in *Mother India* uncritically. Ignoring the contributions of generations of both Indian and foreign women and men, Daly elevated Mayo as the most important voice articulating a feminist critique of indigenous patriarchy in India.[11]

[9]The introduction to a 1970 reprint of *Mother India* (1927; rpt., London: Howard Baker Pub. Ltd, 1970) commends Mayo's "grimly factual" account and concludes: "For this is India as it truly was—and as parts of it still are—in all its helplessness, hopelessness and horror." Also see *Mother India* (New Delhi: Ammol, 1986); and *Mother India* (New York: Greenwood, 1984).

[10]Harold R. Isaacs, *Scratches on Our Minds: American Images of China and India* (New York: John Day, 1958), p. 271. Also see A.M. Rosenthal, " 'Mother India' Thirty Years Later," *Foreign Affairs* 4 (July 1957): pp. 620–30; and Milton Singer, "Passage to More than India: A Sketch of Changing European and American Images," *When a Great Tradition Modernizes* (London: Pall Mall Press, 1972), pp. 11–38.

[11]Mary Daly, *Gyn/Ecology* (Boston: Beacon Press, 1979), esp. p. 119. For a general critique of the use of the "third world woman" in some feminist texts in the West, see Chandra Talpade Mohanty, "Under Western Eyes: Feminist Scholarship and Colonial Discourses," in *Third World*

Although others, like Elisabeth Bumiller, have found it hard to ignore the overtly racist and imperialist tone of *Mother India*, they nevertheless reiterate the view of Mayo as a pioneering, if somewhat flawed, U.S. feminist who was concerned with the condition of women in India. In the preface to *May You Be the Mother of a Hundred Sons: A Journey among the Women of India* (1990), therefore, Bumiller acknowledges Mayo as an inspiration for her own writing on Indian women.[12] There is, indeed, a broader revisionism afoot among some scholars, not all of whom are writing from the United States, for reappraising the nationalist criticism of Mayo and resurrecting Mayo's reputation in the name of feminist-inspired scholarship.[13]

The *Mother India*–based myth of Mayo as a feminist crusader has persisted despite Manoranjan Jha's *Katherine Mayo and India* (1971)—the only full-length scholarly treatment of the *Mother India* controversy—which demonstrated the political motives behind Mayo's book and reconstructed Mayo's connections to the official British imperial propaganda machine.[14] One reason

---

Women and the Politics of Feminism, ed. C.T. Mohanty, A. Russo, and L. Torres (Bloomington: Indiana University Press, 1991), pp. 51–80.

[12]Elisabeth Bumiller, *May You Be the Mother of a Hundred Sons* (New York: Random House, 1990), pp. 21–22. Bharathi Mukerjee's critical response to Bumiller's reference to Mayo is discussed in Nina Mehta's review, "Stranger in a Strange Land," *Women's Review of Books* 8, no. 3 (1990): pp. 19–20. The view that Mayo was at worst a misguided imperial feminist is also reiterated in Liz Wilson "Who Is Authorized to Speak? Katherine Mayo and the Politics of Imperial Feminism in British India," *Journal of Indian Philosophy* 25 (1997): pp. 139–51.

[13]For a recent example of such revisionsm, see William W. Emilsen, "Gandhi and Mayo's 'Mother India,' " *South Asia* 10, no. 1 (1987): pp. 69–82; and for the debate occasioned by Emilsen's argument, see P. Athiyaman and A.R. Venkatachalapathy, "On Gandhi, Mayo and Emilsen," *South Asia* 12, no. 2 (1989): pp. 83–88; and W. Emilsen, "A Note on Mayo, Athiyaman and Venkatachalapathy," *South Asia* 12, no. 2 (1989): pp. 88–93.

[14]Manoranjan Jha, *Katherine Mayo and India* (New Delhi: People's Publishing House, 1971). I remain indebted to Jha's pioneering work for my discussion of the production of *Mother India*.

for this persistence, of course, is that much of this new interest in *Mother India* has been marked by an appalling lack of familiarity with, and a failure to engage seriously with, the existing scholarship on colonial India or on Indian women. Another reason, however, is the isolation in which Mayo's engagement with India has been typically examined. For the lingering myths about the nature of Mayo's contribution in *Mother India* not only underestimate her role as a partisan for British imperialism in India but also reveal an ignorance of Mayo's involvement in domestic U.S. politics. Mayo's lack of sympathy with feminists in the United States, for example, raises interesting questions about her later apotheosis as a feminist crusader for Indian women. The continuity between Mayo's domestic and imperial politics—too often a casualty of overly rigid disciplinary constraints that tend to compartmentalize scholarship along supposedly discrete national lines—provides a fuller background for understanding *Mother India*. The contribution of *Mother India*, indeed, needs to be understood in the multiple contexts of United States, British, and Indian politics. The following three sections thus attempt to situate *Mother India* and the controversy that it generated within these multiple contexts. Section 1 traces the political background—both "domestic" and "imperial"— for the production of *Mother India;* section 2 locates *Mother India* within the history of the imperialist/nationalist debate on the "woman question" in colonial India; and, finally, section 3 examines the outcome of the *Mother India* controversy for the woman question and its implications for the development of Indian nationalism and Indian feminism in late colonial India.

Katherine Mayo (1867–1940), born in Ridgeway, Pennsylvania, was no stranger to public controversy before she acquired international recognition as the author of *Mother India*.[15] Even be-

[15]For biographical information on Katherine Mayo, see Mary E. Handlin, "Mayo, Katherine," in *Notable American Women: 16–7-1950*, ed. Edward T. James, Janet Wilson James, and Paul S. Boyer, vol. 2 (Cambridge: Belknap Press of Harvard University, 1971), pp. 515–17.

fore *Mother India*, Mayo was already well-known as the author
of several books. The spirit of *Mother India*, indeed, was in
keeping with much of Mayo's other writings on various domestic and imperial issues. For, despite the fact that Mayo was
associated early in her career as a research assistant with such
liberal political figures as Oswald Garrison Villard, one of the
cofounders of the National Advancement for Colored People,
her reputation as a writer in the United States was built on
championing very different kinds of political causes.[16] On the
surface, at least, Mayo's writing career shared much with the
well-established late-nineteenth- and early-twentieth-century
tradition of "muckraking," which produced the kind of journalistic exposés that had resulted in many a Progressive-era reform in the United States.[17] Unlike much of this muckraking
tradition, however, Mayo's pen was typically mobilized in support of some of the same powerful, establishment interests
that were often the targets of muckraking exposés.

Mayo's early involvement with state police reform in the
United States, as Gerda Ray has demonstrated, established the
class, gender, and racial ideologies that colored much of
Mayo's career.[18] Mayo and Newell orchestrated a highly successful campaign for the creation of a rural State Police Force in
New York against a background of stiff opposition, especially
from socialists and labor groups. In the course of this campaign Mayo published several books on the Pennsylvania State

[16]Mayo served as Villard's assistant for his book *John Brown, 1800–
1855* (Boston: Houghton, Mifflin and Co., 1910). For Mayo and Villard's
correspondence, see, apart from the *K.M. Papers*, the *Oswald Garrison
Villard Papers*, Houghton Library, Harvard University. For an account of
Villard's life, see O.G. Villard, *Fighting Years: Memoirs of a Fighting Editor*
(New York : Harcourt Brace and Co., 1939).

[17]The origin of the term *muckraking* is associated with President Theo-
dore Roosevelt, who, however, used the term pejoratively. For a brief
and accessible introduction to, and a few sample documents of, the phenomenon of "muckraking" journalism, see *Muckraking: Three Landmark
Articles*, edited, with an introduction, by Ellen F. Fitzpatrick (Boston:
Bedford Books of St. Martin's Press, 1994).

[18]Gerda Ray, "From Cossack to Trooper: Manliness, Police Reform,
and the State," *Journal of Social History* 28, no. 3 (Spring 1995): pp. 565–86.

Police Force, the earliest of the state forces in the United States and the model for the creation of the New York state constabulary. The reputation of the Pennsylvania force, however, had already come under a cloud for its highly partisan role in the settlement of labor disputes in the state. During the strike at the Wilkes-Barre Railway Company, for example, the unsavory conduct of the force had resulted in a vast number of citizen complaints about the force.[19] Mayo's books glossed over such complaints and extolled the virtues of the Pennsylvania force in highly embellished stories. Even a member of the Pennsylvania force, who was one of Mayo's several informants for her glamorized stories about the state police, commented to her in private: "The story is very good, but in places highly colored. You are making the State Policemen too ideal in your stories."[20] The commanding officer of another of the companies of the Pennsylvania State Police was more blunt in acknowledging Mayo's contribution: "We are very grateful to you for keeping our skeletons safely stowed away in their respective closets."[21] One of Mayo's correspondents, a Cleveland high school teacher, who would wonder if Mayo had not been too "one-sided" in her later portrayal of Filipinos and Indians, raised similar questions about her work on the Pennsylvania State Police: "is it a wholly commendable and impartial force or whether as labor men often say, it becomes an instrument of the employers to break the Unions in strike."[22] Subtlety and balance, obviously, were not among Mayo's virtues as a writer.

Mayo's books, as Ray has suggested, were highly successful as propaganda for the state police precisely because of the gendered and racial urgency that she gave her stories on the

[19]Letter to Mayo, 19 Feb. 1917, in Folder no. 13, Ser. 1, Box 2, *K.M. Papers.*

[20]Letter from Captain "D" Troop, Pennsylvania State Force, dated 24 Dec. 1917, in Folder no. 15, Ser. 1, Box 2, *K.M. Papers.*

[21]Letter from Commander of Pennsylvania State Force, Troop "A" to Mayo, dated 29 Oct. 1917, in Folder No. 14, Ser. 1, Box 2, *K.M. Papers.*

[22]Letter to Mayo, 30 Aug. 1927, in Folder no. 36, Ser. 1, Box 5, *K.M. Papers.*

Pennsylvania force. In making her case for the state police force, Mayo effectively invoked the twin specters of hordes of male immigrants and "Negroes," who lacked "manly" self-control, and of defenseless Anglo-Saxon women, who needed the manly protection of the state police.[23] Against the violence that Mayo associated with immigrants and African Americans, the members of the state police force were portrayed by Mayo as the upholders of law and order and, indeed, of civilization itself. Mayo's books on the state police, *Justice to All: History of the Pennsylvania State Police* (1917), *The Standard Bearers: True Stories of Heroes of Law and Order* (1918), and *Mounted Justice* (1922), were justly credited for having laid the foundations for the state police force.[24]

Yet Mayo's books on the state police force also put her at odds with many reformist and feminist circles in the United States. While her books enjoyed the support of powerful politicians and public figures, they elicited a much more critical response from reformers sympathetic to the interests of labor as well as from many liberal women's groups and feminists in the United States. Mayo herself was quite dismissive of criticism of her books from such quarters. Later, indeed, Mayo would dismiss feminist criticism in the United States of *Mother India* by alluding to her long estrangement from U.S. feminists, who had earlier reviled her heroes of the Pennsylvania State Police as "brutal state cossacks."[25]

Mayo, in fact, received a much more sympathetic hearing from conservative women's groups, for whom contemporary feminist activism was tainted by the evils of "bolshevism."[26] As

[23]My discussion here is indebted to Ray, "From Cossack to Trooper," esp. pp. 570–72.

[24]*Justice to All: History of the Pennsylvania State Police* (New York: G.P. Putnam, 1917); *The Standard Bearers: True Stories of Heroes of Law and Order* (New York: Houghton Mifflin and Co., 1918); and *Mounted Justice* (New York: Houghton Mifflin and Co., 1922).

[25]See Mayo's comment in the *Philadelphia Record*, n.d., in Folder no. 214, Ser. 4, Box 41, *K.M. Papers.*

[26]For a discussion both of the work of reformist women and of the backlash against them, see Robyn Muncy, *Creating a Female Dominion in American Reform, 1890–1935* (New York: Oxford University Press, 1991).

a reformer, Mayo appealed much more to women's organizations that had a history of "red-baiting" feminists in the United
States than to liberal women's activists. The dominant trend of
women's activism vis-à-vis the state in the late nineteenth and
early twentieth centuries, according to Paula Baker, consisted
of the "domestication of politics," the results of such women's
campaigns as maternal and child welfare legislation and protec-
tive factory legislation.[27] Mayo's constituency in the United
States, despite her subsequent reincarnation as a champion of
social welfare legislation in Mother India, was drawn largely
from conservative women's organizations that were opposed
to the type of social welfare legislation associated with feminist
activism in the United States. The Massachusetts Public Interest League, for example, had mounted a successful opposition
to the Child Labor Amendment as a subversive "feminist" and
"bolshevist" measure.[28] It was organizations like the Massachusetts Public Interest League that became some of the strongest supporters among women's groups in the United States for
Mayo's Mother India. The Massachusetts Public Interest League
and the equally conservative Daughters of the American Revolution welcomed Mother India warmly and invited Mayo to
address their respective organizations. Margaret Robinson of
the Massachusetts Public Interest League identified in Mayo,
notwithstanding Mayo's ostensible support for social welfare
legislations in India, a kindred soul who was opposed to the
subversive activities of feminists and bolshevists in the United
States and of "native" nationalists abroad. Robinson con-
gratulated Mayo for having produced a book that would be
"useful to counteract communist propaganda about India."
"Our League," she wrote, "is doing valuable work in educating
women as to the menace of subversive forces working through-

[27]See Paula Baker, "The Domestication of Politics: Women and American Political Society, 1780–1920," American Historical Review 89 (June
1984): pp. 620–47.
[28]For the controversy over the Child Labor Amendment in the 1920s,
see Walter I. Trattner, Crusade for the Children: A History of the National
Child Labor Committee and Child Labor Reform in America (Chicago: Quad-
rangle Books, 1970).

out the world." Robinson was concerned quite specifically with the impact of Theosophists and of women, such as Annie Besant in particular, who were putting the "degrading religion of India on a par with or above the Christian religion."[29]

By contrast, the more liberal women's organizations that supported maternity and child welfare legislation in the United States remained much more skeptical of Mayo's contribution in *Mother India*. As the account of one of Mayo's supporters reveals, feminists in the United States, whom he accused of combining support for birth control with love for the "Negro" and the "Hindoo," were more likely to question Mayo's new role as a champion of women and children in *Mother India*.[30] Mayo's own sympathies—reflected as well in her obsession with the impact of bolshevist propaganda in India—were in keeping with the conservative women's groups who kept their distance from feminists. It is perhaps all the more ironic, then, that today some latter-day feminists in the United States have been trying to reclaim Mayo's *Mother India* for a progressive feminist politics.

Mayo also shared common fears for an allegedly beleaguered white Anglo-Saxon Protestant establishment in the United States with organizations such as the Massachusetts Public Interest League and the Daughters of the American Revolution.[31] Mayo, herself a member of the Society of May-

[29]M. Robinson to Mayo, 4 Aug. 1927, in Folder no. 37, Ser. 1, Box 5, *K.M. Papers*.

[30]Letter from Harvey Watts to Mayo, dated 12 Jan. 1928, in Folder 42, Ser. 1, Box 6, *K.M. Papers*. For Mayo's estrangement from U.S. feminists, also see the contrast that her supporters made between the position of Mayo and that of Gertrude Ely of the National League of Women Voters, who was also visiting India in 1927, see J.H. Adams to Mayo, 27 Jan. 1927, in Folder no. 36, Ser. 1, Box 5; and Ely to Mayo, 15 Sept. 1927, Ser. 1, Box 5, *K.M. Papers*. Yet, as many Indian feminists discovered, *Mother India* did hold enormous fascination for women in the United States, see Muthulakshmi Reddi's discussion of the impact of *Mother India* in her own account of her visit to the international women's conference in Chicago in 1933, *Stri Dharma* 17, no. 1 (Nov. 1933): pp. 20–23.

[31]See Mabel Benedict, New Jersey chapter of the Daughters of the American Revolution, to Mayo, 3 Jan. 1928, in Folder no. 42, Ser. 1, Box

flower Descendants, was hostile toward certain minority groups within the United States and toward the immigration of others to the United States. Her disdain for Catholics, for example, had already aroused controversy in her books on the Pennsylvania State Police force. Mayo's story "The Honor of the Force," which appeared first in the *Saturday Evening Post* and was later reprinted in *The Standard Bearers*, provoked a barrage of letters from irate Catholics who found the piece and its depiction of the Catholic priest, Father Cantelmi, deliberately anti-Catholic. The Acting Superintendent of the Pennsylvania State Force, George Lumb, who in the wake of the controversy urged Mayo to verify her facts, explained the reasons behind the controversy in the following manner: "I think that the psychological reason [at the] back of this storm of protest is not the fact in the case, but the manner in which the Priest was described by your facile hand; the shovel hat, the flaunting robes and sardonic leer on his saturnine countenance have done more to arouse the people of his faith against your story than the [facts of the case]."[32] Mayo's publishers, Houghton Mifflin and Company, asked her to remove the libelous passages about Father Cantelmi from her story before it was reprinted in *The Standard Bearers*.[33] The "East Indians," who accounted for a much less visible presence in the United States, would be subjected to similar treatment by Mayo's "facile hand."[34]

The fear that expatriate Indians in the United States were a source of potential threat to the dominant religious and cultural

---

5, *K.M. Papers.* For a general background to the politics of organizations, such as the Daughters of the American Revolution, during the 1920s, see William O'Neill, *Feminism in America: A History* (New Brunswick: Transaction, 1989), p. 229.

[32]George Lumb to Mayo, 2 Apr. 1918, in Folder no. 17, Ser. 1, Box 3, *K.M. Papers.*

[33]Houghton Mifflin and Co. to Mayo, 10 Apr. 1918, in Folder no. 17, Ser. 1, Box 3, *K.M. Papers.*

[34]For a history of "East Indians" in the United States, see Joan Jensen, *Passage from India: Asian Indian Immigrants in North America* (New Haven: Yale University Press, 1988).

fabric of the nation was a strong motivating factor for Mayo in the writing of *Mother India*. Mayo, like the Massachusetts Public Interest League, was wary of a growing trend in the United States, which she associated especially with women's clubs, of flirting with notions about Eastern spiritual superiority over the West. Mayo feared that Americans were succumbing to the superficial charm of eloquent speakers, especially visiting Indians, who apparently made quite an impression on the lecture circuits in the United States. The favorable reception of recent visitors to the United States, such as the Indian Nobel laureate Rabindranath Tagore, seemed to confirm the suspicions of Mayo and her like-minded friends.[35] Tagore's unfavorable comparison of Western materialism with Eastern spirituality were especially galling to Mayo and her friends. F.C. Mortimer of the *New York Times* described Tagore in a letter to Mayo as "a dog that bites the hand that feeds him." To Mortimer, therefore, the real achievement of *Mother India* lay precisely in its response to the sort of propaganda associated with men like Tagore: "probably India is much like the other Eastern lands in morals and manners, but unlike the others it has claimed a 'spiritual' superiority to the West and usually this claim has been admitted. You have put an end to *that*."[36] Mayo herself reiterated often enough that her aim in writing *Mother India* was to provide the American public with the "true" picture of Indian civilization as a counter to the nationalist propaganda about a superior Indian spirituality that was being swallowed by the "India-lovers" in the United States.

Mayo, like the many supporters of the Asian Exclusion Acts in the United States, was equally concerned about the prospect of citizenship rights for expatriate Indians. While commenting on her reasons for writing *Mother India* at a private meeting in London, Mayo was reported to have confessed—a report that

[35]For a discussion of Tagore's reception in the United States, see Ranajan Borra, "Rabindrananth Tagore: Cultural Ambassador of India to the U.S.," in *Women, Politics and Literature*, ed. Clinton B. Seely (East Lansing, Mich.: Asian Studies Center, 1981), pp. 138–45.

[36]F.C. Mortimer to Mayo, n.d., in Folder no. 36, Ser. 1, Box 5, *K.M. Papers*.

she later denied—that her concerns had been aroused in particular by the introduction in the U.S. Senate of the Hindu Citizenship Bill.[37] Senator Royal Copeland's Hindu Citizenship Bill of 1927 was itself a response to the lobbying efforts of expatriate Indian organizations and their U.S. sympathizers against recent efforts to deny Indians rights as U.S. citizens. In the landmark Bhagat Singh Thind case in 1923, the U.S. Supreme Court had upheld the denaturalization of forty-two of the approximately seventy to a hundred Indians who had been naturalized as U.S. citizens between 1907 to 1923. Copeland's bill sought to classify Indians in the United States as "white persons," on grounds of that racialized genealogy that traced both Europeans and Indians back to a so-called Aryan racial stock.[38] Whether or not efforts such as the Copeland Bill had actually prompted Mayo to write *Mother India*, there is no denying that Mayo was certainly aware of, and highly critical of, the activities of expatriate Indians in the United States both on behalf of their struggle against British rule in India and for citizenship rights for Indians residing in the United States.

It was, indeed, a tribute to Mayo's public relations skills that she was able to utilize these same expatriate Indian organizations to generate prepublication publicity for *Mother India*. Mayo and her supporters, taking advantage of the fact that her views on Indians were still not widely known beyond the circle of her friends, had the publishers deliberately prepare innocuous prepublication notices for *Mother India*. These notices were then passed on to an unsuspecting Sailendra Nath Ghose, Secretary of the Indian Freedom Foundation in New York, who had invited Mayo to a banquet in honor of Senator Copeland.

[37]See Emily Lutyens to Mayo, 19 May 1928; and for Mayo's reply, Mayo to Lutyens, 25 May 1928 and 6 June 1928, in Folder no. 46, Ser. 1, Box 6, *K.M. Papers*.
[38]The Copeland Bill received considerable attention in the nationalist press in India; see *Forward*, 6 July 1927, p. 5; and 9 Aug. 1927, pp. 9–10. For a discussion of the racial ideologies adopted by expatriate Indians in the United States, see Sucheta Mazumdar, "Racist Responses to Racism: The Aryan Myth and South Asians in the U.S.," *South Asia Bulletin* 9, no. 1 (1989): pp. 47–55.

The notices were for distribution to the names on his organization's mailing list.[39] It was only after *Mother India* was published that Mayo began to speak out much more openly against citizenship rights for Indians. Her article on this topic, "When Asia Knocks at the Door," painted a grim picture of the kind of neighbor the Indian would make if allowed to reside permanently in the United States.[40]

Given Mayo's views on Indians, at least some of her friends were understandably wary of her decision to visit India and write about British rule in India. Mayo's interest in East Indians dated back to her stay in the early part of her life in Dutch Guiana (later Suriname) in South America. Mayo had encountered communities of indentured Indian laborers in Suriname and in the neighboring colony of British Guiana (later Guyana).[41] Many of her early journalistic contributions provided a paternalistic, as well as a disparaging, look at the culture of the "Hindu" laborers. Mayo's particular antipathy toward Hindus was sufficiently pronounced for her former mentor, Villard, to warn Mayo not to let her prejudices against the Hindus cloud her judgment in her writings.[42] E.C. Carter, who was formerly with the Y.M.C.A. in India and who had provided Mayo information for her book *That Damn Y* (1920), was equally nervous about giving Mayo letters of introduction to his friends in India, lest her proposed book on India end up being simply "pro-British" instead of "pro-humanity."[43] Interestingly, it was while working on her book on the Y.M.C.A. that Mayo encountered, and then became obsessed with countering, the claims

[39]Ghose to Mayo, 20 Apr. 1927, in Folder no. 36, Ser. 1, Box 5; Field to Ghose, 19 May 1927; no name, 22 May 1927, in Folder no. 36, Ser. 1, Box 5, *K.M. Papers*.

[40]See Folder no. 211, Ser. 4, Box 40, *K.M. Papers*.

[41]See especially "My Law and Thine," *Atlantic* 109 (Feb. 1912): pp. 239–44.

[42]Villard to Mayo, 21 July 1911, in Folder no. 2555, *Oswald Garrison Villard Papers*; cited in Jha, *Katherine Mayo and India*, p. 19.

[43]Carter to Mayo, 17 Nov. and 30 Nov. 1925, in Folder no. 35, Ser. 1, Box 5, *K.M. Papers*.

of some Indian women who blamed the British government for perpetuating the social "backwardness" of India.[44]

Mayo's *Mother India*, indeed, was shaped as much by her belief in the salutary role of Anglo-U.S. imperialism as by the concerns of domestic U.S. politics. Mayo had always favored a strong Anglo-U.S. imperial alliance that would jointly keep at bay the demands of various "natives" and their liberal sympathizers for the devolution of greater political responsibility into the hands of the indigenous peoples themselves. This had been the central message of Mayo's book *The Isles of Fear: The Truth about the Philippines* (1925), which was echoed later in *Mother India*. The former had painted a picture of the dismal failure of experiments at self-government among the Filipinos. The book was written with the blessing of the U.S. Governor-General in the Philippines, Leonard Wood, who wrote to Mayo that he "appreciate[d] tremendously having the Philippine situation written up."[45] The resulting polemic against Filipino politicians angered nationalists in the Philippines but met with the full approval of Wood, who acknowledged that Mayo "has done more than [she] realized to help out the situation here."[46] Mayo's critique of Filipino self-rule also attracted attention in Britain, especially in circles that had a say in shaping British policy toward India. Lionel Curtis, the founder of the reform-minded Round Table group and one of the architects of the Government of India reforms of 1919, was sufficiently impressed by Mayo to contribute a preface for the British edition of *The Isles of Fear.*[47]

[44]See reply to Mayo's query on a "Mrs. Row" in a letter from Stanley Reed, *Times of India*, Bombay to Mayo, 13 Jan. 1921, in Folder no. 24, Ser. 1, Box 4, *K.M. Papers.*

[45]L. Wood to Mayo, 29 Jan. 1923, in Folder no. 24, Ser. 1, Box 4, *K.M. Papers.*

[46]Wood to F.B. Kirkbride, 29 Sept. 1925, in Folder no. 34, Ser. 1, Box 5, *K.M. Papers.*

[47]See preface by Lionel Curtis in Katherine Mayo, *The Isles of Fear* (London: Faber and Gwyer, 1925), pp. ix–xii. For a discussion of Lionel Curtis and the Round Table Group, see Deborah Lavin, *From Empire to*

Mayo's decision to follow up her book on the Philippines with a book on India could not have come at a better time for British policy-makers on India. The "official mind" in Britain, especially after the move toward self-governing institutions by the Government of India Act of 1919, was preoccupied precisely with questions about the future direction of imperial policy in India. The concern over the direction of political changes in India came at a time when, for a variety of reasons, British officials were also becoming increasingly sensitive to international, and especially U.S., public opinion about British rule in India. The British government's surveillance of the nationalist activities of Indians in the United States, however, was severely limited after World War I as a result of both budgetary constraints and the new political climate in India.[48] One solution to the problem had been the creation of a special Secret Services Fund operated by the British Foreign Office in London that paid for an agent in the United States to engage in propaganda on behalf of the British Government in India. By 1924, however, the Foreign Office and the Government of India were dissatisfied with their agent in the United States, R. Rustomjee, and ended their financial arrangement with him. Yet the Director of Public Information in India, on his return from a visit to the United States, recommended the continuation of the fund for another plan that would provide "better value for our money."[49] The Foreign Office in London and the British Embassy in Washington, D.C., had already been in secret correspondence for some years about a plan for

---

International Commonwealth: A Biography of Lionel Curtis (Oxford: Clarendon Press, 1995).

[48]For British concern about anti-British propaganda by Indians in the United States, see Home Political 1922 30-III, 1922, National Archives of India, New Delhi. For a general history of British surveillance of Indian nationalists, see Richard J. Poplewell, "The Surveillance of Indian 'Seditionists' in North America, 1905–1915," in Intelligence and International Relations, ed. C. Andrew and J. Noakes (Exeter: University of Exeter Press, 1987); and Intelligence and Imperial Defence: British Intelligence and the Defence of the Indian Empire, 1904–1924 (London: Frank Cass, 1995).

[49]See Home Political F 35/III, 1924.

enlisting local journalists in the United States, with special attention to the inclusion of women, who would undertake an independent journey to India to present the British point of view to the American public at home.[50] It was around this time that Mayo and Newell chose to visit India and present British rule in India to the American public. Both women had been associated with the British Library of Information in New York, which was the major organization for British propaganda work in the United States and was under the supervision of the British Embassy in Washington, D.C.[51] Together, moreover, Mayo and Newell possessed the substantial financial means to undertake the kind of "independent" journey to India that had been envisaged by officials of the Foreign Office in Britain.

The exact nature and extent of the British government's official involvement in Mayo's project remains clouded in secrecy. Although there is no doubt that *Mother India* was produced with the full knowledge and blessing of the relevant colonial authorities concerned with India, government representatives were forced on several occasions to deny any official involvement in Mayo's project in response to questions raised in the British Parliament and in the Central Legislative Assembly in India. The representatives of the government claimed to have provided Mayo with nothing more than what was available to any foreign traveler in India.[52] The official line, however, was undercut when Mayo herself began to refer to her relationship with the British government in a very different light. Ignoring the disclaimer that she had printed in *Mother India*, Mayo committed the political blunder of later acknowledging publicly her tremendous indebtedness to the British government without whose help she now admitted she could not have written her book. This blunder both embarrassed British officials and cost Mayo their cooperation for

[50]Cited in Jha, *Katherine Mayo and India*, pp. 10–11.

[51]For the role of the British Library of Information in New York on behalf of propaganda for the British government in India, see *Home Political F. 177, 1924*; *Home Political 311/1925*; and *Home Political 269, 1926*.

[52]See *Home Political 10/74, 1927*; and *Home Political 20/II, 1928*. Also see *Home Political 22/36/34, 1934*.

her subsequent books on India,[53] for her admission placed British officials and various government agencies in India in a very awkward situation.

The newly created Bureau of Public Information in India, which was at the mercy of the Central Legislative Assembly, with its elected Indian majority to vote funds annually for its continued existence, was the most hard hit by the controversy.[54] Mayo's faux pas also made British officials in New York and in London more nervous about extending any further cooperation to Mayo for her subsequent books on India. Hugh MacGregor, who was the Information Officer at the India Office in London, sympathized with the nervousness of British officials in their future dealings with Mayo. MacGregor, however, decided that for the India Office it was much safer, given the nature of Mayo's work, to continue to play some role in her future projects rather than leave her entirely to her own devices. MacGregor, therefore, first "lectured" Mayo on her blunder in referring to government help for *Mother India* and, then, as a condition for his continued support for her subsequent projects "obtained from her the promise that in no circumstances will references again be made to official sources of help."[55] The British and colonial Indian government's denial of any official involvement in Mayo's project was thus a disingenuous half-truth.

The production of *Mother India*, in fact, was characterized by government support—whether "official" or "unofficial"— from the very outset. Before embarking for India, Mayo had met with Earl Winterton, the Under-Secretary of State for India

[53]For the fallout caused by Mayo's blunder, see *Secretary of State Private Office Papers: Personal Files: Katherine Mayo File*, India Office Library and Records (henceforth cited as *Personal Files: K.M.*).

[54]See L.F. Rushbrook Williams (director of Bureau of Public Information in India), *Inside Both Indias, 1914–1938* (Gloucester: Earle and Ludlow, n.d), p. 38; in *Rushbrook Williams Papers*, Centre for South Asian Studies, University of Cambridge, Cambridge.

[55]See letters from Hugh MacGregor, India Office, to Stephens, director of Public Information, Government of India, dated 25 Jan. 1935 and 19 Feb. 1935, in *Personal Files: K.M.*

in London, who expressed his "personal sympathies" with Mayo's objectives but "desired to take council whether [these objectives] would be best effected by full official recognition or by quieter means."[56] Although the meeting concluded with the understanding that Mayo would show Winterton a copy of her manuscript before publication, Mayo, on the advice of officials in India with which Winterton himself concurred, decided eventually against such a step. In February 1927 Mayo wrote Winterton from New York: "I feel . . . that it will be happier for you, and stronger for the book, if you can all say, after it comes out, that you had no knowledge of its nature, that you were never afforded a reading or even a synopsis of the text, that your connection with it is limited to travel courtesy offered to a strange American and to the civility of answering requests for published statistics."[57] While a denial along these lines enabled British officials to persist in maintaining their innocence regarding *Mother India*, it did not allay the justifiable suspicions of Mayo's critics about the extent of government involvement in her project.

The further point, moreover, is that Mayo kept key colonial officials in both Britain and India apprized of the nature and scope of her book on India. Mayo was constantly in close consultation with officials at various levels, from the junior to the most senior. She did not hesitate to disclose to them that her aim was to help the British cause in India through her book in any way they deemed desirable. Immediately upon her arrival in India, for example, Mayo wrote to Sir Basil Blackett, the Finance Member of the Government of India, explaining her objectives in undertaking her project on India:

Briefly we want to be useful to our own country, and we think that our own country's greatest need is a better understanding of and closer sympathetic relationship with Great Britain. Against such understanding and sympathy there is in America, a constant effort—sometimes open, some-

[56]Mayo's Diary entry for 22 Oct. 1925, in Folder no. 113, Ser. 2, Box 13, *K.M. Papers.*
[57]Mayo to Winterton, 6 Feb. 1927, in Folder no. 36, Ser. 1, Box 5, *K.M. Papers.*

times subtle and covered; and its greatest ally is the ignorance of the public on the points attached. . . . The British administration in India is always conspicuous among these. And it therefore occurred to us that if we could do, in India some such work as we did in the Philippines, we might cut some ground from under the feet of the trouble-makers—But to that end, it was, of course, necessary to choose some circumscribed field, and out of that to choose a few striking and representative examples, to sustain statistics and a general argument. A non-political, non-controversial field would be best, in order to work aside from grounds already occupied by prejudices implanted by the enemy propaganda. . . . And the fact that we come of our own pleasure committed to no one at home or abroad, we have also found in like cases to be an asset—I went to the India Office as well as to the Health Ministry in London to explain this, and to ask for their approval in undertaking this errand.[58]

Mayo's political objectives were so blatant that even sympathetic government officials who came into contact with her team in India often expressed their discomfort at her obvious partisanship. The Lieutenant Governor of the United Provinces (U.P.), Sir William Marris, to whom Mayo had letters of introduction from London, expressed his concern to Mayo's secretary, Harry Field. Field, in turn, tried to warn Mayo of the impression she was creating among some British officials in India:

[The Lieutenant Governor] is really perturbed about you, dear, he says that you appeared to them all, here, to be like a good hound on a scent running it down in a splendid manner . . . or like an excellent barrister preparing a brief . . . against India. He couldn't give any viewpoint against you except "playing cricket" and "it is their country and they have a right to rule it." He said that many of your questions pointed to a preconceived opinion . . . and all lead one way.[59]

At no stage of Mayo's project, indeed, were colonial officials ever in doubt about the general outcome of the disingenuous "research" that Mayo was undertaking into the conditions in India.

The biggest irony, perhaps, is that, despite *Mother India's*

[58]Mayo to Blackett, 25 Dec. 1925, in Folder no. 7, *Sir Basil Blackett Papers*, India Office Library and Records.
[59]Field to Mayo, n.d., in Folder no. 226, Ser. 4, Box 42, *K.M. Papers*.

subsequent fame as a book revealing the problems of child marriage and premature maternity in India, Mayo had intended to write a very different book on India. Mayo's initial plan was to focus on public health in India, especially on epidemics such as cholera, which were arguably man-made. For, as Mayo had written to Blackett on arrival in India, she chose "cholera rather than plague, because cholera is concerned with people rather than rats."[60] Mayo claimed that the idea had been suggested to her by her friends Dr. Victor Heiser and Dr. George Vincent of the International Health Board of the Rockefeller Foundation, although the foundation itself later disclaimed any official connection with Mayo's project.[61] On her way to India Mayo floated the plan for her book on public health in India with the Health Ministry in London and with international health officials in Geneva. The health officials in Geneva were the first to express skepticism toward her plan to base her entire case against India around the supposed public health menace that India posed to the world.[62] Mayo obviously paid some heed to this warning; henceforth, she let it be known to sympathetic British officials that she was open to their suggestions for an alternative focus for her book.[63] Even

[60]Mayo to Blackett, 25 Dec. 1925, in Folder no. 7, *Sir Basil Blackett Papers.*

[61]For a discussion of the Rockfeller Foundation's involvement with Mayo, see Jha, *Katherine Mayo and India,* pp. 66–67. The International Health Board of the Rockefeller Foundation and Dr. Victor Heiser had also been active in the creation of a colonial discourse on public health in the Philippines; see Warwick Anderson, "Colonial Pathologies: American Medicine in the Philippines, 1898–1921" (Ph.D. diss., University of Pennsylvania, 1992). Also see Richard Brown, *Rockefeller Medicine Men: Medicine and Capitalism in America* (Berkeley: University of California Press, 1979); and John Ettling, *The Germ of Laziness: Philanthropy and Public Health in the New South* (Cambridge: Harvard University Press, 1981). I am grateful to Leslie Reagan for the references on the Rockefeller Foundation and public health discourse in the United States.

[62]Diary entry for 18 Nov. 1925, in Folder no. 113, Ser. 2, Box 13, *K.M. Papers.*

[63]Mayo to Blackett, 25 Dec. 1925, in Folder no. 7, *Sir Basil Blackett Papers.* For a discussion of disease and the public health discourse on

after settling upon a new focus, however, Mayo never aban-
doned entirely her initial focus on public health. The theme of
public health, after all, had proved highly successful in her
earlier polemic against Filipino self-rule in *Isles of Fear*.[64] In the
chapter in *Mother India* entitled "World Menace" Mayo covered
similar grounds about the public health hazards posed by Indians. Mayo and Newell retained the habit of presenting *Mother
India*, even after its publication, as primarily a public health
document that had revealed the unsanitary and unhygienic
practices of Indians to the world.

The theme for which Mayo's *Mother India* became most well-
known—the general "sex-obsession" of the Hindus and its particular manifestation in child marriage and premature maternity in India—was, in fact, suggested to her by a British official
of the Central Intelligence Division in India, J.H. Adams. Adams, who was originally with the North West Frontier Police in
India, was on deputation from February 1923 with the central
intelligence division. In 1925 he was sent to the India Office,
with money out of the Secret Service Funds operated from London, on a mission kept secret in India. The comment in the files
of the Government of India on Adams's duties at the India
Office simply state: "it is essential that the nature of Mr. Adams'
duties at the India Office should be kept secret."[65] It is interesting that later the same year the India Office was recommending
Adams to Mayo as a companion on board her ship out to India.[66] Mayo acknowledged in private the tremendous debt she

India, see David Arnold, "The Indian Ocean as a Disease Zone, 1500–
1950," *South Asia* 12 , no. 2 (1991): pp. 1–21.

[64]For a useful discussion of the theme of public health and sanitary
issues in the "civilizing mission" adopted by the United States in the
Philippines, see Warwick Anderson, "Excremental Colonialism: Public
Health and the Poetics of Pollution," *Critical Inquiry* 21, no. 3 (Spring
1995): pp. 640–69. For a discussion of the public health theme, especially
concerning the training of midwives and maternal health, see Sandhya
Shetty, "(Dis)Locating Gender: Space and Medical Discourse in Colonial
India," *Genders* 20 (1994): pp. 188–230.

[65]*Home Political F. 375, 1924.*

[66]J.W. Hose, India Office, to Mayo, 20 Nov. 1925, in Folder no. 32, Ser.
1, Box 5, *K.M. Papers.*

owed Adams for providing her with the central argument of her book. She wrote: "it was by no accident that you came and gave me that one idea at the beginning of my journey—if I write a general book, write a couple of chapters in this, it makes escape from the point more possible. Shall I make this just a complete bomb—self contained and exclusive?"[67] Mayo's central argument that India's problems were the result of its "sex-ridden" culture was elaborated in the first two parts of *Mother India*. Parts 3, 4, and 5, however, went on to discuss other matters; Mayo obviously could not resist the temptation of maximizing her case against Indian self-rule by including a miscellaneous grab bag of Indian social ills. Yet it was the "bomb" about Indian sexual practices in the first third of the book that remained the heart of her argument.

Mayo's horrific description of the actual conditions of childbirth—presided over by the allegedly filthy, louse-infested, unscientific Indian *dai*, or midwife—presented in the eponymous chapter of the book, together with the terrible consequences of child marriage on Indian women and children, were generally agreed to constitute the main contribution of the book. It was Mayo's description of such practices that led the anonymous reviewer in the London *New Statesman*, a journal that had hitherto been sympathetic to some of the demands of the Indian nationalist movement, to declare that *Mother India* had revealed "the filthy personal habits of even the most highly educated classes in India—which, like the degradation of Hindu women, are unequaled among the most primitive African or Australian savages." This reviewer at least concluded that "[Mayo] makes the claim for Swaraj [self-rule] seem nonsense and the will to grant it almost a crime."[68] Even Edward Thompson, a liberal critic of many aspects of British rule in India, was

[67]Note from Mayo to Adams, n.d., in Folder 181, Ser. 4, Box 34, *K.M. Papers*. Newell wrote: "Miss Mayo's original idea was a book on the problems of Public Health as seen through the eyes of the League of Nations—but 'Mother India' was the result"; see Note by Newell in Folder no. 32, Ser. 1, Box 5, *K.M. Papers*.

[68]C.S. [Clifford Sharpe], "India as It Is," *New Statesman* (16 July 1927): pp. 448–49.

moved by the first two parts of Mayo's book: "the first 134 pages of the book are as true as they are terrible . . . the last 250 pages make it prolonged nagging." Thompson's only real criticism of the book was that Mayo had allowed the "general condemnation" of Indian nationalism in the latter half of the book to detract from the powerful critique contained in the first half.[69] It would thus appear that Adams, who at the time was on a secret assignment with the India Office, had indeed provided Mayo with a vehicle far more potent than her original discussion of cholera and public health for making her case against India.

The winning formula that had worked so well in *Mother India*, however, proved difficult for Mayo to sustain in any of her subsequent books on India. For, although Mayo did much to capitalize on her newfound reputation as a champion of the rights of women in India, her efforts were overshadowed by her constant need to find other potentially even more volatile vehicles—such as Hindu-Muslim conflict—for pursuing her case against Indian self-rule. Mayo had very quickly recognized the potential of Hindu-Muslim divisions in India for making her attack against Indian nationalism. The only change that Mayo made to subsequent editions of *Mother India*, for example, was to substitute *Hindu* for *Indian* so as to present her attack in the book as directed specifically and pointedly against the Hindu population of India.[70] Mayo also tried to encourage translations of her book into Urdu with a view toward driving a wedge between Hindu and Muslim public opinion on *Mother India*. This strategy was especially pronounced in Mayo's subsequent books on India. In *Slaves of the Gods* (1929), a collection of short stories meant to illustrate the arguments of *Mother India*, Mayo decided to portray the social ills of India as confined to Hindus in particular. In private communications about the book, for example, she admitted to changing the Muslim names of characters in the original stories in order

[69]*Bookman* (Sept. 1927): p. 323. For Thompson's view of *Mother India*, see also the review of his *The Reconstruction of India* in *Women's Leader and Common Cause* 22, no. 36 (10 Oct. 1930): pp. 265–66.

[70]See Note, 12 Feb. 1928, in Folder 43, Ser. 1, Box 6, *K.M. Papers*.

deliberately to make "Hindus out of them."[71] Even more blatant, perhaps, was Mayo's deliberate manipulation of the "communal card" in *Volume II* (1931), a collection of excerpts from the report of the Age of Consent Committee appointed by the Government of India to explore the need to raise the age of consent for sexual intercourse in India; and in *The Face of Mother India* (1935), a pictorial representation of India and of Indian women.

Mayo's exploitation of communal (religious sectarian) politics in the two latter books were so obvious that even her erstwhile allies found it hard to overlook. The British feminist Eleanor Rathbone, who had been a great supporter of *Mother India* and had been inspired by the book to take upon herself the responsibility for ameliorating the suffering of the child-brides of India, could not help rebuking Mayo for having deliberately misinterpreted evidence on child marriage in *Volume II*. This later book, according to Rathbone, had lost its usefulness because Mayo was too keen to show that the evils of child marriage were a specifically Hindu phenomenon.[72] Even the colonial government, on its own initiative, decided to ban *The Face of Mother India* from India because, as one official explained, the "whole thesis of it is Hindu-Muslim antagonism."[73] MacGregor of the India Office, who had earlier concluded that it was in the interest of his office to cooperate with Mayo on the *Face of Mother India*, admitted to Mayo that the "anti-Hindu and pro-Muslim bias [of the book was] too pronounced" for the government to permit its sale in India.[74] Cornelia Sorabji, a friend and confidante of Mayo's and one of the

[71]Letter from Mayo to J.C. Pringle, n.d., in Folder no. 215, Ser. 4, Box 42, *K.M. Papers.*

[72]Letter from Rathbone to Mayo, n.d., in Folder no. 97, Ser. 1, Box 11, *K.M. Papers.* For Rathbone's criticism of Mayo for deliberately exempting the British and the Muslim population from any blame for the effects of child marriage and premature maternity in India, see also Rathbone to Lothian, 29 Nov. 1931, in Folder 7, Box 93, *Eleanor Rathbone Papers,* Fawcett Library, London Guildhall University.

[73]Stephens to MacGregor, 27 Jan. 1936, *Personal Files: K.M.*

[74]Letter from MacGregor to Mayo, n.d., in Folder no. 78, Ser. 1, Box 10, *K.M. Papers.*

only prominent Indian women to publish a sympathetic review of *Mother India*, had already decided against having her
photograph used in the *Face of Mother India* for fear that its
obvious bias against Hindus would alienate her from her orthodox Hindu friends and clients in India.[75] Mayo was thus unable to sustain again what the "accident" of her association
with Adams had once made possible in *Mother India*: her mas-
querade as a genuine crusader against the treatment of women
and children in India.

There was, indeed, little in Mayo's career either before or
after *Mother India* that lends credence to her subsequent reputation as a feminist crusader. Mayo's career in the United States
prior to *Mother India* as well as the particular route by which
she happened to arrive at the special focus of *Mother India*
suggest that her contribution to women and to feminism have
been accidental at best: an arbitrary and contingent instrument
deployed to advance a colonial agenda.

The subsequent myth of *Mother India*, indeed, was the
product of a long history of the deployment of the "woman
question" in the struggle between imperialism and nationalism in India. It was the terms of this struggle—much more
than anything in the book itself—that framed *Mother India* as
a contribution to the woman question in India. As several
scholars have pointed out, the woman question in colonial
India had already become an ideological battleground between Indian nationalists and British imperialists long before
Mother India was published.[76] It was not surprising, therefore,
that the first two parts of *Mother India* that dealt quite specifically with conditions affecting the status of women in India
became the focus of attention and generated the most heated

[75]Letters from Sorabji to Mayo, dated 2 May 1935, in Folder no. 75,
Ser. 1, Box 9; dated 31 Dec. 1935, in Folder no. 76, Ser. 1, Box 10, *K.M.
Papers*.

[76]See Joanna Liddle and Rama Joshi, "Gender and Imperialism in
British India," *South Asia Research* 5, no 2 (1985): pp. 147–65; and Lata
Mani, "Contentious Traditions: The Debate on Sati in Colonial India,"
Cultural Critique 7 (1987): pp. 119–56.

exchanges about the respective merits of British imperialism and Indian nationalism.

There was a long precedent for the appropriation of the woman question for the purposes of the moral justification of British imperialism. As far back as James Mill's *History of British India* (1817), the practices found among particular groups and in particular regions of India, such as the self-immolation of widows (popularly known as *sati*), female infanticide, the veiling of women (*purdah*), child marriage, and enforced widowhood, were treated as emblematic of all India and of Indian culture as a whole.[77] As such, therefore, these practices afforded a basis not only for the ideological justification of the "civilizing mission" of British imperialism in India but also for arguments about the "barbarity" of Indian culture. The framing of the woman question in these terms, however, created a negative climate for social reforms for women in India. For, on the one hand, such a limited frame focused only on Indian cultural practices, and thus conveniently ignored any negative impact that colonialism had on the condition of women in India. And, on the other, it provoked defensive Indian responses by converting specific reforms for women into occasions for an overall criticism of Indian culture. Indeed, British imperialists often used the condition of Indian women as a particularly handy stick with which to beat Indian proto-nationalists and nationalists. Hence, in various imperial conflicts, as in the "white mutiny" of 1882 against a bill that would have given Indian civil servants criminal jurisdiction over European British subjects in the Indian countryside, the British opponents of the bill used the position of Indian women to argue that Indian men were as yet "unfit" for any concessions of political or legal equality from the government.[78]

[77]For a discussion of James Mill's *History of British India* and the ideological justification of imperialism, see A.R.H. Copley, "Projections, Displacement and Distortion in 19th Century Moral Imperialism—A Re-Examination of Charles Grant and James Mill," *Calcutta Historical Journal* 7, no. 2 (Jan.–June 1983): pp. 1–27.

[78]See Mrinalini Sinha, " 'Chathams, Pitts and Gladstones in Petti-coats': The Politics of Gender and Race in the Ilbert Bill Controversy," in

Increasingly, moreover, imperialists found it expedient to deflect the political demands of Indians with admonitions that India would be better served if Indians redirected attention from political to social reforms. The imperialist strategy of pitting social against political reform did little to strengthen the hands of Indian social reformers, especially since after 1857 official policy itself was reluctant to support social reform measures for fear of alienating powerful orthodox interests from loyalty to the British Crown.[79] Yet, despite the ambivalent record of the colonial government on reforms for women in India, the woman question remained an important pillar in the ideological justification of British imperialism in India.

The woman question had an equally long history in the ideological work of elite proto-nationalism and nationalism in India. The figure of the "Aryan woman" of the ancient past— who was defined as superior to Western and Westernized women as well as to lower-caste/-class women in India—had long occupied a central place in the cultural nationalist project of reconstructing a "golden past" from which contemporary Indian society had allegedly fallen.[80] The figure of this ideal Aryan woman was used alternatively by Indian reformers to argue for reforms in the position of women in contemporary Indian society and by opponents of reforms to resist any change in the status quo. Once again the condition of women was tied to the evaluation of what constituted Indian culture and of the Indian past as a whole. The implications of the popular investment in the figure of the Indian woman was

---

Western Women and Imperialism: Complicity and Resistance, ed. Nupur Chaudhuri and Margaret Strobel (Bloomington: Indiana University Press, 1992), pp. 98–118.

[79]For a history of social reform in India, see S. Natarajan, *A Century of Social Reform in India* (Bombay: Asia Publishing House, 1962); and Charles Heimsath, *Indian Nationalism and Hindu Social Reform* (Princeton: Princeton University Press, 1964).

[80]See especially Uma Chakravarti, "Whatever Happened to the Vedic Dasi? Orientalism, Nationalism, and a Script for the Past" in *Recasting Women: Essays in Indian Colonial History,* ed. Kumkum Sangari and Sudesh Vaid (New Brunswick: Rutgers University Press, 1990), pp. 27–87.

further manifest in the nationalist iconography of the nation itself as Mother India.[81] In fact, the discourse of official nationalism in India, as Partha Chatterjee has suggested, had invested the figure of the modern Indian woman as the site of national autonomy in response to the "derivative" nature of its own project. Indian nationalism thus sought to overcome its derivativeness vis-à-vis the West through a convenient ideological split whereby it acknowledged Indian inferiority to the West in the "material" realm and located Indian autonomy in an alternative "spiritual" realm supposedly untouched by the West.[82] Hence, both the tremendous nationalist investment in the figure of the Indian woman, who, as the traditional guardian of the spiritual realm, became the very embodiment of Indianness and the exaggerated nationalist claims about the superiority of Indian spirituality over Western materialism.

The impact of the ideological resolution of Indian nationalism on actual reforms for women—not unlike the impact of British imperialism—was ambiguous at best. On the one hand, it provided Hindu revivalists, especially in the second half of the nineteenth century, with a patriotic language through which they could articulate their patriarchal resistance to legislative initiatives aimed at improving the condition of women. This was evident, for example, in the cries against "colonial

[81]See Jasodhara Bagchi, "Representing Nationalism: Ideology of Motherhood in Colonial Bengal," *Economic and Political Weekly* 25, nos. 42–43 (20–27 Oct.1990): pp. WS65–WS71; Tanika Sarkar, "Nationalist Iconography: Images of Women in Nineteenth Century Bengali Literature," *Economic and Political Weekly* 2, no. 47 (21 Nov. 1987): pp. 2011–15; Samita Sen, "Motherhood and Mothercraft: Gender and Nationalism in Bengal," *Gender and History* 5, no. 2 (Summer 1993): pp. 231–33; C.S. Lakshmi, "Mother, Mother-Community and Mother-Politics in Tamil Nadu," *Economic and Political Weekly* 25, nos. 42–43 (20–27 Oct. 1990): pp. WS72–WS83.

[82]Partha Chatterjee, "Colonialism, Nationalism and Colonized Women: The Contest in India," *American Ethnologist* 16, no. 4 (Nov. 1989): pp. 662–83; and "The Nationalist Resolution of the Woman Question," in Sangari and Vaid, *Recasting Women*, pp. 233–53. For Chatterjee's analysis of Indian nationalist thought more generally, see *Nationalist Thought and the Colonial World*.

interference" that marked the fierce Hindu resistance to the Age of Consent Act of 1891.[83] On the other hand, however, it also made possible the gradual emergence of a fragile new consensus—shared even by many of the leading Hindu revivalists of the late nineteenth and early twentieth centuries—in favor of certain limited reforms for women, albeit within strictly nationalist parameters. In short, certain limited reforms in the contemporary status of women in India were now incorporated as an integral part of the nationalist agenda.

Mother India was aptly framed so as to exploit both the imperialist and nationalist investments in the woman question for making its own case against Indian self-government. It owed its entire discussion of the plight of Indian women, in fact, to the central tropes that had already been long established in imperialist writings on women in India. *Mother India,* for example, defined the problems of women in India only in relation to "timeless" Hindu cultural practices. Its diagnosis of the problems of Indian women ignored both the historical and material factors that were behind particular cultural practices and the shifting impact of these practices on women. By overlooking the role of the colonial state in its diagnosis of women's condition in India, moreover, the book neglected conveniently any discussion of the decline in status of women of certain classes and groups in India as a direct result of specific colonial interventions in the Indian economy and in Indian culture.[84] Further-

[83]See esp. Amiya Sen. "Hindu Revivalism in Action—The Age of Consent Bill Agitation in Bengal," *Indian Historical Review* 7, nos. 1–2 (July 1980–Jan. 1981): pp. 160–84; and Tanika Sarkar, "Rhetoric against Age of Consent: Resisting Colonial Reason and Death of a Child-Wife," *Economic and Political Weekly* 28, no. 36 (4 Sept. 1993): pp. 1869–78; and "The Hindu Wife and the Hindu Nation: Domesticity and Nationalism in Nineteenth-Century Bengal," *Studies in History* 8, no. 2 (1992): pp. 213–35.

[84]For at least two instances in which colonial interventions negatively affected the existing position of certain classes and groups of women in India, see Lucy Carroll,"Law, Custom and Statutory Social Reform: The Hindu Widow's Remarriage Act of 1856," in *Women in Colonial India,* ed. J. Krishnamurthy (Delhi: Oxford University Press, 1989), pp. 1–26; and Nirmala Bannerjee, "Working Women in Colonial Bengal: Modernization and Marginalization," in Sangari and Vaid, *Recasting Women,* pp. 269–301.

more, *Mother India* paid attention only to the contributions of British men and women in the "upliftment" of Indian women. Neither the colonial government's repeated opposition to a number of reform measures, including bills sponsored by Indian legislators for raising the age of consent and abolishing child marriage, nor the many reform initiatives for women undertaken by Indian men and women themselves held much interest for the author of *Mother India*. As such, therefore, *Mother India* was designed to confirm the familiar imperialist trope that Gayatri Chakravorty Spivak has captured in the phrase "white men [and white women] saving brown women from brown men."[85] What set *Mother India* apart, perhaps, was that it provided one of the most systematic elaborations for the old imperialist theme that connected the continued political backwardness of India to the condition and treatment of Indian women. Mayo argued that practices such as child marriage and premature maternity had taken their toll on the physical and mental development of the "race" as a whole and had rendered the Hindu physically incapable of holding the "reins of government." For Mayo, in fact, the very character of Indian nationalism was related to the fatal "sexual exaggerat[ion]" she found prevalent in India. Hence, Bengal, according to Mayo, was the "seat of bitterest political unrest—the producer of India's main crop of anarchists, bomb throwers, and assassins" because it was also among the "most sexually exaggerated regions of India" (p. 160). Mayo's relentless effort to tie her entire discussion of Indian women in *Mother India* to the twin arguments about the benevolence of British rule and the unfitness of Indians for self-rule was, if anything, a rather crude restatement of arguments that had long been deployed with varying degrees of sophistication in various imperialist writings on Indian women.

The very crassness of Mayo's imperial propaganda, however, had the inadvertent effect of limiting *Mother India*'s potential for exploiting fully its challenge to nationalist recuperations of the woman question in India. Mayo had clearly

[85]Gayatri Chakravorty Spivak, "Can the Subaltern Speak? Speculations on Widow Sacrifice," *Wedge* 7–8 (Winter–Spring, 1985): p. 121.

intended not only to shore up the myth of British benevolence or paternalism in India, especially in regard to Indian women, but also to expose nationalist myths about the glories of Indian womanhood. Nowhere, perhaps, was Mayo's specific attack on nationalist myths about Indian womanhood more evident than in her choice for the title of the book. The title, *Mother India*, alluded both to the nationalist glorification of India as "Mother India" and to Mayo's own horrific description of what the actual Indian mother had to undergo during childbirth. Mayo explained her reasons for having chosen this title in a story addressed to "The Women of Hindu India" that appeared in her collection *Slaves of the Gods:*

> The title was chosen with an object. Its purpose was to awaken your intelligent patriotism and the consciousness of your men, by making inescapable the contrast between, on the one hand, florid talk of devotion and "sacrifice" poured out before an abstract figure, and on the other hand, the consideration actually accorded to the living woman, mother of the race.[86]

The implications of the title were not lost on her contemporaries. They responded to Mayo's challenge with books with some of the following titles: *Father India* (1927); *Sister India* (1928); *My Mother India* (1930); *A Son of Mother India Answers* (1928); *Long Live India: What a Son Has to Say about Mother and Father India* (1932); *My Mother's Picture* (1930); *An Englishman Defends Mother India* (1929); *The Truth about Mother India* (1928); *Unhappy India* (1928); *The True India* (1939); *Mother India by Those Who Know Her Better than Miss K. Mayo* (1927); *Miss Mayo's Cruelty to Mother India* (n.d.); *Mother India Ka Jawab* (The Reply to Mother India) (1928); *Mother India Aur Uska Jawab* (Mother India and Her Reply) (1928); and *Bharata-Mateci Sreshthata* (The Truth about Mother India) (1928). Mayo's *Mother India*, as a good number of her nationalist critics recognized, intended to take the critique of women's position into the heart of the nationalist camp itself.

Yet Mayo herself had made it easy for her critics to escape the

[86]K. Mayo, *Slaves of the Gods* (New York: Harcourt Brace and Co., 1929), p. 237.

full import of her challenge to nationalist versions of the woman question. Hence, even many social reformers and women activists in India found little they could use in Mayo's book and dismissed it as an imperialist diatribe against Indian nationalism. It was, indeed, left largely to Mayo's pro-imperialist supporters to try and salvage *Mother India*'s implications for the position of women in India. Thus, Sorabji urged Mayo to abjure political conclusions and to change the title of her book in subsequent editions so that the book did not provide easy grounds for its own dismissal as just another pro-imperialist argument.[87] Yet Mayo, who had chosen the woman question in *Mother India* precisely for purposes of her attack on Indian nationalism and a defense of British imperialism in India, resisted any such dilution of this central message of her book.

Even within the rather limited terms of the dominant imperialist/nationalist debate on the woman question, Mayo's text could add little to the existing social reform literature in India. For *Mother India* neither broke any new ground in its revelations of the condition of women in India nor provided any new explanations for the problems facing Indian women. Mayo's revelations about the condition of women in India were already well-known in the social reform literature of the time. Much of this literature was often even more critical of existing social practices in India than *Mother India*. Mayo's dubious generalizations, crude exaggerations, and relentless emphasis on the sexual connotations of myriad Hindu cultural practices was probably more disabling than enabling for the work of social reformers and women activists in India. While it was to be expected that Mayo's use of statistics would be open to dispute and varying interpretations, her gross exaggeration of her figures often strained all credibility. Hence, Adams, Mayo's longtime mentor, had to correct Mayo that 10 and not 90 per cent of Indians, as reported in *Mother India*, suffered

[87]See Cornelia Sorabji to Lady Richmond, 6 Oct. 1927, in Folder no. 42, *Cornelia Sorabji Papers*, India Office Library and Records. Also see letters from Sorabji to Mayo, dated 1 and 6 Sept. 1927, in Folder no. 38, Ser. 1, Box 5, *K.M. Papers*.

from venereal disease![88] Other highly sensationalized claims in
Mother India about the sexual degeneracy of Indians also under-
mined many of the problems touched upon in the book. Mayo
claimed, for example, that it was general practice for mothers
in India to stimulate their children sexually to keep them from
crying and for Indian parents routinely to condone the use of
young boys for the sexual pleasure of older men (p. 86). Such
claims only made *Mother India* into an easy target for her critics.

If *Mother India*, nevertheless, became an important episode
in the history of the woman question in colonial India, that was
because of the particular historical moment of its appearance.
Because *Mother India* burst on the scenes at a critical turning
point in the histories of both British imperialism and Indian
nationalism, it became the focus for a redeployment of the
woman question in India. The changes in British imperial policy toward India in the 1920s had created new conditions for the
strategic redeployment of the woman question in India in fur-
thering the imperialist agenda. The momentous declaration of
E.M. Montagu, the Secretary of State for India, in 1917 had
ushered in a dramatic shift in imperial thinking on India. With
this declaration British official policy in India recognized for the
first time, at least in principle, the development of self-
governing institutions for India, even though the nature and
pace of this change was kept firmly in government hands. The
political reforms proposed in the Government of India Act of
1919 were designed to embody this new imperial order. Even
these limited changes, however, provoked tremendous anxiety
among die-hard imperialists about the future of the British Empire in India. The hard-line imperialist position was defined
against what it perceived as the growing support for the nationalist cause in India among sections of the British public, espe-

[88]Adams to Mayo, 19 Jan. 1928, in Folder 42, Ser. 1, Box 6, *K.M.
Papers*. Several women doctors, both British and Indian, challenged
Mayo's figures on women and children, see Dr. Margaret Balfour's letter
to the *Times of India*, quoted in *Bengalee*, 11 Oct. 1927, p. 4; also see the
objections raised by Dr. Alice Pennell (Cornelia Sorabji's sister) about
Mayo's statistics, cited in Sorabji to Richmond, n.d., in Folder no. 42,
Cornelia Sorabji Papers.

cially around the Labour Party. Hence, the outgoing Conservative Government in Britain, in an effort to put its own stamp on the pace of political change in India, announced the formation of the Indian Statutory Commission to examine the workings of the new political reforms in November 1927, a year earlier then had been provided for under the provisions of the Act of 1919. Mayo's imperialist collaborators had all along hoped that her book would be completed in time to influence the debate in the British Parliament over the composition of the Statutory Commission.[89] Her supporters would have been gratified to find that free copies of *Mother India* had, indeed, been distributed to every Member of Parliament in Britain by private initiative before the start of the deliberations over the composition of the Statutory Commission, also known as the Simon Commission.[90] The almost unanimous support that all the major political parties in Britain, including the Labour Party, gave to the appointment of an "all-white" Simon Commission to investigate political reforms in India—one that deliberately excluded all Indians—may well have been influenced, as nationalist leaders charged, by the impact of *Mother India*. British imperialists were keenly aware of the impact of *Mother India* as a caution to liberal sentiments in a Britain threatening to concede too much to the political aspirations of the Indians. Hence, imperialist-feminist Eleanor Rathbone was especially eager to see a cheaper edition of *Mother India* made available to members of the Labour Party in Britain who, she believed, "badly need the corrective of [Mayo's] book because of their tendency to espouse self-government anywhere."[91] The tremendous

[89]See Adams to Mayo, 10 Jan. 1927, in Folder no. 36, Ser. 1, Box 5, *K.M. Papers*. For a general history of the Statutory Commission, see S.R. Bakshi, *Simon Commission and Indian Nationalism* (Delhi: Munshiram Manoharlal, 1977).

[90]Lady Lyttleton, who undertook to find out the identity of the donor of *Mother India*, discovered that the book had been distributed by a private individual; see Letter to the Editor, *Times*, 14 Jan. 1928; and Report in the *New York Times*, 14 Jan. 1928, p. 6.

[91]Letter from Rathbone to Mayo, dated 24 August 1927, in Folder no. 37, Ser. 1, Box 5, *K.M. Papers*. For a similar sentiment about the impor-

attention that *Mother India's* portrayal of Indian women received from imperialists, then, was directed as much at pro-Indian sentiments in Britain as at nationalists in India.

The 1920s were also the period when Indian nationalism itself came of age. With it came new imperatives that seemed to demand a fresh deployment of the woman question in India. The emergence of Gandhi on the all-India scene in 1919 and the adoption by the Indian National Congress in 1920 of Gandhi's Non-Cooperation Movement, with its goal of *Swaraj*, had breathed new life into the nationalist movement in India. After the dramatic days of the Non-Cooperation Movement, however, Gandhi had himself withdrawn suddenly from active political struggle in favor of social reform work. Much of the 1920s, in fact, were dominated by the seemingly more mundane concerns of Indian politicians of various persuasions who were engaged in readjusting and realigning their relation to the Congress and to one another within the new constitutional framework of the Government of India Act of 1919. This period also witnessed a reconsolidation and exacerbation of various rival politics based on differences of class, caste, religion, and region within the broader anticolonial struggle. It was against this background that the Indian National Congress in December 1927, at the urging of a group of young radicals led by Jawaharlal Nehru, for the first time entertained a resolution supporting the idea of "complete independence" for India. While as yet a minority demand, strongly resisted by the majority of the Congress that favored "dominion status" for India within the British Empire, this demand would become by 1929 the official platform of the Indian National Congress. The debate on the woman question during the *Mother India* controversy would become a vehicle for Indian nationalism to stake its claim as the only truly modernizing force in colonial Indian society, wresting that claim away from the colonial govern-

tance of making *Mother India* available to the Trades Unions and the Labour Party in Britain, see Sorabji to Richmond, 6 Oct. 1927, in Folder no. 42, *Cornelia Sorabji Papers.* Also see Mesbahuddin Ahmed, "Indian Political Divisions and the British Labour Party (1919–1924): Some Reflections," *Journal of Indian History* (1982): pp. 161–77.

ment, on the one hand, and asserting it against rival political movements within India, on the other.[92] Mayo's foray into the woman question, then, received more than its share of attention from Indian nationalists as well. It was, indeed, the changing imperatives of British imperialism and Indian nationalism in the 1920s that helped make a book, which was hardly original in its subject or exceptional in its argument, the center of an unprecedented international controversy.

The massive imperialist/nationalist controversy over *Mother India* left the woman question in India transformed. The controversy, indeed, had the effect of consolidating the claims of the organized women's movement in India and of middle-class Indian women to represent what came to be touted as the "authentic voice of modern Indian womanhood" in debates over the condition of women in India.[93] The controversy thus marked an important turning point in the history of the woman question in colonial India: henceforth, the contributions of middle-class Indian women and of the organized women's movement in India would prove more difficult to ignore.

It is ironic, however, that a book that scarcely acknowledged the agency of Indian women themselves became the means for providing greater visibility to the contributions of the organized women's movement in India. The controversy

[92]See Mrinalini Sinha, "The Lineage of the 'Indian' Modern: Rhetoric, Agency, and the Sarda Act in Late Colonial India," in *Gender, Sexuality and Colonial Modernities*, ed. Antoinette Burton (London: Routledge, 1999).

[93]The quotation is from the foreword, written by Sarojini Naidu, for a collection of essays by Indian women, published in the wake of the *Mother India* controversy, see *Women in Modern India: Fifteen Papers by Indian Women Writers*, ed. Evelyn C. Gedge and Mithan Choksi (Bombay: D.B. Tarporewala Sons and Co., 1929). For an analysis of the historical production of a so-called authentic voice of modern Indian womanhood in late colonial India, see Mrinalini Sinha, "Gender in the Critiques of Colonialism and Nationalism: Locating the 'Indian Woman,' " in *Feminists Revision History*, ed. Ann-Louise Shapiro (New Brunswick: Rutgers University Press, 1994), pp. 246–75; reprinted in *Feminism and History*, ed. Joan Wallach Scott (Oxford: Oxford University Press, 1996), pp. 477–504.

over *Mother India* had coincided with the gradual incorporation of more elite and middle-class Indian women into the public life of the new nation-in-the-making.[94] By the mid-1920s Indian women, albeit a very tiny fraction thereof, had secured the right to vote and to be elected to the provincial legislatures from the new Indian legislators in most of the provinces of British India.[95] Although the first two women candidates who stood for election to the newly constituted legislative councils were defeated, a representative of the Women's Indian Association (WIA) was nominated to the Madras Legislative Council. Dr. Muthulakshmi Reddi, the first Indian woman legislator, also became the first woman ever to be elected as deputy president of a legislative body.[96] The number of women municipal councillors and Justices of Peace, especially in the "advanced" provinces of Madras and Bombay, was also on a steady rise. The Indian National Congress, the leading nationalist organization in India, had already appointed its first Indian woman president, Sarojini Naidu, in 1925. The principle of equality on the basis of sex in future political settlements was further affirmed by the All-Parties Constitution or the Nehru Report of 1928.

Women's organizations themselves were becoming more active on an all-India level on behalf of various reforms for women. The predominantly southern-based Women's Indian

[94]For an overview of the role of women in colonial Indian politics, see Geraldine Forbes, *The New Cambridge History of India IV.2: Women in Modern India* (Cambridge: Cambridge University Press, 1996).

[95]The 1920s were an important period for the history of elite women's involvement in public life in India, see *Annual Reports of the Women's India Association*, especially for the years 1920 to 1930 (National Archives of India, Fawcett Library, and Adyar Library and Research Centre in Madras). Also see M.E. Cousins, *What Women Have Gained by the Reforms* (Madras: Besant Press, n.d.); *The Awakening of Asian Womanhood* (Madras: Ganesh and Co., 1922); and K. Chattopadhyay et al., *The Awakening of Indian Women* (Madras: Everyman's Press, 1939).

[96]See Mrs. Reddy (also written as "Reddi"), *Autobiography of Dr. (Mrs.) S. Muthulakshmi Reddy (A Pioneer Woman Legislator)* (Madras: M. Reddi, 1964); and *The Pathfinder: Dr. Muthulakshmi Reddy*, ed. Dr. Aparna Basu (New Delhi: AIWC Pub., 1987).

Association (WIA) had increased its profile across the country in the campaign for women's franchise. Throughout the 1920s, moreover, the WIA and its several branch organizations all over the country held meetings and passed resolutions on behalf of various private bills that had been successively introduced in the Central Legislative Assembly in Delhi to raise the age of marriage and of consent for girls in India.[97] Reddi introduced similar reform bills for women in the Madras Legislative Council. The WIA, moreover, sponsored the first All-India Women's Education Conference (AIWC) in 1926. The first conference, a gathering of some two thousand mainly upper-caste and middle-class women, was held in Poona in January 1927 with the express aim of addressing proposals for the education of women in India. Recognizing the negative impact of child marriage and premature maternity on female education, however, the conference also passed unanimous resolutions against child marriage and in favor of raising the age of consent for Indian girls. The AIWC in Poona laid the foundations for what became one of the most ambitious all-India organizational structures to represent the views of women on social and educational reforms in India.[98] The new level of involvement of Indian women in the national life of India was significant enough to attract the attention of the Simon Commission, which commented on this development in its report on the political and constitutional developments in India.[99]

[97]For the WIA's involvement in child marriage reform even before *Mother India*, see *Stri Dharma* 8, no. 9 (July 1925), pp. 132–33; and no. 11 (Sept. 1925): p. 163; *Annual Reports of the WIA*, especially for the years 1924–25 and 1925–26; and "Social Welfare Measures," 1921–28, File no. 7, *Muthulakshmi Reddi Papers*, Nehru Memorial Museum and Library, New Delhi.

[98]See *AIWC Papers, File nos. 1–12*, Nehru Memorial Museum and Library, New Delhi; and AIWC Diamond Jubilee 1927–87. For the history of the AIWC, see Aparna Basu and Bharati Ray, *Women's Struggle: A History of the All India Women's Conference, 1927–1990* (New Delhi: Manohar, 1990).

[99]The Statutory Commission or the Simon Commission Report stated that "the beginning of a movement among certain Indian women is one of the most encouraging signs of India's progress"; quoted in *Stri Dharma*

This emerging all-India women's movement and nascent middle-class Indian feminism that had been slighted and ignored in Mayo's *Mother India* brought their weight to bear on the controversy. The responses of Indian women to *Mother India*, both as individuals and in the independent women's movement, were overwhelmingly critical of the book. Leading women politicians were conspicuous by their presence at the largest protest meeting held against *Mother India* in India at the Calcutta Town Hall. Sarojini Naidu, arguably the most influential female figure in the nationalist and the women's movements in India, sent a telegram of support that was read at the Calcutta Town Hall meeting.[100] Women also met separately in their *mahila samitis* and in other women's organizations all over the country to pass resolutions condemning *Mother India*. Indian women took the opportunity to condemn Mayo not only in various meetings held in India and abroad but also in dozens of reviews and letters in the general as well as in specifically women's journals and newspapers. A wide spectrum of women's journals in English and in vernacular languages in India expressed criticism of Mayo's self-appointed role as the champion of Indian women. Kamala Sathianadhan's sarcastic editorial in the *Indian Ladies Magazine* captured the resentment that many middle-class Indian women felt toward Mayo's contribution:

16, no. 12 (Oct. 1933): p. 628. Sir John Simon had himself attended the second AIWC session held in Delhi. His private notes on his impressions of the India women's movement were later adopted in the commission's report: "The women's movement in India holds the key of progress. . . . the work that has been done by Indian women themselves in breaking down opposition, in rousing interest, and in letting light into dark places is beyond all praise"; see Folder no. 86, *Sir John Simon Papers*, India Office Library and Records.

[100]Among those present at the meeting were Sarala Devi Chaudhrani, Latika Basu, and Jyotirmoyee Ganguly; see *Bengalee*, 6 Sept. 1927, p. 3. Also see *Amrita Bazar Patrika*, 6 Sept 1927, p. 6. Sarojini Naidu's telegram to the meeting read: "The mouths of liars rot and perish with their own lies, but the glory of Indian womanhood shines pure and as the morning star"; quoted in *Forward*, 7 Sept. 1927, p. 5.

We honour Miss Mayo for her courage in not caring for resentments and accusations; we congratulate her on her public spirit in "shouldering the task" of "holding the mirror" to that part of the human race which is a "physical menace" to the world; we do not question her ability or her cleverness in writing this book; but we do deny her the self-presumption that she is "in a position to present conditions and their bearings," and we do not for a minute admit her "plain speech" as the "faithful wounds of a friend"; for she is no friend of ours.[101]

The editors of *Chand,* a popular Hindi-language paper for women, similarly chided Mayo for her gross exploitation of the condition of Indian women for her own political agenda.[102]

Several women activists, including Reddi, issued strong statements criticizing *Mother India* on behalf of organized women in India.[103] Women activists, indeed, did much to engage Indian women themselves in responding to *Mother India.* Among the several books written in response to *Mother India,* for example, there were a number that were written by women and for women in India: Charulata Devi wrote *The Fair Sex of India: A Reply to "Mother India"* (1929); Chandravati Lakhanpal, the author of the prize-winning book *Striyon ki Stithi* (The Situation of Women) (1934), wrote *Mother India Ka Jawab* (*The Reply to Mother India*) (1928); Uma Nehru, a frequent contributor to the women's journal *Stri Darpan,* wrote *Mother India Aur Uska Jawab: Miss Mayo ki "Mother India" [Sachitra Hindi Anuwad] jis me Srimati Uma Nehru likhit bhumika tatha paschimi samajavad ke vishay me Miss Mayo se do do bate* (Mother India and Its Reply: A True Translation of Miss Mayo's "Mother India" with a Dialogue between Mrs. Uma Nehru and Miss Mayo on Western

[101]Quoted in Padmini Sengupta, *The Portrait of an Indian Woman* (Calcutta: Y.M.C.A., 1956), pp. 179–80. For a fuller discussion of the role of Indian women in the *Mother India* controversy, see Mrinalini Sinha, "Reading *Mother India*: Empire, Nation, and the Female Voice," *Journal of Woman's History* 6, no. 2 (Summer 1994): pp. 6–44.

[102]"Bharat-Mata (Mother India)," *Chand* (Nov. 1927): pp. 7–16.

[103]Reddi responded to Mayo's thesis, especially Mayo's obsession with sex, in some detail; see "Comment on Miss Mayo's Book about Indians" and "Miss Mayo Answered" in "Speeches and Writings," vol. 2, pts. 1–2, *Muthulakshmi Reddi Papers.*

Civilization) (1928); and Padmabai Sanjeeva Rau, an active educationist and Theosophist, wrote *Women's Views on Indian Problems* (1927) as a direct challenge to Mayo's *Mother India*. Cornelia Sorabji's positive review of *Mother India* in the *Englishman* stands out as an exception to the more common pattern of Indian women's public response to Mayo.[104] As president of the Federation of University Women in India, however, Sorbaji faced a revolt from hostile female graduates in Calcutta for her reluctance to denounce Mayo's *Mother India* publicly.[105] The dominant response to *Mother India* among the active and articulate section of middle-class women in India was noted by the male author of *Sister India:* "the women of India have held meetings in every part of India and have unanimously protested against *her* description of their trouble."[106]

Although Indian women's responses to *Mother India* did reflect the full range of positions found in the general nationalist critiques of *Mother India*, the position of the independent women's movement in India was consistent with its goals on reforms for women. The position adopted by the women's movement on *Mother India* was a delicate balance between condemnation of the book itself and recognition of the urgent need for the reform of women's position in India. The biggest women's protest meeting against *Mother India*, which was sponsored by the WIA together with several other women's organizations and was held in Triplicane in Madras, reflected this sentiment. The resolutions passed at the meeting denied

[104]Cornelia Sorabji, "Mother India—The Incense of Service: What Sacrifice Can We Make?" *Englishman*, pt. 1, 31 Aug. 1927, pp. 6–7; and pt. 2, 1 Sept. 1927, pp. 6–9. Most other Indian women who had met Mayo during her visit to India, such as Mona Bose and Dorothy Roy, quickly distanced themselves from her book; see Sinha, "Gender in the Critiques of Colonialism and Nationalism."

[105]See letters from Sorabji to Lady Richmond, 12 Apr. 1928; 18 Apr. 1928; 26 Apr. 1928; 19 July 1928, in Folder no. 43, *Cornelia Sorabji Papers*. Also Letter from Sorabji to Mayo, dated 21 Nov. 1928, in Folder no. 50, Ser. 1, Box 7, *K.M. Papers*.

[106]World Citizen (S.G. Warty), *Sister India: A Critical Examination of and a Reasoned Reply to Miss Katherine Mayo's Mother India* (Bombay: Sister India Office, 1928) p. 143.

that "Indian womanhood as a whole is in a state of slavery, superstition, ignorance and degradation as Miss Mayo falsely concludes from individual instances and from statistics unproportioned to other balancing figures." But, at the same time, the conference recognized the existence of several social evils in India and urged the need for legislation that would prohibit child marriage, early parentage, enforced widowhood, dedication of girls to temples, and commercialized immorality in India.[107] The speech of Jayalakshmi Kumar at the Indian women's protest meeting bears quoting at some length:

> If [Mayo] had done something for us, lived with us and tried to understand us with sympathy in order to help, we would gladly welcome her comment. But her setting out on a quest for finding fault with a great country, simply because others overpraised it, cannot meet with any sympathy. . . . She deals in her book with child marriage and suggests all kinds of loathsome things as contributing towards this custom. But this was uncalled for, as the enlightened are trying their utmost to stop this evil. . . . She talks of the British being unable to pressure natives to accept reform. That is exactly our complaint; the natives of the land can compel with impunity where a foreigner cannot and that is why we want political freedom so that we may compel social improvement. . . . *Let us endeavour to change the really bad social customs [in India] and let that be our protest against all such books.*[108]

The emphasis on social reform together with condemnation of *Mother India* characterized the response of organized women and their journals, such as the *Stri Dharma*, the official voice of the WIA.

The response of the women's movement to Mayo's *Mother India* was perhaps most clearly manifest in the efforts to secure the passage of the long-delayed Child Marriage Restraint

[107]*Stri Dharma* 10, no. 12 (Oct. 1927): p. 18; and the report of the WIA protest meeting in *Hindu* (29 Sept. 1927) in "India," vol. 2, in Folder 207, Ser. 4, Box 37, *K.M. Papers*. The protest of the women's movement in India and the resolutions passed at the protest meeting were sent to various sympathetic women's journals in Britain; see *Jus Suffragi: The International Women Suffrage News* 22 (Nov. 1927): p. 27. I am grateful to Angela Woollacott and Carrol Pursell for this reference.
[108]*Stri Dharma* 10, no. 12 (Oct. 1927): p. 182; my emphasis.

Bill or Sarda Bill in India. The passage of the Child Marriage Restraint Act in 1929 was rightly seen as a triumph of the fledgling all-India women's movement.[109] Women's organizations in India had lobbied for child marriage reform well before the publication of *Mother India*, but support from the government had not been forthcoming. The women's movement thus seized upon the publicity over *Mother India* to gain support for the Sarda Bill both from the colonial government and from male nationalist leaders. The frustration that women activists felt, especially against the unsympathetic attitude of the colonial government, was echoed in Reddi's speech, "Government's Attitude towards Indian Social Reforms," at the Indian Social Reform Conference held in Madras in December 1927:

we all know what the government's attitude was when Mr. Sarda's Bill was introduced. Even at this stage, in spite of our meetings, in spite of our memorials and petitions, the government member Honorable Crerar brought a dilatory motion to delay such a good and urgent legislation on the plea of religious neutrality. Cannot the enlightened British government follow in the footsteps of the progressive native states even if they do not want to go against the orthodox feelings? Even we women have become discontent and have begun to grumble at the attitude of our government which is indifferent and unsympathetic to social legislation.[110]

The same conference also criticized *Mother India* and expressed the hope that the publicity surrounding the book would at least force the colonial government out of its long apathy. Women activists and social reformers, therefore, simultaneously distanced themselves from *Mother India* and utilized the publicity surrounding the book to their advantage: to embarrass an apathetic government into reversing its obstructionist attitude to-

[109]For a history of child marriage reforms in India, see Geraldine Forbes,"Women and Modernity: The Issue of Child Marriage in India," *Women's Studies International Quarterly* 2 (1979): pp. 407–9; and Barbara Ramusack, "Women's Organizations and Social Change: The Age of Marriage Issue in India," in *Women and World Change*, ed. Naomi Black and A.B. Cottrell (London: Sage Pub., 1981), pp. 198–216.

[110]See "Speeches and Writings," vol. 2, pt. 2, *Muthulakshmi Reddi Papers*.

ward various bills addressing the problem of child marriage that had been sponsored by Indian legislators.

The publicity surrounding *Mother India,* moreover, also helped keep nationalist politicians in line over the Sarda Bill. On occasion, for example, Reddi threatened to embarrass male politicians who were dragging their feet on this important piece of social reform legislation with revelations that could match Mayo's tales of horror in *Mother India.*[111] Women activists lobbied Indian politicians in the assembly to support Sarda's bill by urging them to neutralize the charges leveled at all Indians in *Mother India.* The representatives of the women's organizations met with, and secured the support of, the leaders of all the important Indian political parties in the assembly, such as Motilal Nehru, M.R. Jayakar, and Muhammad Ali Jinnah, for the Sarda Bill. Gandhi, who as a staunch non-cooperationist was boycotting the assembly, also issued a call to Indians in the assembly to support the Sarda Bill as a national duty. The debates on the Sarda Bill in the Legislative Assembly were some indication of the success of a strategy that identified social reform as the most fitting nationalist rejoinder to *Mother India.*

The Sarda Act, indeed, was considered not a contribution of Mayo's *Mother India* but the most fitting nationalist riposte—fashioned in large part as a result of the efforts of Indian women activists themselves—to Mayo's *Mother India.*[112] The organized women's movement had been actively involved in the eventual passage of the Sarda Bill. Although the women's movement had failed to persuade the viceroy to nominate at least two Indian women to the all-male Central Legislative Assembly to participate in the debate over the Sarda Bill, it secured the nomination of one of its members, Rameshwari Nehru, to the Age of Consent Committee appointed by the government to investigate the effects of premature sexual

---

[111]See "Social Welfare Measures," pt. 1, File no. 8, *Muthulakshmi Reddi Papers.*

[112]The WIA and the AIWC, however, recommended a higher age of marriage than was adopted in the Sarda Bill.

intercourse and the need to raise the age of consent.[113] Women's organizations remained galvanized throughout the deliberations of the Sarda Bill in the assembly and during the investigations of the Age of Consent Committee. The women of the Arya Samaj in Simla, for example, picketed outside the meetings of the assembly held in Simla, carrying placards in support of the Sarda Bill; another three hundred women from the AIWC attended the discussions of the Sarda Bill in the assembly in Delhi; and the AIWC sent an official delegation to present evidence before the Age of Consent Committee during its investigations in Patna. The efforts of the women's movement helped to demonstrate that public opinion, at least among the organized and articulate section of Indian women, opposed child marriage and was in favor of a higher age of consent for girls in India.

It was thus with the help of the Indian women's movement that the first important piece of social reform legislation for women in India since the Age of Consent Act of 1891 was passed in 1929. The attempts of Mayo and her supporters in the West to give all credit for the Sarda Act to *Mother India* was felt as a deliberate slight by both nationalists and women activists in India.[114] The official records of the Indian women's movement, as well as the personal accounts written by Indian women active in the efforts to secure child marriage reform, acknowledge no debt to Mayo's *Mother India* for the Sarda Act.[115] In fact, Harbilas

[113]*Legislative Department 3-II/28. A, 1928*; and *Home Judicial File no. 382/27, 1927.*

[114]For a sample of some Western press coverage that credited Mayo for the passage of the Sarda Act, see *New York Times,* 10 Feb. 1928, p. 13.; for Britain, see *Edinburgh Evening News,* 10 Feb. 1928; *Star,* 10 Feb. 1928; and *Reynolds Illustrated News,* 12 Feb. 1928, in "Great Britain," vol. 2 in Folder 207, Ser. 4, Box 38, *K.M. Papers.*

[115]For women's accounts of their contribution to the passage of the Sarda Bill, see Kamaladevi Chattopadhyay, *Inner Recesses, Outer Spaces: Memoirs* (New Delhi: Navrang, 1986), pp. 113–17; Dhanvanthi Rama Rau, *An Inheritance: The Memoirs of Dhanvanthi Rama Rau* (London: Harper and Row, 1977), p. 151; Jahan Ara Shahnawaz, *Father and Daughter* (Lahore: Nigarishat,1971), pp. 97–98; Hansa Mehta, *Indian Women* (Delhi: Butala and Co.,1981), p. 63; and Amrit Kaur, *Challenge to Women* (Allahabad:

Sarda, the architect of the act, had the following to say of Mayo's connection to his measure:

A few there are, however, who do not belong to India, and who are unhappy over the abolition of child marriage. Their chief representative is Miss Mayo and they fear that when child marriage disappears their profession of ruling the country on which they flourish shall have gone. By belittling the enormous importance of the new law, they betray their hostility to the advancement of the country.[116]

If anything, then, Mayo was seen by the main actors in the campaign for the Sarda Bill as an opponent rather than a supporter of the abolition of child marriage from India.

The growing self-assertion of the women's movement in India during the *Mother India* controversy was especially marked in its relation to Western women's organizations. Some Western feminists, especially in Britain, had seized upon Mayo's book as an opportunity to articulate an imperialist-feminist agenda for their own movement. The British women's movement, having recently won the right to vote for women in Britain, felt free to redirect its energies to the "white woman's burden."[117] Eleanor Rathbone, president of the National Union of Societies for Equal Citizenship (NUSEC), emerged in the wake of the *Mother India* controversy as the most influential voice in Britain in favor of taking up the imperial responsibility for the women of India.[118]

New Literature, 1946), p. 5. Also see File nos. 7, 8, 12, *AIWC Files;* and "Social Welfare Measures," File nos. 8, 9, and 10, *Muthulakshmi Reddi Papers.*

[116]Quoted in *Stri Dharma* 13, no. 3 (Jan. 1930): pp. 77–78.

[117]For the history of British feminism's investment in the "upliftment" of Indian women, see Antoinette Burton, "The White Woman's Burden: British Feminists and 'The Indian Woman,' 1865–1915," in Chaudhuri and Strobel, *Western Women and Imperialism,* pp. 137–57; and *Burdens of History: British Feminists, Indian Women, and Imperial Culture, 1865–1915* (Chapel Hill: University of North Carolina Press, 1994).

[118]For background on Eleanor Rathbone, see Mary D. Stocks, *Eleanor Rathbone: A Biography* (London: Victor Gollancz Ltd., 1949); and Susan Pederson "Rathbone and Daughter: Feminism and the Father at the Fin-de-Siècle," *Journal of Victorian Culture* 1, no. 1 (Spring 1996): pp. 98–117. For a discussion of Rathbone's relation to Indian women in particular, see

Inspired by Mayo's depiction of the plight of Indian women, Rathbone spent the next decade focusing her energies, and those of her organization, on the problems of Indian women. *Mother India* was the inspiration for many of Rathbone and the NUSEC's initiatives for Indian women: the *Women's Leader and Common Cause*, which was the official organ of the NUSEC and was edited by Rathbone's companion Elizabeth Macadem, gave extensive publicity to, and published favorable reviews of, *Mother India*; Rathbone herself wrote a powerful defense of Mayo in "Has Katherine Mayo Slandered Mother India?"; the NUSEC, under Rathbone, organized two controversial conferences in London, inspired by *Mother India*, on the position of Indian women; Rathbone set up the Office of the Women of India Survey to undertake further investigation into the conditions of Indian women as depicted in *Mother India*; she lobbied British officials using *Mother India* to demonstrate the necessity of nominating a representative of the British women's organizations to the Simon commission to examine the implications of political reform for Indian women; and, finally, Rathbone also used the revelations in *Mother India* to impress upon British women's organizations and the British Parliament the significance of the passage of the Age of Marriage Act in Britain, which would raise the legal age of marriage for girls in Britain as an example to India, which urgently needed the benefits of such a legislative measure.[119]

Rathbone, however, quickly discovered that even her seemingly well-intentioned efforts on behalf of Indian women were met with skepticism from the Indian women's movement because of her explicit alliance with Mayo's *Mother India*. The representatives of the Indian women's movement who were present in London took every opportunity not only to distance

---

Barbara Ramusack, "Cultural Missionaries, Maternal Imperialists, Feminist Allies: British Women Activists in India, 1865–1945," in Chaudhuri and Strobel, *Western Women and Imperialism*, pp. 119–36.

[119]See article by E.F.R., "Mother India: Its Claim on the Women's Movement," *Women's Leader and Common Cause*, no. 26, 5 Aug. 1927, pp. 231–32; see also *Women's Leader and Common Cause*, no. 47, 30 Dec. 1927, pp. 373–74.

themselves from *Mother India* but also to challenge Rathbone's efforts to assume responsibility for Indian women in total ignorance of the initiatives of Indian women themselves.[120] Indian women sought, and utilized, the platforms provided by other women's organizations in Britain that were willing to recognize the Indian women's movement. The British Commonwealth League, founded by Australian feminists in Britain, provided representatives of the Indian women's movement in London, such as Dorothy Jinarajadasa, Hannah Sen, Dhanvanthi Rama Rao, and Mrinalini Sen, a forum for publicizing their position during the *Mother India* controversy.[121] M. Chave Collisen, the president of the British Commonwealth League, had herself been suitably impressed during her visit to India, in the aftermath of the *Mother India* controversy, by the work being done for Indian women by Indian women themselves.[122] The combined efforts of sympathetic British women and Indian women in London helped to keep the challenge to Rathbone's imperialist-

[120]For Indian women's opposition to Rathbone's various initiatives inspired by *Mother India*, see Sinha, "Reading *Mother India*"; and "Gender in the Critiques of Colonialism and Nationalism." The conflict between Rathbone and Dhanvanthi Rama Rau at the Oct. 1929 conference in London received extensive coverage both in the general press and in the women's press in Britain and India; see *Statesman*, 9 Oct. 1929, p. 9; and 28 Nov. 1929, p. 8; *Times*, 8 Oct. 1929, p. 9; and 9 Oct. 1929, p. 9; *Stri Dharma* 13, nos. 1–2 (Dec. 1929): pp. 1–5; and *Women's Leader and Common Cause* 21, no. 38 (25 Oct. 1929): p. 286.

[121]See *Annual Reports British Commonwealth League*, Fawcett Library. The British Commonwealth League had a reputation in the women's movement in India for not being "imperialist"; see *Stri Dharma* 8, no. 12 (Oct. 1925): p. 181. Other British women's organizations that were also considered relatively sympathetic to the women's movement in India included the Women's International League for Peace and Freedom and the International Alliance for Suffrage and Equal Citizenship.

[122]*Conference Report: Women and the Future, 5–6 June, 1929, British Commonwealth League*, Fawcett Library. For the "new internationalism" represented by such organizations as the British Commonwealth League during the interwar period, see Angela Woollacott, "Inventing Commonwealth and Pan-Pacific Feminisms: Australian Women's Internationalist Activism in the 1920s–30s," *Gender and History* 10, no. 3 (Nov. 1998): pp. 425–48.

feminist initiatives before the public. Indeed, organized Indian women, eager to command respect within international feminist circles, took every opportunity to assert the position of the Indian women's movement. The delegation of Indian women to the International Congress of Women for Suffrage and Equal Citizenship in Berlin in 1929, for example, took special delight in defeating Rathbone's resolution on the age of marriage for boys and girls. Despite opposition from the entire British delegation, an amendment to Rathbone's resolution proposed by Dhanvanthi Rama Rau was passed, calling for an even higher age of marriage for boys.[123] The differences that arose during the *Mother India* controversy between Indian women activists and British women activists, like Rathbone, prompted representatives of the Indian women's movement in London to form the Indo-British Mutual Welfare League in 1929 to inform British women of the activities of organized women in India and to serve as a channel for Indian women to respond to friendly gestures from abroad. Hannah Sen, who was one of the founding members of this organization, traced the impetus for such an organization directly to the experiences of Indian women in London during the *Mother India* controversy.[124]

It was in large part due to the success with which Indian women were able to disseminate their position on *Mother India* to feminist circles in London that Rathbone was forced to take their position more seriously. Eventually, Rathbone, who was arguably one of the more influential names in the contemporary women's movement in Britain, recognized that her efforts to align the British women's movement with Mayo's *Mother India*, rather than with the burgeoning women's movement in India, was counterproductive to her own agenda: the claim that the British women's movement's interest in India was motivated not by politics but by concern for the welfare of women in India. Rathbone's *Child Marriage: The Indian Mino-*

[123]The women's movement in India saw this as a nationalist triumph; see Report of the conference in the *Stri Dharma* 12, no. 10 (Aug. 1929): pp. 434–35.

[124]Hannah Sen in *Stri Dharma* 13, no. 3 (Jan. 1930): pp. 83–85.

taur (1934) reflected how far she had been willing to come from her early association with Mayo's *Mother India*. While Rathbone's book shared *Mother India*'s general account of the causes and effects of child marriage in India, it neither let the colonial government off the hook for its obstructionist policy toward social reform in India nor failed to acknowledge the contributions of Indians themselves in addressing the problems of child marriage.[125] *Child Marriage* was well received by the women's movement in India and served to dispel some of Rathbone's reputation in India as an "English Katherine Mayo." By distancing herself from *Mother India*, Rathbone was able eventually to establish a partnership with select Indian women on women's issues in India as well as to build a career as a champion for the cause of Indian women in the British Parliament. Although Rathbone's imperialist views precluded any long-term alliance with the Indian women's movement, the *Mother India* controversy made Rathbone, and feminists in Britain more generally, much more sensitive to the contributions of the Indian women's movement.[126] The *Mother India* controversy thus served to provide greater recognition both in India and abroad for the role of middle-class Indian women and of the organized women's movement in the debate on the woman question in India.

The relative success of Indian women's interventions during the *Mother India* controversy, however, was a product both of the maturity of the women's movement itself and of its

[125]*Child Marriage: The Indian Minotaur* (London: George Allen and Unwin, 1934). Rathbone described her intentions to "adopt 'Mayo tactics' i.e. to write something that puts the truth as crudely and offensively as Miss Mayo does, but with this difference, that the responsibility should be placed where I believe it belongs, that is not only on Hindus but also on Mohammedans and on the British in India"; see Rathbone to Lothian, 29 Nov. 1931, in Folder 7, Box 93, *Eleanor Rathbone Papers*. The women's movement in India, however, approved of Rathbone's book; see the favorable mention in the *Stri Dharma* 17, no. 1 (Nov. 1933): pp. 20–23.

[126]For the differences that arose between Rathbone and the major women's organizations in India over the issue of women's franchise, see Rathbone's correspondence with Indian women in Box 93, *Eleanor Rathbone Papers*.

implications for the broader nationalist struggle for hegemony in late colonial India. For the "modernizing" of Indian gender relations already occupied a central place in the ideological struggle of "official" Indian nationalism both against British colonialism and against indigenous rivals in India. The platform of the nationalist movement had thus incorporated certain limited reforms for women, explained variously in terms of the necessity for modernizing certain outdated social practices affecting Indian women or of reviving the ancient freedoms that Indian women supposedly enjoyed in some golden past, as part of the nationalist agenda. Consequently the position of some of the most influential male-nationalist leaders on *Mother India* was often not very different from that of the women's movement. The actual range of nationalist responses to *Mother India*, of course, was vast. On one end of the scale were those who strongly vilified Mayo and denied defensively that there was any basis for a critique of women's position in India. There were also those who responded to Mayo's criticism in kind by turning their own critical lens on the "sex problems" of the United States and Britain. The most famous of this latter subgenre of nationalist responses to *Mother India* was K .L. Gauba's *Uncle Sham: The Strange Tale of a Civilization Run Amok* (1929), written, as the author himself proclaimed, as a *tu quoque* critique of U.S. society but without the benefit of even a three-month tour of the country![127] Still others quibbled with this or that aspect of Mayo's interpretation of the position of women in India only to avoid confronting the problems of Indian women. On the other end of the scale, however, were men like Gandhi and K. Natarajan, the famous editor of the *Indian Social Reformer*, who criticized Mayo's imperial agenda without ever denying that tremendous work still remained to be done to reform the position of women in India.[128] Men like

[127]*Uncle Sham* (Ludhiana: Times of India Corp. Ltd, 1929). See also p. 64 and pp. 116–18, *Oral History Transcript, K.L. Gauba*, pt. 1, Nehru Memorial Museum and Library.

[128]For Gandhi's famous review of *Mother India*, see *Young India* (15 Sept. 1927), in *The Collected Works of Mahatma Gandhi* (Ahemedabad:

Gandhi, Natarajan, Tagore, and Jawaharlal Nehru, to name a few, had responded to *Mother India* in ways that did not minimize the urgent need for reform. During the campaign for the Sarda Bill, therefore, women activists could count on support from important nationalist leaders against both the intransigence of the religious orthodoxy in India and the timidity of the colonial government. However superficial was the commitment of some political leaders to the Sarda Bill, as the representatives of the women's movement were to find out soon after the passage of the bill, Indian nationalism had emerged as a much more responsive ally for women's reform then British imperialism, despite Mayo's argument to the contrary in *Mother India*.

The alliance that was forged between Indian nationalism and Indian feminism in response to *Mother India* was instrumental in not only providing greater visibility for the independent women's movement in India but also in validating Indian nationalism's claim of displacing colonialism as the agent of modernity in late colonial India. The latter point was not lost on nationalist politicians, who were quick to recognize the strategic potential of foregrounding the so-called authentic voice of modern Indian womanhood in countering Mayo's attack on Indian nationalism. When Gandhi and the Congress hierarchy in India were urged to send a representative to the United States to undo the damage done to the nationalist cause by Mayo's *Mother India*, the choice of India's first "unofficial ambassador" to the United States fell on a woman. Sarojini Naidu was dispatched to the United States at the recommendation of Gandhi and the Congress leaders to counter Mayo's libel with a description of the "true" nature of Mother India. Naidu's mission in the United States was to make a case for the Indian nation as much as for Indian women. Hence, the topics for her extensive lecture tour in the United States included "The Political Situation in India" as well as "Interpretation of

Navajivan Publishing House, 1969), vol. 34, pp. 539–47. For K. Natarajan's response to *Mother India*, see *Miss Mayo's Mother India: A Rejoinder* (Madras: G.A. Natesan and Co., 1928).

the Ideals of Indian Womanhood."[129] The accommodation of individual women, and even of the independent women's movement, in the dominant nationalist response to *Mother India* helped in the efforts of Indian nationalism to establish its credentials—against British colonialism—as the truly modernizing force in late colonial India.

The further point about the alliance between the nationalist and women's movement in the *Mother India* controversy, however, was its effect on the marginalization of other socially radical critiques of gender, caste, and class hierarchies in India. The position of the anti-caste Self-Respect Movement, founded by E.V Ramaswami, also known as "Periyar," on *Mother India* is instructive in this regard. The Self-Respect Movement, as several scholars have suggested, took the critique both of Brahmanical domination and male domination in colonial Indian society much further than did either Gandhian nationalism or the middle-class women's movement.[130] The controversy over *Mother India* coincided with the final break between Periyar, a former Congressite and Gandhian, and Gandhi. The break was crystallized during Gandhi's tour of the south in 1927, at a time

[129]See Tara Ali Baig, *Sarojini Naidu* (New Delhi: Publications Division, Ministry of Information and Broadcasting, 1974), pp. 99–100; and Padmini Sengupta, *Sarojini Naidu* (Bombay: Asia Publishing House, 1966), pp. 197 and 209–11. For sample press coverage of Naidu's visit to the United States, see *Statesman*, 30 Jan. 1929, p. 10; *Stri Dharma* 11, no. 11 (Sept. 1928): p. 247; *New York Times*, 14 Oct. 1928, p. 14; 28 Oct. 1928, p. 6; and 3 March 1929, p. 15. Naidu herself recounts her experiences as India's ambassador to the United States; see Correspondence with Sarojini Naidu, 1928 and 1929, pts. 1–2, *Padmaja Naidu Papers*, Nehru Memorial Museum and Library.

[130]See E.V.R. Periyar, *Self-Respect Marriages* (Madras: Periyar Self Respect Propaganda Institute, 1983); also see Prabha Rani, "Women's Indian Association and the Self Respect Movement in Madras, 1925–1936: Perceptions on Women" (paper presented at the Third National Women's Studies Conference, Punjab University, Chandigarh, Oct. 1986); S. Anandhi, "Women's Question in the Dravidian Movement c. 1925–1948," *Social Scientist* 19, nos. 5–6 (1991): pp. 24–41; and Natalie Pickering, "Recasting the Indian Nation: Dravidian Nationalism Replies to the Women's Question," *Thatched Patio* (May–June 1993): pp. 1–20.

when he was reading *Mother India* and drafting his own famous response to the book, the "Drain Inspector's Report."[131] Gandhi met with representatives of the women's movement and of the Self-Respect Movement, including Periyar. While Gandhi accepted the request of the women's movement to speak out against the evils of child marriage and temple prostitution during his tour of the south, he refused the request of Periyar and the Self-Respecters to withdraw his public support for the *varnashramadharma*—that is, Gandhi's own idealized interpretation of the caste system.[132] The final break with Gandhi over his support for an idealized version of the caste system made Periyar and his supporters skeptical of the implications of Gandhian *Swaraj* for the lower castes as well as for women in India. It was against this background, then, that the Self-Respecters adopted a much more sympathetic response to Mayo's *Mother India* than did the representatives of either Gandhian nationalism or middle-class Indian feminism.

The nuances of the Self-Respect Movement's position on *Mother India*, however, were often lost in the overly simplistic polarization that reduced all positions to either the imperialist or the nationalist camp. For, despite its relative sympathy with *Mother India*, the point of the Self-Respect Movement's position was not to endorse Mayo's imperial views but to challenge the implicit gender, caste, and class hierarchies in the modernizing agenda of Indian nationalism. The Self-Respect Movement's stand on *Mother India*, however, drew strong public ire at the 1927 Social Reform Conference in Madras.[133] The Non-Brahman

[131]See *The Collected Works of Mahatma Gandhi* (Ahmedabad: Navajivan Trust, 1969), vol. 34, no. 429, p. 503; and no. 438, p. 521.

[132]For the early history of Periyar and the Self-Respect Movement, see N.K. Mangalamurugesan, *Self-Respect Movement in Tamil Nadu, 1920–1940* (Madurai: Koodal Publishers, 1981); and B.S. Chandrababu, *Social Protest and Its Impact on Tamil Nadu: with Reference to the Self Respect Movement (from 1920s to 1940s)* (Madras: Emerald Publishers, 1993).

[133]The controversy over Arya's disruption at the Social Reform Conference spilled over into the pages of the *Hindu*, as O. Kandasami Chettiar, the Congress representative, and Reddi exchanged barbs over their responsibilities for the disruption of the conference; see "Speeches and Writings," vol. 2, pt. 2, *Muthulakshmi Reddi Papers*.

Self Respecter, S.N. Arya, was the only speaker at the conference, which was held together with the annual meeting of
the Indian National Congress, to defend *Mother India* publicly
and to laud Mayo for helping the cause of social reform,
especially of child marriage reform in India. Arya's defense of
Mayo disrupted the conference and caused considerable embarrassment to Muthulakshmi Reddi, who was one of the
conference organizers. Arya's mention of Mayo in connection
with the Sarda Bill threatened to jeopardize support for the
bill. Mayo and her supporters eagerly watched such developments in the hope of recruiting new allies for their own case
in favor of British imperialism in India.[134] Yet, unlike Mayo,
the various Non-Brahman Youth Leagues in Madras were
genuinely concerned with promoting reform and supported
Reddi and other activists during the passage of the Sarda Bill
against the intransigence of orthodox Hindus. The nuances of
the Self-Respect Movement's position were evident in the discussions on *Mother India* in the pages of the *Kudi Arasu*, the

[134]Mayo and her supporters took note of, and made inquiries about,
the report of the conference published in the *Hindu*; see Field to Hayes,
Madras, 17 Apr. 1928, in Folder no. 45, Ser. 1, Box 6, *K.M. Papers*. Mayo
was more successful in her correspondence with Bhagat Ram, representative of the *Audi Achhut (Depressed Classes) Sabha* of Ferozepur Cantt (Punjab). Bhagat Ram became Mayo's frequent correspondent; he praised her
Mother India and was extremely critical of the nationalist position in India;
see, for example, Folder 42, Ser. 1, Box 6, *K.M. Papers*. Bhagat Ram's
favorable review of *Mother India* and his attack on leaders of the women's
movement and nationalist movement in India for being critical of Mayo
received attention in imperialist circles in Britain; see Bhagat Ram, "The
Hardships of Women in Hinduism," *Women's Leader and Common Cause*
20, no. 27 (10 Aug. 1928): pp. 219–20; and Bhagat Ram, "Miss Mayo's
'Mother India,' " in the papers of the Duchess of Atholl, an ardent opponent of self-government for India, in File no. 1, *Atholl Papers*, India Office
Library and Records. Mayo's efforts to use Dr. Ambedkar, who had
emerged as the national leader for the Depressed Classes in India, were
less successful. Dr. Ambedkar requested, and succeeded in getting,
Mayo to correct the wrong she had done him in her book *Volume 2*; see
Ambedkar to Mayo, 24 Feb. 1931, in Folder no. 57, Ser. 1, Box 8, *K.M.
Papers*.

official voice of the movement. These discussions were later published by Kovai Ayamutthu, a longtime Periyar follower, in *Meyo Kutru Moyya Poyya* (Mayo's Charges—True or False) (1929). Periyar, who wrote the preface for Ayamutthu's book, endorsed the views contained therein as representing those of the Self-Respect Movement as a whole. On the one hand, Ayamutthu offered a vigorous defense of Mayo from charges of falsehood and praised her for exposing both the tyranny of man over woman and of Brahman over non-Brahman in India.[135] Yet, on the other hand, Ayamutthu's chapter on "British Rule" also made clear that he did not share Mayo's unqualified optimism about the role of British rule in India. The stand of the Self-Respect Movement on *Mother India* did not fit the dominant terms of the controversy. Insofar as the dominant terms of the *Mother India* controversy sought preemptively to collapse the position of the Self-Respect Movement within an imperialist/nationalist logic, however, it made possible an escape from the combined gender, caste, and class critique of Indian nationalism by Periyar and his followers.

What the success of the redeployment of the woman question in the *Mother India* controversy achieved, then, was the consolidation of a certain type of nationalism and feminism in the nationalist and women's movements of the time. For the *Mother India* controversy had cemented an alliance between Indian nationalism and Indian feminism that would have far-reaching implications for both.[136] This, of course, neither precluded criticism of the patriarchal aspects of Indian nationalism by leaders of the women's movement nor of the "Westernized" and elitist character of the women's movement by leaders of the nationalist movement. What it did underscore, however, was a shared commitment to certain ideas about the

[135]K. Ayamutthu, *Meyo Kutru Moyya Poyya* (Kanchipuram: Kumaran Printing Press, 1929).

[136]For a discussion of one implication of this resolution of the woman question, whose origins could be traced to the controversy over *Mother India*, see Rosie Thomas, "Sanctity and Scandal: The Mythologization of Mother India," *Quarterly Review of Film and Video* 11 (1989): pp. 11–30.

Indian nation, its past and its future, among the predominantly elite and upper-caste composition of both movements. The following comment on *Mother India* by Reddi, who unlike many of her peers in the women's movement never joined the Congress, reveals the contours of the shared understanding of "Indianness" that fueled the imagination of many of the leaders of the nationalist and of the independent women's movement alike: "[I] want to impress on all people of Miss Mayo's type that Hindu religion does not sanction the practice of all those social ills that are at present preying upon our society, and it is the centuries of foreign invasions, oppression and subordination that must account for the present deplorable condition of India."[137] It was the meaning that was attached to the historical legacy of Hinduism and, through a frequent slippage, of Indianness that eventually separated the nationalist movement and the independent women's movement not just from Mayo's imperialist critique of Hindu culture but also from the Self-Respect Movement's critique of an idealized Aryan/Hindu past.[138] Even when the women's movement asserted greater autonomy from the nationalist movement or appealed to universal humanist values over traditional Hindu values in promoting women's rights in colonial India, it remained committed to versions of an idealized golden past as the prototype for the modern Indian nation.[139] It was this shared understanding of the Indian past by the nationalist and women's movements that reinforced the re-

[137]M. Reddi, "Miss Mayo Answered," "Speeches and Writings," vol. 2, pt. 2, *Muthulakshmi Reddi Papers*. For a discussion of the impact of such selected interpretations of the Indian past, see V. Geetha and S.V. Rajadurai, "One Hundred Years of Brahminitude: Arrival of Annie Besant," *Economic and Political Weekly* 30, no. 28 (15 July 1995): pp. 1768–79.

[138]For an analysis of Periyar's relationship to the "Indian" past, see M.S.S. Pandian, " 'De-nationalising' the Past: 'Nation' in E.V. Ramasamy's Political Discourse," *Economic and Political Weekly* 28, no. 2 (16 Oct. 1993): pp. 2282–87.

[139]This point has been made by Gail Omvedt; see "Feminism and the Women's Movement in India," *Working Paper No. 16*, Research Centre for Women's Studies, S.N.D.T. Women's University, Bombay, 1987.

spective positions of the two movements in the *Mother India* controversy against both British imperialism and more socially radical movements in India. The results were that an elite Indian nationalism managed to secure political cover from challenges posed by other modern movements in India, and a middle-class Indian feminism remained distant from combined gender, caste, and class analyses of Indian society. The historical legacy of the imperialist/nationalist controversy over *Mother India*, therefore, lies as much in the elite/upper-caste nationalism and the liberal feminism that emerged as the dominant ideologies of the nationalist and independent women's movements, respectively, as in the gradual discrediting of the ideological justification of British imperialism in late colonial India.

Criteria for the Selections from *Mother India*

I have included Parts 1 and 2 of *Mother India* in their entirety. The first two parts contain the central argument of Mayo's book, for they deal most directly with the woman question and its implications for Indian nationalism.

I have edited Parts 3, 4, and 5 with an eye toward including both a general sampling of the range of topics covered in *Mother India* and particular points and passages relevant to understanding the nature of the book and the controversy that it generated.

The themes that have received special attention in making these selections from *Mother India* are Mayo's discussions of the condition of women and of so-called untouchables in India.

The text of *Mother India* that is reprinted here is faithful to the original and has not been changed in any way. The spellings of words have been left untouched even when alternative spellings exist. The forty-one illustrations that accompanied the original U.S. edition of *Mother India*, however, have been omitted here.

I have annotated the text in a few places and added the notes as editor's footnotes (*).

Select Contemporary Responses to *Mother India*

At the end of the book I have included excerpts from four contemporary responses to *Mother India*. Two of these responses
were written originally in English; one has been translated
from Hindi and another from Tamil. They reflect the position
of the organized women's movement and of the anti-caste
Self-Respect Movement in India on Katherine Mayo's *Mother
India*. In my selection I have been motivated by the goal of
making available responses that typically have received far less
attention than the responses of imperialist feminists in the
West and male nationalists in India.

Mother India

Katherine Mayo

To

THE PEOPLES OF INDIA
AND TO
THAT INDIAN FIELD LABORER
WHO ONCE, BY AN ACT OF
HUMANITY, SAVED
MY LIFE[†]

[†]Mayo's earlier description of this episode paints a rather unflattering picture of the indentured Indian labourer who had evidently rescued her. See
Katherine Mayo, "Bushed", *Scribner's Magazine* 49 (June 1911): 754–61.

Foreword

It would be a great pleasure to thank, by name, the many persons, both Indian and English, who have so courteously facilitated my access to information, to records, and to those places and things that I desired to see for myself. But the facts [sic] that it was impossible to forecast the conclusions I should reach, and that for these conclusions they are in no way responsible, make it improper to embarrass them now by connecting them personally therewith.

For this reason the manuscript of this book has not been submitted to any member of the Government of India, nor to any Briton or Indian connected with official life. It has, however, been reviewed by certain public health authorities of international eminence who are familiar with the Indian field.

I may, on the other hand, express my deep indebtedness to my two friends, Miss M. Moyca Newell and Harry Hubert Field, the one for her constant and invaluable collaboration, the other for a helpfulness, both in India and here, beyond either limit or thanks.

K.M.

REDFORD HILLS
NEW YORK

PART I

Introduction

THE BUS TO MANDALAY

Calcutta, second largest city in the British Empire, spread along the Ganges called Hooghly, at the top of the Bay of Bengal. Calcutta, big, western, modern, with public buildings, monuments, parks, gardens, hospitals, museums, University, courts of law, hotels, offices, shops, all of which might belong to a prosperous American city; and all backed by an Indian town of temples, mosques, bazaars and intricate courtyards and alleys that has somehow created itself despite the rectangular lines shown on the map. In the courts and alleys and bazaars many little bookstalls, where narrow-chested, near-sighted, anæmic young Bengali students, in native dress, brood over piles of fly-blown Russian pamphlets.

Rich Calcutta, wide-open door to the traffic of the world and India, traffic of bullion, of jute, of cotton—of all that India and the world want out of each other's hands. Decorous, sophisticated Calcutta, where decorous and sophisticated people of all creeds, all colors and all costumes go to Government House Garden Parties, pleasantly to make their bows to Their Excellencies, and pleasantly to talk good English while they take their tea and ices and listen to the regimental band.

You cannot see the street from Government House Gardens, for the walls are high. But if you could, you would see it filled with traffic—motor traffic, mostly—limousines, touring cars, taxis and private machines. And rolling along among them now and again, a sort of Fifth Avenue bus, bearing the big-lettered label, "Kali Ghat."

This bus, if you happen to notice it, proceeds along the parkside past the Empire Theater, the various clubs, St. Paul's Cathedral, past the Bishop's House, the General Hospital, the London Missionary Society's Institution, and presently comes

to a stop in a rather congested quarter, which is its destination
as advertised.

"Kali Ghat"—"place of Kali"—is the root-word of the
name Calcutta. Kali is a Hindu goddess, wife of the great god
Siva, whose attribute is destruction and whose thirst is for
blood and death-sacrifice. Her spiritual domination of the
world began about five thousand years ago, and should last
nearly four hundred and thirty-two thousand years to come.

Kali has thousands of temples in India, great and small.
This of Calcutta is the private property of a family of Brahmans who have owned it for some three centuries. A round
hundred of these, "all sons of one father," share its possession
today. And one of the hundred obligingly led me, with a Brahman friend, through the precincts. Let him be called Mr. Haldar, for that is the family's name.

But for his white petticoat-drawers and his white toga, the
usual Bengali costume, Mr. Haldar might have been taken for
a well-groomed northern Italian gentleman. His English was
polished and his manner entirely agreeable.

Five hundred and ninety acres, tax free, constitute the
temple holding, he said. Pilgrims from far and near, with
whom the shrine is always crowded, make money offerings.
There are also priestly fees to collect. And the innumerable
booths that shoulder each other up and down the approaches,
booths where sweetmeats, holy images, marigold flowers,
amulets, and votive offerings are sold, bring in a sound income.

Rapidly cleaving a way through the coming and going
mass of the devotees, Mr. Haldar leads us to the temple
proper. A high platform, roofed and pillared, approached on
three sides by tiers of steps of its own length and width. At
one end, a deep, semi-enclosed shrine in which, dimly half-
visible, looms the figure of the goddess. Black of face she is,
with a monstrous lolling tongue, dripping blood. Of her four
hands, one grasps a bleeding human head, one a knife, the
third, outstretched, cradles blood, the fourth, raised in
menace, is empty. In the shadows close about her feet stand
the priests ministrant.

On the long platform before the deity, men and women prostrate themselves in vehement supplication. Among them stroll lounging boys, sucking lollypops fixed on sticks. Also, a white bull-calf wanders, while one reverend graybeard in the midst of it all, squatting cross-legged on the pavement before a great book, lifts up a droning voice.

"He," said Mr. Haldar, "is reading to the worshipers [sic] from our Hindu mythology. The history of Kali."

Of a sudden, a piercing outburst of shrill bleating. We turn the corner of the edifice to reach the open courtyard at the end opposite the shrine. Here stand two priests, one with a cutlass in his hand, the other holding a young goat. The goat shrieks, for in the air is that smell that all beasts fear. A crash of sound, as before the goddess drums thunder. The priest who holds the goat swings it up and drops it, stretched by the legs, its screaming head held fast in a cleft post. The second priest with a single blow of his cutlass decapitates the little creature. The blood gushes forth on the pavement, the drums and the gongs before the goddess burst out wildly. "Kali! Kali! Kali!" shout all the priests and the suppliants together, some flinging themselves face downward on the temple floor.

Meantime, and instantly, a woman who waited behind the killers of the goat has rushed forward and fallen on all fours to lap up the blood with her tongue —"in the hope of having a child." And now a second woman, stooping, sops at the blood with a cloth, and thrusts the cloth into her bosom, while half a dozen sick, sore dogs, horribly misshapen by nameless diseases, stick their hungry muzzles into the lengthening pool of gore.

"In this manner we kill here from one hundred and fifty to two hundred kids each day," says Mr. Haldar with some pride. "The worshipers [sic] supply the kids."

Now he leads us among the chapels of minor deities—that of the little red goddess of smallpox, side by side with her littler red twin who dispenses chicken pox or not, according to humor; that of the five-headed black cobra who wears a tiny figure of a priest beneath his chin, to whom those make offerings who fear snakebite; that of the red monkey-god, to whom

wrestlers do homage before the bout; that to which rich merchants and students of the University pray, before confronting
examinations or risking new ventures in trade; that of "the
Universal God," a mask, only, like an Alaskan totem. And
then the ever-present phallic emblem of Siva, Kali's husband.
Before them all, little offerings of marigold blossoms, or of red
wads of something in baskets trimmed with shells, both of
which may be had at the temple booths, at a price, together
with sacred cakes made of the dung of the temple bulls.

Mr. Haldar leads us through a lane down which, neatly
arranged in rows, sit scores of more or less naked holy men
and mendicants, mostly fat and hairy and covered with ashes,
begging. All are eager to be photographed. *Saddhus*—reverend
ascetics—spring up and pose. One, a madman, flings himself
at us, badly scaring a little girl who is being towed past by a
young man whose wrist is tied to her tiny one by the two ends
of a scarf. "Husband and new wife," says Mr. Haldar. "They
come to pray for a son."

We proceed to the temple burning-ghat. A burning is in
progress. In the midst of an open space an oblong pit, dug in
the ground. This is now half filled with sticks of wood. On the
ground, close by, lies a rather beautiful young Indian woman,
relaxed as though in a swoon. Her long black hair falls loose
around her, a few flowers among its meshes. Her forehead,
her hands and the soles of her feet are painted red, showing
that she is blessed among women, in that she is saved from
widowhood—her husband survives her. The relatives, two or
three men and a ten-year-old boy, standing near, seem
uninterested. Crouching at a distance, one old woman, keen-
ing. Five or six beggars like horse-flies nagging about.

Now they take up the body and lay it on the pile of wood
in the pit. The woman's head turns and one arm drops, as
though she moved in her sleep. She died only a few hours
ago. They heap sticks of wood over her, tossing it on until it
rises high. Then the little boy, her son, walks seven times
around the pyre, carrying a torch. After that he throws the
torch into the wood, flames and smoke rush up, and the
ceremony is done.

"With a good fire everything burns but the navel," explains Mr. Haldar. "That is picked out of the ashes by the temple attendants, and, with a gold coin provided by the dead person's family, is rolled in a ball of clay and flung into the Ganges. We shall now see the Ganges."

Again he conducts us through the crowds to a point below the temple, where runs a muddy brook, shallow and filled with bathers. "This," says Mr. Haldar, "is the most ancient remaining outlet of the Ganges. Therefore its virtues are accounted great. Hundreds of thousands of sick persons come here annually to bathe and be cured of their sickness just as you see those doing now. Also, such as would supplicate the goddess for other reasons bathe here first, to be cleansed of their sins."

As the bathers finished their ablutions, they drank of the water that lapped their knees. Then most of them devoted a few moments to grubbing with their hands in the bottom, bringing up handfuls of mud which they carefully sorted over in their palms. "Those," said Mr. Haldar, "are looking for the gold coins flung in from the burning-ghat. They hope."

Meantime, up and down the embankment, priests came and went, each leading three or four kids, which they washed in the stream among the bathers and then dragged back, screaming and struggling, toward the temple forecourt. And men and women bearing water-jars, descending and ascending, filled their jars in the stream and disappeared by the same path.

"Each kid," continued Mr. Haldar. "must be purified in the holy stream before it is slain. As for the water-carriers, they bring the water as an offering. It is poured over Kali's feet, and over the feet of the priests that stand before her."

As Mr. Haldar took leave of us, just at the rear of the outer temple wall, I noticed a drain-hole about the size of a man's hand, piercing the wall at the level of the ground. By this hole, on a little flat stone, lay a few marigold flowers, a few rose-petals, a few pennies. As I looked, suddenly out of the hole gushed a flow of dirty water, and a woman, rushing up, thrust a cup under it and drank.

"That is our holy Ganges water, rendered more holy by having flowed over the feet of Kali and her priests. From the floor of the shrine it is carried here by this ancient drain. It is found most excellent against dysentery and enteric fever. The sick who have strength to move drink it here, first having bathed in the Ganges. To those too ill to come, their friends may carry it."

So we found our waiting motor and rolled away, past the General Hospital, the Bishop's House, the various Clubs, the Empire Theater, straight into the heart of Calcutta in a few minutes' time.

"Why did you go to Kali Ghat? That is not India. Only the lowest and most ignorant of Indians are Kali worshipers [sic]," said an English Theosophist, sadly, next day.

I repeated the words to one of the most learned and distinguished of Bengali Brahmans. His comment was this:

"Your English friend is wrong. It is true that in the lower castes the percentage of worshipers of Kali is larger than the percentage of the worshipers of Vishnu, perhaps because the latter demands some self-restraint, such as abstinence from intoxicants. But hundreds of thousands of Brahmans, everywhere, worship Kali, and the devotees at Kali Ghat will include Hindus of all castes and conditions, among whom are found some of the most highly educated and important personages of this town and of India."

Chapter I

THE ARGUMENT

The area we know as India is nearly half as large as the United States. Its population is three times greater than ours. Its import and export trade—as yet but the germ of the possible—amounted, in the year 1924–25, to about two and a half billion dollars.[1] And Bombay is but three weeks' journey from New York.

Under present conditions of human activity, whereby, whether we will or no, the roads that join us to every part of the world continually shorten and multiply, it would appear that some knowledge of main facts concerning so big and today so near a neighbour should be a part of our intelligence and our self-protection.

But what does the average American actually know about India? That Mr. Gandhi lives there; also tigers. His further ideas, if such he has, resolve themselves into more or less hazy notions more or less unconsciously absorbed from professional propagandists out of one camp or another; from religious or mystical sources; or from tales and travel-books, novels and verses, having India as their scene.

It was dissatisfaction with this status that sent me to India, to see what a volunteer unsubsidized, uncommitted, and unattached, could observe of common things in daily human life.

Leaving untouched the realms of religion, of politics, and of the arts, I would confine my inquiry to such workaday ground as public health and its contributing factors. I would try to determine, for example, what situation would confront a public health official charged with the duty of stopping an epidemic of cholera or of plague; what elements would work

---

[1]*Review of the Trade of India in 1924–25*, Department of Commercial Intelligence and Statistics, Calcutta, 1926, p.51.

for and against a campaign against hookworm; or what forces would help or hinder a governmental effort to lower infant mortality, to better living conditions, or to raise educational levels, supposing such work to be required.

None of these points could well be wrapped in "eastern mystery," and all concern the whole family of nations in the same way that the sanitary practices of John Smith of 23 Main Street concern Peter Jones at the other end of the block.

Therefore, in early October, 1925, I went to London, called at India Office, and, a complete stranger, stated my plan.

"What would you like us to do for you?" asked the gentlemen who received me.

"Nothing," I answered, "except to believe what I say. A foreign stranger prying about India, not studying ancient architecture, not seeking philosophers or poets, not even hunting big game, and commissioned by no one, anywhere, may seem a queer figure. Especially if that stranger develops an acute tendency to ask questions. I should like it to be accepted that I am neither an idle busybody nor a political agent, but merely an ordinary American citizen seeking test facts to lay before my own people."

To such Indians as I met, whether then or later, I made the same statement. In the period that followed, the introductions that both gave me, coupled with the untiring courtesy and helpfulness alike of Indian and of British, official or private, all over India, made possible a survey more thorough than could have been accomplished in five times the time without such aid.

"But whatever you do, be careful not to generalize," the British urged. "In this huge country little or nothing is everywhere true. Madras and Peshawar, Bombay and Calcutta—attribute the things of one of these to any one of the others, and you are out of court."

Those journeys I made, plus many another up and down and across the land. Everywhere I talked with health officers, both Indian and British, of all degrees, going out with them into their respective fields, city or rural, to observe their tasks and their ways of handling them. I visited hospitals of many sorts' and localities, talked at length with the doctors, and studied conditions and cases. I made long sorties in the open country from the North-West Frontier to Madras, sometimes accompanying a district commissioner on his tours of checkered duty, sometimes "sitting in" at village councils of peasants, or at Indian municipal board meetings, or at court sessions with their luminous parade of life. I went with English nurses into bazaars and courtyards and inner chambers and over city roofs, visiting where need called. I saw, as well, the homes of the rich. I studied the handling of confinements, the care of children and of the sick, the care and protection of food, and the values placed upon cleanliness. I noted that personal habits of various castes and grades, in travel or at home, in daily life. I visited agricultural stations and cattle-farms, and looked into the general management of cattle and crops. I investigated the animal sanctuaries provided by Indian piety. I saw the schools, and discussed with teachers and pupils their aims and experience. The sittings of the various legislatures, all-India and provincial, re-paid attendance by the light they shed upon the mind-quality of the elements represented. I sought and found private opportunity to question eminent Indians—princes, politicians, administrators, religious leaders; and the frankness of their talk, as to the mental and physical status and conditions of the peoples of India, thrown out upon the background of my personal observation, proved an asset of the first value.

And just this excellent Indian frankness finally led me to think that, after all, there are perhaps certain points on which—south, north, east and west—you *can* generalize about India. Still more: that you can generalize about the only matters in which we of the busy West will, to a man, see our own concern.

John Smith of 23 Main Street may care little enough about the ancestry of Peter Jones, and still less about his religion, his philosophy, or his views on art. But if Peter cultivates habits of living and ways of thinking that make him a physical menace not only to himself and his family, but to all the rest of the block, then practical John will want details.

"Why," ask modern Indian thinkers, "why, after all the long years of British rule, are we still marked among the peoples of the world for our ignorance, our poverty, and our monstrous death rate? By what right are light and bread and life denied?"

"What this country suffers from is want of initiative, want of enterprise, and want of hard, sustained work," mourns Sir Chimanlal Setalvad.[2] "We rightly charge the English rulers for our helplessness and lack of initiative and originality," says Mr. Gandhi.[3]

Other public men demand: "Why are our enthusiasms so sterile? Why are our mutual pledges, our self-dedications to brotherhood and the cause of liberty so soon spent and forgotten? Why is our manhood itself so brief? Why do we tire so soon and die so young?" Only to answer themselves with the cry: "Our spiritual part is wounded and bleeding. Our very souls are poisoned by the shadow of the arrogant stranger, blotting out our sun. Nothing can be done—nothing, anywhere, but to mount the political platform and faithfully denounce our tyrant until he takes his flight. When Britain has abdicated and gone, then, and not till then, free men breathing free air, may we turn our minds to the lesser needs of our dear Mother India."

Now it is precisely at this point, and in a spirit of hearty sympathy with the suffering peoples, that I venture my main generality. It is that:

The British administration of India, be it good, bad, or indifferent, has nothing whatever to do with the conditions above indicated. Inertia, helplessness, lack of initiative and originality, lack of staying power and of sustained loyalties, sterility of enthusiasm, weakness of life-vigor itself—all are traits that truly characterize the Indian not only of today, but of long-past history. All, furthermore, will continue to characterize him, in increasing degree, until he admits their causes

[2]*Legislative Assembly Debates*, 1925, Vol. VI, No. 6, p. 396.

[3]*Young India*, March 25, 1926, p. 112. This is Mr. Gandhi's weekly publication from which much hereinafter will be quoted.

and with his own two hands uproots them. His soul and body are indeed chained in slavery. But he himself wields arld hugs his chains and with violence defends them. No agency but a new spirit within his own breast can set him free. And his arraignments of outside elements, past, present, or to come, serve only to deceive his own mind and to put off the day of his deliverance.

Take a girl child twelve years old, a pitiful physical specimen in bone and blood, illiterate, ignorant, without any sort of training in habits of health. Force motherhood upon her at the earliest possible moment. Rear her weakling son in intensive vicious practices that drain his small vitality day by day. Give him no outlet in sports. Give him habits that make him, by the time he is thirty years of age, a decrepit and querulous old wreck—arld will you ask what has sapped the energy of his manhood?[†]

Take a huge population, mainly rural, illiterate and loving its illiteracy. Try to give it primary education without employing any of its women as teachers—because if you do employ them you invite the ruin of each woman that you so expose. Will you ask why that people's education proceeds slowly?

Take bodies and minds bred and built on the lines thus indicated. Will you ask why the death rate is high and the people poor?

Whether British or Russians or Japanese sit in the seat of the highest; whether the native princes divide the land, reviving old days of princely dominance; or whether some autonomy more complete than that now existing be set up, the only power that can hasten the pace of Indian development toward freedom, beyond the pace it is traveling today, is the power of the men of India, wasting no more time in talk, recriminations, and shifting of blame, but facing and attacking, with the best resolution they can muster, the task that awaits them in their own bodies and souls.

[†]This has been closely paraphrased from the correspondence between Mayo and J.H. Adams about finding a central argument for Mayo's book See Notes, Folder 181 Katherine Mayo Papers, Series 4, Box no. 34.

This subject has not, I believe, been presented in common print. The Indian does not confront it in its entirety; he knows its component parts, but avoids the embarrassment of assembling them or of drawing their essential inferences. The traveler in India misses it, having no occasion to delve below the picturesque surface into living things as they are. The British official will especially avoid it—will deprecate its handling by others. His own daily labors, since the Reforms of 1919, hinge upon persuasion rather than upon command; therefore his hopes of success, like his orders from above, impose the policy of the gentle word. Outside agencies working for the moral welfare of the Indian seem often to have adopted the method of encouraging their beneficiary to dwell on his own merits and to harp upon others' shortcomings, rather than to face his faults and conquer them. And so, in the midst of an agreement of silence or flattery, you find a sick man growing daily weaker, dying, body and brain, of a disease that only himself can cure, and with no one, anywhere, enough his friend to hold the mirror up and show him plainly what is killing him.

In shouldering this task myself, I am fully aware of the resentments I shall incur: of the accusations of muck-raking; of injustice; of material-mindedness; of lack of sympathy; of falsehood perhaps; perhaps of prurience. But the fact of having seen conditions and their bearings, and of being in a position to present them, would seem to deprive one of the right to indulge a personal reluctance to incur consequences.

Here, in the beginning of this book, therefore, stands the kernel of what seems to me the most important factor in the life and future of one-eighth of the human race. In the pages to come will be found an attempt to widen the picture, stretching into other fields and touching upon other aspects of Indian life. But in no field, in no aspect, can that life escape the influences of its inception.

Chapter II

"SLAVE MENTALITY"

"Let us not put off everything until Swaraj[1] is attained and thus put off Swaraj itself," pleads Gandhi. "Swaraj can be had only by brave and clean people."[2]

But, in these days of the former leader's waned influence, it is not for such teachings that he gains ears. From every political platform stream flaming protests of devotion to the death to Mother India; but India's children fit no action to their words. Poor indeed she is, and sick—ignorant and helpless. But, instead of flinging their strength to her rescue, her ablest sons, as they themselves lament, spend their time in quarrels together or else lie idly weeping over their own futility.

Meantime the British Government, in administering the affairs of India, would seem to have reached a set rate of progress, which, if it be not seriously interrupted, might fairly be forecast decade by decade. So many schools constructed, so many hospitals; so many furlongs of highway laid, so many bridges built; so many hundred miles of irrigation canal dug; so many markets made available; so many thousand acres of waste land brought under homestead cultivation; so many wells sunk; so much rice and wheat and millet and cotton added to the country's food and trade resources.

This pace of advance, compared to the huge needs of the country, or compared to like movements in the United States or in Canada, is slow. To hasten it materially, one single element would suffice—the hearty, hard-working and intelligent devotion to the practical job itself, of the educated Indian. Today, however, few signs appear, among Indian public men,

[1]Self-government.
[2]*Young India*, Nov. 19, 1925, p. 399.

of concern for the status of the masses, while they curse the one power which, however little to their liking, is doing practically all of whatever is done for the comfort of sad old Mother India.

The population of all India is reckoned, in round numbers, to be 319,000,000.[3] Setting aside Indian States ruled by Indian princes, that of British India is 247,000,000. Among these people live fewer than 200,000 Europeans, counting every man, woman and child in the land, from the Viceroy down to the haberdasher's baby. The British personnel of the Army, including all ranks, numbers fewer than 60,000 men. The British Civilian cadre, inclusive of the Civil Service, the medical men, the engineers, foresters, railway administrators, mint, assay, educational, agricultural and veterinary experts, etc., etc., totals 3,432 men. Of the Indian Police Service, the British membership approximates 4,000. This last figure excludes the subordinate and provincial services, in which the number of Europeans is, however, negligible.

Representing the British man-power in India today, you therefore have these figure:

Army	60,000
Civil Services	3,432
Police	4,000

	67,432

This is the entire local strength of the body to whose oppressive presence the Indian attributes what he himself describes as the "slave mentality" of 247,000,000 human beings.

But one must not overlook the fact that, back of Britain's day, India was ever either a chaos of small wars and brigandage, chief preying upon chief, and all upon the people; or else she was the flaccid subject of a foreign rule. If, once and again, a native king arose above the rest and spread his sway, the reign of his house was short, and never covered all

[3]*The Indian Year Book, Times* Press, Bombay, 1926, p. 13.

of India. Again and again conquering forces came sweeping through the mountain passes down out of Central Asia. And the ancient Hindu stock, softly absorbing each recurrent blow, quivered—and lay still.

Many a reason is advanced to account for these things, as, the devitalizing character of the Hindu religion, with its teachings of the nothingness of things as they seem of the infinitude of lives—dreams all—to follow this present seeming. And this element, beyond doubt, plays its part. But we, as "hard-headed Americans," may, for a beginning, put such matters aside while we consider points on which we shall admit less room for debate and where we need no interpreter and no glossary.

The whole pyramid of the Hindu's woes, material and spiritual—poverty, sickness, ignorance, political minority, melancholy, ineffectiveness, not forgetting that subconscious conviction of inferiority which he forever bares and advertises by his gnawing and imaginative alertness for social affronts—rests upon a rock-bottom physical base. This base is, simply, his manner of getting into the world and his sex-life thenceforward.

In the great orthodox Hindu majority, the girl looks for motherhood nine months after reaching puberty[4]—or anywhere between the ages of fourteen and eight. The latter age is extreme, although in some sections not exceptional; the former is well above the average.[†] Because of her years and upbringing and because countless generations behind her have been bred even as she, she is frail of body. She is also completely unlettered, her stock of knowledge comprising

[4]Cf. *post.*, p. 44

[†]Dr. Margaret Balfour, a leading medical practitioner for women in India, wrote to the *Times of India* stating that Mayo's claim was not typical. Balfour offered statistics from her own experience of medical practice among women in India to argue that motherhood at such an early age was not as common as Mayo would have her readers believe. See Balfour's letter reprinted in K. Natarajan, *Miss Mayo's Mother India: A Rejoinder* (Madras: G.A. Natesan and Co., 1928), pp. 95–96.

only the ritual of worship of the household idols, the rites of placation of the wrath of deities and evil spirits, and the detailed ceremony of the service of her husband, who is ritualistically her personal god.

As to the husband, he may be a child scarcely older than herself or he may be a widower of fifty, when first he requires of her his conjugal rights. In any case, whether from immaturity or from exhaustion, he has small vitality to transmit.

The little mother goes through a destructive pregnancy, ending in a confinement whose peculiar tortures will not be imagined unless in detail explained.

The infant that survives the birth-strain—a feeble creature at best, bankrupt in bone-stuff and vitality, often venereally poisoned, always predisposed to any malady that may be afloat—must look to his child-mother for care. Ignorant of the laws of hygiene, guided only by the most primitive superstitions, she has no helpers in her task other than the older women of the household, whose knowledge, despite their years, is little greater than hers. Because of her place in the social system, child-baring and matters of procreation are the woman's one interest in life, her one subject of conversation, be her caste high or low. Therefore, the child growing up in the home learns, from earliest grasp of word and act, to dwell upon sex relations.

Siva, one of the greatest of the Hindu deities, is represented, on highroad shrines, in the temples, on the little alter of the home, or in personal amulets, by the image of the male generative organ, in which shape he receives the daily sacrifices of the devout. The followers of Vishnu, multitudinous in the south, from their childhood wear painted upon their foreheads the sign of the function of generation.[5†]

[5]Fanciful interpretations of this symbol are sometimes given.

[†]Several Indian critics took particular objection to Mayo's interpretation of these symbols. See M.K. Gandhi, "Drain Inspector's Report", *Young India* (15 Sept. 1927) in *The Collected Works of Mahatma Gandhi* (Ahmedabad: Navajivan Publishing House, 1969), vol. 34, pp. 539–47; and Muthulakshmi Reddi, "Miss Mayo Answered", *Muthulakshmi*

And although it is accepted that the ancient inventors of these and kindred emblems intended them as aids to the climbing of spiritual heights, practice and extremely detailed narratives of the intimacies of the gods, preserved in the hymns of the fireside, give them literal meaning and suggestive power, as well as religious sanction in the common mind.[6]

"Fools," says a modern teacher of the spiritual sense of the phallic cult, "do not understand, and they never will, for they look at it only from the physical side."[7]

But, despite the scorn of the sage, practical observation in India forces one to the conclusion that a religion adapted to the wise alone leaves most of the sheep unshepherded.

And, even though the sex-symbols themselves were not present, there are the sculptures and paintings on temple walls and temple chariots, on palace doors and street-wall frescoes, realistically demonstrating every conceivable aspect and humor of sex contact; there are the eternal songs on the lips of the women of the household; there is, in brief, the occupation and pre-occupation of the whole human world within the child's vision, to predispose thought.

It is true that, to conform to the International Convention for the Suppression of the Circulation of and Traffic in Obscene Publications, signed in Geneva on September 12, 1923, the Indian Legislature duly amended the Indian Penal Code and Code of Criminal Procedure; and that this amendment duly prescribes set penalties for "whoever sells, lets to

---

[6]*Hindu Manners, Customs and Ceremomies*, Abbé J.A. Dubois, 1821. Edited and corrected by H.K. Beauchamp. Clarendon Press, Oxford, 1924, pp. 111–12, 628–31, etc.

[7]Swami Vivekanada, in *Bhakti Yoga*. For a brief and liberal discussion of the topic see Chapter XIII in *The Heart of Aryavarta*, by the Earl of Ronaldshay, Constable & Co., Ltd., London, 1925.

Reddi Papers Speeches and Writings, Volume II, Part 2 (included in the contemporary responses section at back of this volume). For a discussion of how nationalist responses to *Mother India* were implicated in the alternative construction of a "respectable sexuality" in India, see Mrinalini Sinha, "Nationalism and Respectable Sexuality in India", *Genders* 21 (1995): 30–57.

hire, distributes, publicly exhibits ... conveys ... or receives profit from any obscene object, book, representation or figure." But its enactment unqualified, although welcome to the Muhammadans, would have wrought havoc with the religious belongings, the ancient traditions and customs and the priestly prerogatives dear to the Hindu majority. Therefore the Indian Legislature, preponderantly Hindu, saddled the amendment with an exception, which reads:[8]

This section does not extend to any book, pamphlet, writing, drawing or painting kept or used *bona fide* for religious purposes or any representation sculptured, engraved, painted or otherwise represented on or in any temple, or on any car used for the conveyance of idols, or kept or used for any religious purpose.

In many parts of the country, north and south, the little boy, his mind so prepared, is likely, if physically attractive, to be drafted for the satisfaction of grown men, or to be regularly attached to a temple, in the capacity of prostitute. Neither parent as a rule sees any harm in this, but is, rather, flattered that the son has been found pleasing.

This, also, is a matter neither of rank nor of special ignorance. In fact, so far are they from seeing good and evil as we see good and evil, that the mother, high caste or low caste, will practice upon her children—the girl "to make her sleep well," the boy "to make him manly," an abuse which the boy, at least, is apt to continue daily for the rest of his life.[†]

[8]*Indian Penal Code*, Act No. VIII of 1925, Section 292.

[†]Several contemporary readers of *Mother India* were especially intrigued by the exact content of this abuse (presumably genital founding). One of Mayo's correspondents, a Mrs Ruby Kruyster who was using *Mother India* as a text book among her friends in the U.S. and in India, wrote to Mayo: "Many who are now studying this splendid work have asked me to explain p. 33 [this page]. I request you to tell me what brutal abuse it is that Indian mothers practice on their children, male and female, and what are the signs which the poor unfortunate children bear on their bodies." Letter dated 19 November 1927, *Katherine Mayo Papers*, Folder no. 40, Series 1, Box 5. Her Indian critics remained especially appalled by this accusation. The 'pornographic' appeal of *Mother India*, however, contributed to its popularity. One journal

This last point should be noticed. Highest medical authority in widely scattered sections attests that practically every child brought under observation, for whatever reason, bears on its body the signs of this habit. Whatever opinion may be held as to its physical effects during childhood, its effect upon early thought-training cannot be overlooked. And, when constantly practiced during mature life, its devastation of body and nerves will scarcely be questioned.

Ancient Hindu religious teachings are cited to prove that the marriage of the immature has not original Scriptural sanction. Text is flung against text, in each recurrence of the argument. Pundits radically disagree. But against the fog evoked in their dispute stand sharp and clear the facts of daily usage. Hindu custom demands that a man have a legitimate son at the earliest possible moment—a son to perform the proper religious ceremonies at and after the death of the father and to crack the father's skull on the funeral pyre, according to his caste's ritual. For this reason as well as from inclination, the beginning of the average boy's sexual commerce barely awaits his ability. Neither general habit nor public opinion confines that commerce to his wife or wives.

Mr. Gandhi has recorded that he lived with his wife, as such, when he was thirteen years old, and adds that if he had not, unlike his brother in similar case, left her presence for a certain period each day to go to school, he "would either have fallen a prey to disease and premature death, or have led [thenceforth] a burdensome existence."[9]

Forced up by western influences, the subject of child marriages has been much discussed of latter years and a sentiment of uneasiness concerning it is perceptibly rising in the Indian mind. But as yet this finds small translation into act,

[9]*Young India*, Jan. 7, 1926.

---

in the U.S., for example, claimed that only "a quarter of the books' readers were interested in India, the other three-fourth found it pornographic", quoted in Manoranjan Jha, *Katherine Mayo and India* (New Delhi: People's Publishing House, 1971), p. 79.

and the orthodox Hindu majority fights in strength on the side of the ancient practice.

Little in the popular Hindu code suggests self-restraint in any direction, least of all in sex relations. "My father," said a certain eminent Hindu barrister, one of the best men in his province, "taught me wisely, in my boyhood, how to avoid infection."

"Would it not have been better," I asked, "had he taught you continence?"

"Ah—but we know that to be impossible."

"No question of right or wrong can be involved in any aspect of such matters," a famous Hindu mystic, himself the venerated teacher of multitudes, explained to me. "I forget the act the moment I have finished it. I merely do it not to be unkind to my wife, who is less illumined than I. To do it or not to do it, signifies nothing. Such things belong only to the world of illusion."

After the rough outline just given small surprise will meet the statement that from one end of the land to the other the average male Hindu of thirty years, provided he has means to command his pleasure, is an old man; and that from seven to eight out of every ten such males between the ages of twenty-five and thirty are impotent.[†] These figures are not random, and are affected by little save the proviso above given; a cultivator of the soil, because of his poverty and his life of wholesome physical exertion during a part of the year, is less liable than the man of means, or the city dweller. A sidelight will be found by a glance down the advertisement space of Indian-owned newspapers. Magical drugs and mechanical contrivances, whether "for princes and rich men only," or the humbler and not less familiar "32 Pillars of Strength to prop up your decaying body for One Rupee[10] only," crowd the columns and support the facts.

[10]The market value of the rupee fluctuates with other international exchanges. But for the purpose of this book, one rupee is taken to be worth

[†]The source for Mayo's information here was John Coatman, Director of Public Information in India; see Notes, Folder 233, *Katherine Mayo Papers* Series 4, Box 44.

In the Punjab alone, between December 29, 1922, and December 4, 1925, Government prosecuted vernacular papers eleven separate times for carrying ultra-indecent advertisements. In seven cases the publications were Hindu, thrice Muhammadan, once Sikh. The fines imposed ranged from twenty-five to two hundred rupees, in one case plus ninety days rigorous imprisonment. And it should be duly noted that such prosecutions are never undertaken save where the advertisement gives the grossest physical details in plain and unmistakable language.

Following the eleventh prosecution, Government sent out a note to the press informing the editors of this last conviction with its relatively high fine, and advising them to scrutinize advertisements before publication. Upon this suggestion the editorial comment of the *Brahman Samachar*[11] emitted an informing ray:

Government wants that such advertisements should not be published and that the editors should go through them before publishing them. It would have been better if the Information Bureau had published the obscene advertisement along with its report so that the subject matter and the manner of writing of the advertisement would have become known.

Mr. Gandhi in his newspaper has, it is true, recorded his disapproving cognizance. "Drugs and mechanical contrivances," he writes, "may keep the body in a tolerable condition, but they sap the mind."[12]

But a far more characteristic general attitude was that evidenced in the recent action of a Hindu of high position whereby, before giving his daughter in marriage, he demanded from his would-be son-in-law a British doctor's certificate attesting that he, the would-be son-in-law, was venereally infected. The explanation is simple: a barren wife casts embarrassment upon her parents; and barren marriages, although commonly laid to the wife, are often due to the

33⅓ cents, three rupees one dollar, United States currency.

---

[11] A Hindu paper of Lahore issue of Feb. 16, 1926.

[12] *Young India*, Sept. 2, 1926, p. 309.

husband's inability. The father in this case was merely taking practical precaution. He did not want his daughter, through fault not her own, to be either supplanted or returned upon his hands. And no reproach whatever attaches to the infected condition. No public opinion works on the other side.

In case, however, of the continued failure of the wife—any wife—to give him a child, the Hindu husband has a last recourse; he may send his wife on a pilgrimage to a temple, bearing gifts. And, it is affirmed, some castes habitually save time by doing this on the first night after the marriage. At the temple by day, the woman must beseech the god for a son, and at night she must sleep within the sacred precincts. Morning come, she has a tale to tell the priest of what befell her under the veil of darkness.

"Give praise, O daughter of honor!" he replies. "It was the god!"

And so she returns to her home.

If a child comes, and it lives, a year later she re-visits the temple, carrying, with other gifts, the hair from her child's head.[13]

Visitors to the temples today sometimes notice a tree whose boughs are hung with hundreds of little packets bound in dingy rags; around the roots of that tree lies a thick mat of short black locks of human hair. It is the votive tree of the god. It declares his benefits. To maintain the honor of the shrine, the priests of this attribute are carefully chosen from stout new brethren.

Every one, seemingly, understands all about it. The utmost piety, nevertheless, truly imbues the suppliant's mind and contents the family.

As to the general subject, enough has now, perhaps, been said to explain and to substantiate the Hindu's bitter lament of his own "slave mentality."

It may also suggest why he develops no real or lasting leaders, and why such men as from time to time aspire to that

[13]Cf. *Hindu Manners, Customs and Ceremonies*, pp. 593–4.

rank are able only for a brief interval to hold the flitting minds of their followers.

The Indian perceives, to a certain degree, the condition; but he rarely goes all the way to the bottom thereof. Nor does he recognize its full significance and relate it to its consequences. "Why do our best men—those who should lead us—die so young?" he repeats despondently, implying that the only possibly answer is: "Karma—Kismet—an enigmatic fate." "The average life of our inhabitants is 23 years," says the Hindu Doctor Hariprasad[14]—and lays the blame to bad sanitation. Another characteristic Indian view is expressed by Manilal C. Parekh,[15] treating with dismay of [sic] the inroads of tuberculosis—an infection that finds ideal encouragement in the unresisting bodies and depleting habits of the people:

One need not think just now of the causes of this frightful increase... The present writer wishes Swaraj to come to India as early as possible in order that the people of the land may be able to deal with this tremendously big problem....

Thus they still contrive to shift the burden and avoid the fact.

Yet it was one of the most distinguished of Indian medical men, a Bombay Brahman, physician and pathologist, who gave me the following appraisal:

My people continually miss the association of their mental and material poverty with their physical extravagance. Yet our undeniable race deterioration, our natural lack of power of concentration, of initiative and of continuity of purpose cannot be dissociated from our expenditure of all vital energy on the single line of sexual indulgence.

Once more, then, one is driven to the original conclusion: Given men who enter the world physical bankrupts out of bankrupt stock, rear them through childhood in influences and practices that devour their vitality; launch them at the dawn of maturity on an unrestrained outpouring of their whole provision of creative energy in one single direction;

[14]*Young India,* Nov. 5, 1925, p. 375.
[15]*Servants of India,* April 8, 1926, p. 124.

find them, at the age when the Anglo-Saxon is just coming into full glory of manhood, broken-nerved, low-spirited, petulant ancients; and need you, while this remains unchanged, seek for other reasons why they are poor and sick and dying and why their hands are too weak, too fluttering, to seize or to hold the reins of Government?

Chapter III

MARBLES AND TOPS

A study of the attitude of the Government of India as to the subject of child-marriage shows that, while steadily exercising persuasive pressure toward progress and change, it has been dominated, always, by two general principles—the first, to avoid as far as possible interference in matters concerning the religion of the governed; the second, never to sanction a law that cannot be enforced.[†] To run counter to the Indian's tenets as to religious duties, religious prohibitions, and god-given rights has ever meant the eclipse of Indian reason in madness, riot and blood. And to enforce a law whose keeping or breaking must be a matter of domestic secrecy is, in such a country as India at least, impossible.

Indian and English authorities unite in the conviction that no law raising the marriage age of girls would be today effectively accepted by the Hindu peoples. The utmost to be hoped, in the present state of public mentality, is, so these experienced men hold, a raising of the age of consent within

[†]Contemporary social reformers in India, however, challenged Mayo's version of the role of the government in promoting reform in India. Margaret Cousins, the Secretary of the Women's India Asociation, explicitly challenged Mayo's efforts to absolve the British of any responsibility for the defeat of the reform measures in the Indian Legislature in her attack on *Mother India* in *The Modern Review* (November 1927), quoted in Ernest Wood, *An Englishman Defends Mother India: A Complete Constructive Reply to 'Mother India'* (Madras: Ganesh and Co., 1929), pp. 60–61. For a history of child-marriage reform in India, see Geraldine Forbes, "Women and Modernity: The Issue of Child Marriage in India", *Women's Studies International Quarterly* 2 (1979): 407–09; and Barbara Ramusack, "Women's Organizations and Social Change: The Age of Marriage Issue in India", in Naomi Black and A.B. Cottrell (eds.) *Women and World Change* (London: Sage Pub., 1981), pp. 198–216.

the marriage bonds. A step in this direction was accomplished in 1891, when Government, backed by certain members of the advanced section of the Indians, after a hot battle in which it was fiercely accused by eminent orthodox Hindus of assailing the most sacred foundations of the Hindu world, succeeded in raising that age from ten years to twelve[†]. In latter-day Legislative Assemblies the struggle has been renewed, non-official Indian Assemblymen bringing forward bills aiming at further advance only to see them, in one stage or another, defeated by the strong orthodox majority.

Upon such occasions, the attitude of the Viceregal Government has consistently been one of square approval of the main object in view, but of caution against the passage of laws so much in advance of public opinion that their existence can serve only to bring law itself into disrepute. This course is the more obligatory because of the tendency of the Indian public man to satisfy his sense of duty by the mere empty passing of a law, without thought or intention or accepted responsibility as to the carrying of his law into effect.

Not unnaturally, Government's course pleases no one. From the one side rise accusations of impious design against the sanctuaries of the faith; from the other come charges as bitter but of an opposite implication.

"What right have you to separate man and wife?" cries an orthodox Brahman Assemblyman. "You may lay your unholy hands on our ancient ideals and traditions, but we will not follow you."[1] Yet, with equal vehemence a second member declares that "every Englishman in the Government of India

---

[1]*Legislative Assembly Debates,* 1925, Vol. V, Part III, p. 2890.

[†]For a discussion of the orthodox Hindu protest against the Age of Consent Act of 1891, see Amiya Sen, "Hindu Revivalism in Action—The Age of Consent Bill Agitation in Bengal", *The Indian Historical Review,* 7: 1–2 (July 1980–Jan. 1981): 160–84; and Tanika Sarkar, "Rhetoric Against Age of Consent: Resisting Colonial Reason and the Death of a Child Wife", *Economic and Political Weekly* 28: 36 (4 Sept. 1993): 1869–78.

seems to be throwing obstacles in the way of other people going forward."[2]

An examination of these debates gives a fair general view of the state of public opinion on the whole topic. Members seem well aware of conditions that obtain. The divergence comes in the weight they assign to those conditions.

Rai Bahadur Bakshi Sohan Lal, member from Jullundur, when introducing a non-official amendment to raise the age of consent within the marriage bond to fourteen years, argued:[3]

The very high rate of fatality amongst the high classes in this country of newly-born children and of young married wives is due to sexual intercourse and pregnancy of the girl before she reaches the age of puberty or full development of her physical organs. The result of such consummation before bodily development not only weakens the health of the girl but often produces children who are weak and sickly, and in a large number of cases cannot resist any illness of an ordinary type, or any inclemency of weather or climate. Thus some of them die immediately after birth or during their infancy. If they live at all, they are always in need of medical attendance, medical advice or medical treatment, to linger on their lives; or in other words they are born more to minister to the medical profession than themselves and their families or their country. Neither can they be good soldiers nor good civilians, neither good outdoor workers nor good indoor workers; neither can they be fit to attack an enemy nor defend themselves against attacks of an enemy, or against the raid of thieves or dacoits.[4] In a few words, his birth is very often the cause of ruining the health, strength and prosperity of his parents without resulting in a corresponding benefit to society. The husband, in the majority of cases, ... has to arrange for his re-marriage several times during his life-time, on account of the successive deaths of his young wives or on account of his wife bearing children who are not long-lived.

Successive debates expose the facts that few or none of the Indian parliamentarians dispute the theoretical wisdom of postponing motherhood until the maturity of the mother; but all agree that it is impossible to effect such a result without prohibiting the marriage of girls of immature age. Yet this they say, with one accord, cannot be done—and for three reasons:

[2]*Ibid.*, 1925, Vol. VI, p. 557.
[3]*Ibid.*, 1922, Vol. II, Part III, p. 2650.
[4]Gang robbers.

First, because immutable custom forbids, premarital pubescence being generally considered, among Hindus, a social if not a religious sin.[5]

Second, because the father dare not keep his daughter at home lest she be damaged before she is off his hands. And this especially in joint-family households, where several men and boys—brothers, cousins, uncles—live under the same roof.

Third, because the parents dare not expose the girl, after her dawning puberty, to the pressure of her own desire unsatisfied.

With these intimate dangers in view a learned Brahman Assemblyman, Diwan Bahadur T. Rangachariar, Member from Madras, spoke earnestly against the un-official bill of 1925 raising the age of consent within the marriage bonds to fourteen years. Any pretense at enforcing such a law would, it was generally conceded, demand the keeping of the wife away from her husband, retaining her in her own father's *zenana*.[6] Said the Madrassi Assemblyman, warning, imploring:[7]

Remember the position of girls in our country between twelve and fourteen. Have we not got our daughters in our house? Have we not got our sisters in our house? Remember that, and remember your own neighbours. Remembering our habits, remembering our usages, remembering the precociousness of our youth, remembering the condition of the climate, remembering the conditions of the country, I ask you to give your weighty judgment to this matter.

Another Brahman member vehemently protests:[8]

The tradition of womanhood in this country is unapproached by the tradition of womanhood in any other country. Our ideal of womanhood is this. Our women regard their husbands—they have been taught from the moment they were suckling their mothers' milk to regard their husbands as their God on earth. ... To the Brahman girl-wife the husband is a greater, truer, dearer benefactor than all the social reformers bundled together! ...

[5]See *Legislative Assembly Debates* of 1925, March 23 and 24 in Vol. V, Part III, and Sept. I, in Vol. VI.

[6]Women's quarters.

[7]*Legislative Assembly Debates*, 1925, Vol. V, Part III, p. 2884.

[8]*Ibid.*, p. 2890 *et seq.*

What right have you to interfere with this ancient, noble tradition of ours regarding the sanctity of wedlock ?... What is the object of this legislation? Do you want to make the women of India strong and their children stalwart? But remember that in trying to do that, you may otherwise be doing a lot of evil, far worse than the evil you seek to remove. ... By all means take care of [the girl's] body; but fail not to train her morals, to train her soul, so as to enable her to look upon her husband as her God, which indeed is the case in India, among Hindus at least.... Don't destroy I beg of you—don't ruin our Hindu Homes.

To reasoning of this sort another member—Mr. Shanmukhan Chetty, of Salem and Coimbatore—hotly retorts:[9]

The fact that a so-called marriage rite precedes the commission of a crime does not and cannot justify that crime. I have no doubt that if you were to ask a cannibal, he would plead his religion for the heinous act he does.

And Dr. S.K. Datta, Indian Christian representative from Calcutta:[10]

If ever there was "a man-made law," this compulsion of young girls to become mothers is one of them.

The bill raising the age of consent to fourteen was finally thrown, out, buried under an avalanche of popular disapproval. In the next Assembly Sir Alexander Muddiman, leader of the Viceroy's Government, brought in an official bill drafted with a view of breaking the *impasse* and securing that degree of advance that would be conceded by the conservative Indian element. This bill, fixing the woman's age of consent within and without the marriage bond respectively at thirteen and fourteen years, was enacted into law as Act XXIX of 1925.

The discussion that it evoked on the floor of the Assembly gave still further light upon the attitude of Indians.

Some speakers pointed to the gradual growth of public opinion as expressed in caste, party and association councils as the best hope of the future. These deprecated legislation as both irritating and useless, calling attention to the fact that the orthodox community, comprising as it does the great majority

[9]*Legislative Assembly Debates*, 1925, Vol. VI, p. 558.
[10]*Ibid.*, 1925, Vol. V, Part III, p. 2839.

of Hindus all over India, would regard legal abolition of child-marriage as, literally, a summons to a holy war.

Similarly, any active attempt to protect the child-wife during her infancy would, it was shown, be held as an attack upon the sacred marital relation, impossible to make effective and sure to let loose "bloodshed and chaos."

Rai Sahib M. Harbilas Sarda, of Ajmer-Merwara maintained, it is true, that[11]

where a social custom or a religious rite outrages our sense of humanity or inflicts injustice on a helpless class of people, the Legislature has a right to step in. Marrying a girl of three or four years and allowing sexual intercourse with a girl of nine or ten years outrages the sense of humanity anywhere.

But Pundit Madan Mohan Malaviya, of Allahabad, thought differently, saying:[12]

I have to face the stern realities of the situation, realities which include a general permission or rather a widespread practice of having marriages performed before twelve and consequently of the impossibility of preventing a married couple from meeting. ... I submit that it is perhaps best that we should reconcile ourselves to leave the law as it is in the case of married people for the present, and to trust to the progress of education and to social reform to raise the age of consummation of marriage to the proper level. ... I am sure, Sir, that a great deal of advance has been made in this matter. In many provinces among the higher classes the marriageable age has been rising. ... It is the poorer classes who unfortunately are the greatest victims in this matter. Early marriages take place among the poorer classes in a larger measure than among the higher classes.

And Mr. Amar Nath Dutt, of Burdwan, combated the action proposed, thus:[13]

We have no right to thrust our advanced views upon our less advanced countrymen.... Our villages are torn with factions. If the age of consent is raised to 13, rightly or wrongly we will find that there will be inquisitions by the police at the instance of members of an opposite faction in the village and people will be put to disgrace and trouble.... I would ask [Government] ... to withdraw the Bill at once. Coming as I do, Sir, from Bengal, I know what is the opinion of the majority of the people there.

[11]*Ibid.*, 1925, Vol. VI, p. 561.

[12]*Ibid.*, pp. 573–4.

[13]*Legislative Assembly Debates*, 1925, Vol. VI, pp. 558–9.

Mr. M.K. Acharya, of South Arcot, also strongly adverse to change, declared that[14]

... what is sought to be done is to make that an offence which is not an offence now, to maʾe that a crime which is not at present a crime, and which we are unable to regard as a crime, whatever may be the feelings of some few people to the country.

To which the same speaker added, a few moments later:[15]

There is very little opinion of any respectable body of men in India which wants this reform very urgently. It may come, and there is no harm in it, in its own course. Really this is ... merely to give Honourable Members some legislative marbles and tops to play with during the time that we happen to be in Simla.[16]

[14]*Ibid.*, p. 551
[15]*Ibid*, p. 556.
[16]Simla is the summer seat of the Central Government.

Chapter IV

EARLY TO MARRY AND EARLY TO DIE

Upon the unfruitful circlings of the Hindus breaks, once and again, a voice from the hardy North. Rarely, for the subject carries small interest there; yet, when it comes, weighted with rough acumen.

Nawab Sir Sahibzada Abdul Qaiyum is, as his name suggests, a Muhammadan. Speaking as of the distant North-West Frontier Province, he said:[1]

I should like to say only a few words on the practical side of it. In my part of the country, we do not have early marriages. So the Bill is not likely to affect us very much. ... I should have thought ... the proper remedy ... fixing the age of marriage for a man at a certain point and for a woman at another point ... [but] I do not think the country is prepared. ... Well, just consider: Who is going to be the prosecutor, who is going to be the investigator, who are going to be the witnesses, and who is going to enforce the verdict? ... Then there is another difficulty ... that you allow a young couple to be married and to live together and give them the opportunity of sharpening their sexual appetite and then prevent them by law from having their natural intercourse simply because they have not reached a certain age. ... Well, suppose this law is enacted, and the young couple are prevented from having intercourse, I should think that in the majority of cases you would thus be sending the young boy into the streets .... but so long as you allow people to be married young, there is no sufficient reason why you should enact laws which may interfere with their private life.

The handling of child-wives, many finally affirm, must, regardless of legal enactment, continue to be guided by natural instincts under the husbands' sacred rights.

Throughout the Hindu argument, however, the general conviction appears that law-making for social advance, while entirely hopeless of enforcement, exerts an educational influence upon the community and is therefore to be regarded with satisfaction as a completed piece of work. "The people

---

[1]*Legislative Assembly Debates*, 1925, Vol. VI, pp. 571–2.

should be éducated," the Indian public man declares. "They should follow the course that I hereby indicate." Having spoken, he washes his hands. His task is done.

The voice of Diwan Bahadur T. Rangachariar, the Madrassi Brahman Assemblyman before quoted, was one of the few raised in criticism of this characteristic viewpoint. Addressing a fellow Assemblyman, proponent of the reform amendment, he says:[2]

May I ask my Honourable friend how many platforms he has addressed in this connection outside this hall? (A voice: "Never.") Has he ever summoned a meeting in his own province and addressed the people on the value of these reforms? Sir, it is easy to avail yourself of the position which you occupy here appealing to an audience where all are wedded to your views and to get them to aid in this legislation. But ... it is not so easy a task to go to the country and convince your own countrymen and countrywomen.

Thus throughout these councils, the weight of responsibility tosses back and forth, a beggar for lodgment. "It is only the Brahmans who marry their girls in infancy." Or, equally, "It is only the low castes that follow such practice"; and, "In any case the evils of early marriages are much exaggerated, interference is unwise, and volunteer social and religious reform associations may be trusted to protect young wives."

But, turning from the shifts and theories of politicians—from their vague affirmations of progress attained, to cold black and white—you are pulled up with a jerk. Says the latest Census of India:[3]

It can be assumed for all practical purposes that every woman is in the married state at or immediately after puberty and that cohabitation, therefore, begins in every case with puberty.

And the significance of the thing is further driven home by the estimate that in India each generation sees the death of 3,200,000 mothers in the agonies of childbirth[4]—a figure greater than that of the united death-roll of the British Empire, including India, France, Belgium, Italy and the United States,

[2]*Ibid.*, 1925, Vol. V, Part III, p. 2847.
[3]*Census of India*, 1921, Appendix VII.
[4]*Legislative Assembly Debates*, 1922, Vol. III, Part I, p. 882.

in the World War; and that the average physical rating of the population is at the bottom of the international list.

To turn again to the Legislative Assembly: Once more, it is a man from the North who speaks—a gray-beard yeoman, tall, straight, lean and sinewy, hard as nails, a telling contrast to the Southerners around him who jeer as he talks—Sardar Bahadur Captain Hira Singh Brar, of the Punjab, old Sikh fighting man.[5]

I think, sir, the real solution for preventing infant mortality lies in smacking the parent who produces such children, and more so, in slapping many of our friends who always oppose the raising of the age to produce healthy children. ... Is it not a sin when they call a baby of nine or ten years or a boy of ten years husband and wife? It is a shame. (Voices: "No, no!") ... a misfortune for this generation and for the future generation. ... Girls of nine or ten, babies themselves who ought to be playing with their dolls rather than becoming wives, are mothers of children. Boys who ought to be getting their lessons in school are rearing a large family of half a dozen boys and girls. ... I do not like to go into society. I feel ashamed, because there is no manhood, there is no womanhood. I should feel ashamed myself to go into society with a little girl of twelve years as my wife. ... We all talk, talk and talk a hundred and one things here, but what hapens? All left in this house, all left on the platform and nothing carried to our homes, nothing happens. ... Healthy children are the foundation of a strong nation. Every one knows that the parents cannot produce healthy children. To be useful we must have long life which we cannot have if early marriage is not stopped. "Early to marry and early to die," is the motto of Indians.

The frank give-and-takes of the Indian Legislature, between Indian and Indian, deal with facts. But it is instructive to observe the robes that those facts can wear when arrayed by a poet for foreign consideration. Rabindranath Tagore, in a recent essay on "The Indian Ideal of Marriage," explains child-marriage as a flower of the sublimated spirit, a conquest over sexuality and materialism won by exalted intellect for the eugenic uplift of the race.[†] His explanation, however, logically implies the assumption, simply, that Indian women must be

[5]*Ibid.*, 1925, Vol. V, Part III, pp. 2829–31.

[†]Rabindranath Tagore replied to these charges with a letter protesting that Mayo had deliberately plucked quotations out of context from his text See Rabindranath Tagore's letter to *Manchester Guardian Weekly* (14 Oct. 1927 quoted in K. Natarajan, *Miss Mayo's Mother India: A Rejoinder* (Madras: G.A. Natesan and Co., 1928) pp. 99–102.

securely bound and delivered before their womanhood is upon them, if they are to be kept in hand. His words are:

The "desire" ... against which India's solution of the marriage problem declared war, is one of Nature's most powerful fighters; consequently, the question of how to overcome it was not an easy one. There is a particular age, said India, at which this attraction between the sexes reaches its height; so if marriage is to be regulated according to the social will [as distinguished from the choice of the individual concerned], it must be finished with before such age. Hence the Indian custom of early marriage.[6]

In other words, a woman must be married before she knows she is one.

Such matter as this, coming as it does from one of the most widely known of modern Indian writers, may serve to suggest that we of the "material-minded West" shall be misled if we too quickly accept the Oriental's phrases as making literal pictures of the daily human life of which he seems to speak.

All thus far written here concerns the fate of children within the marriage bond. The general subject of prostitution in India need not enter the field of this book; but certain special aspects therefore may be cited because of the compass bearings that they afford.

In some parts of the country, more particularly in the Presidency of Madras and in Orissa, a custom obtains among the Hindus whereby the parents, to persuade some favor from the gods, may vow their next born child, if it be a girl, to the gods. Or, a particularly lovely child, for one reason or another held superfluous in her natural surroundings, is presented to the temple. The little creature, accordingly, is delivered to the temple women, her predecessors along the route, for teaching in dancing and singing. Often by the age of five, when she is considered most desirable, she becomes the priests' own prostitute.[†]

[6]*The Book of Marriage*, Keyserling, Harcourt, Brace & Co., New York, 1926, p. 112.

[†]For a discussion of the institution of temple prostitution, see Amrit Srinivasan, "Reform or Conformity? Temple Prostitution and the Community in the Madras Presidency" in *Structures of Patriarchy* (ed.) Bina Agarwal (Delhi: Kali for Women, 1988) and "Reform and Revival: The Devadasi and Her Dance", *Economic and Political Weekly* 20:40 (2 Nov 1985); also S. Anandhi, "Representing Devadasis: 'Dasigal Mosavalai' as a Radical Text", *Economic and Political Weekly* 26: 11–12 (1191): 739–46.

If she survives to later years she serves as a dancer and singer before the shrine in the daily temple worship; and in the houses around the temple she is held always ready, at a price, for the use of men pilgrims during their devotional sojourns in the temple precincts. She now goes beautifully attired, often loaded with the jewels of the gods, and leads an active life until her charms fade. Then, stamped with the mark of the god under whose aegis she has lived, she is turned out upon the public, with a small allowance and with the acknowledged right to a beggar's livelihood. Her parents, who may be well-to-do persons of good rank and caste, have lost no face at all by the manner of their disposal of her. Their proceeding, it is held, was entirely reputable. And she and her like form a sort of caste of their own, are called *devadassis*, or "prostitutes of the gods," and are a recognized essential of temple equipment.[7]

Now, if it were asked how a responsible Government permits this custom to continue in the land, the answer is not far to seek. The custom, like its background of public sentiment, is deep-rooted in the far past of an ultra-conservative and passionately religiose people. Any one curious as to the fierceness with which it would be defended by the people, both openly and covertly, and in the name of religion, against any frontal attack, will find answer in the extraordinary work[8] and in the too-reticent books[9] of Miss Amy Wilson-Carmichael.

A province could be roused to madness by the forcible withdrawal of girl-children from the gods.

"You cannot hustle the East." But the underground workings of western standards and western contacts, and the steady, quiet teachings of the British official through the years have done more, perhaps, toward ultimate change than any coercion could have effected.

---

[7]Cf. *The Golden Bough*, J.G. Frazer, Macmillan & Co., London, 1914. *Adonis, Attis, Osiris*, Vol. I, pp. 61–5.

[8]In Dohnavur, Tinnevelly District, South India.

[9]*Lotus Buds, Things As They Are*, etc., Morgan & Scott, London.

Thus, when one measure came before the Legislative Assembly to raise the age of consent outside the marriage bond it was vigorously resisted by that conspicuous member, the then Rao Bahadur T. Rangachariar. His argument was, that such a step would work great hardships to the temple prostitutes.

And why?

Because, as he explained, the daughters of the *devadassis* cannot be married to caste husbands; so,[10]

as these girls cannot find wedlock, the mothers arrange with a certain class of Zemindars—big landlords—that they should be taken into alliance with the Zemindar.

And the sympathetic legislator goes on in warning that if the girl's age is raised, no *zemindar* will desire her, with the result that a good bargain is lost and the child is planted on her poor mother's hands.

But the interesting point in the debate is not the eminent Brahman's voicing of the mass-sentiment of his people, but the opposition that his words call forth from the seats around him, which are almost at one in their disapproval of an argument that, a generation earlier, would have met another reception.

Then followed the member from Orissa, Mr. Misra, with his views on *devadassis* or ordinary *dassis* or prostitutes:[11]

They have existed from time immemorial. ... They are regarded as a necessity even for marriage and other parties, and for singing songs in invocation of God. ... Much has been said about girls being disposed of to Zemindars and Rajas.[12] ... Zemindars never get any girls from procurers. What happens is this. When Zemindars or Rajas marry, their wives or Ranis bring with them some girls as maid servants. ... Such a thing as procuring of girls does not exist and no gentleman, whether he be a Zemindar or a Raja or an ordinary man, would ever adopt such a nefarious means to procure girls. ... Why should we think so much about these people [minor girls] who are able to take care of themselves?

[10]*Legislative Assembly Debates*, 1923, Vol. III, Part IV, pp. 2807–8.

[11]*Ibid.*, pp. 2826–7.

[12]A Hindu title, inferior to Maharaja.

Mr. Misra's speech, although it dealt with simple facts, evoked another manifestation of western influence, in that it definitely jarred upon many of his colegislators. However true, they did not want it spread in the record. Cries of "Withdraw!" repeatedly interrupted him, and the words of other speakers gave ample proof of stirrings, intellectually, at least, of a new perception in the land.

To translate intellectual perception into concrete act requires yet another subversive mental process, in a people whose religion teaches that freedom from all action is the crown of perfect attainment.

Chapter V

SPADES ARE SPADES

To visualize the effects of child-marriage as outlined by the legislators just quoted, one of the most direct means that the foreigner in India can take is to visit women's hospitals. This I have done from the Punjab to Bombay, from Madras to the United Provinces. This a man can scarcely do, for the reason that, doctor or not, he will rarely be admitted to the sight of a woman patient.

In one of the cities of the northeast is a little *purdah*[1] hospital of great popularity among Indian women. The timid creatures who crowd it are often making thereby their first excursion outside the walls of their own homes, nor would they have ventured now save for the pain that drove them. Muhammadans always, Hindus often, arrive in *purdah* conveyances—hidden in curtained carriages, or in little close-draped boxes barely high enough to hold their crouching bodies, swinging on a pole between bearers like bales of goods. Government clerks' wives they are, wives of officials or of professional men, rich women sometimes, sometimes poor, women of high caste, women of low caste—too desperate, all, for the help they are dying for, to set up against themselves their cherished bars of religious hatreds and caste repulsions.

The hospital consists of a series of little one-story bungalows, partly in wards, partly in single rooms. At the start, years ago, it was slow business getting the women to come; the first season producing a total of nine midwifery cases. But now every bed is full, even the verandas are crowded with cots, and women by scores, for whom there is no space, are pleading for admission.

[1]The seclusion of women as in a harem.

Walking down the aisles you see, against the white plane òf the pillows, dark faces of the non-Aryan stock, lighter faces of Brahmans, fine-cut faces of the northern Persian-Muhammadan strain, coarse faces of the South, all alike looking out from behind a common veil of helplessness and pain. Most of the work, here, is gynecological. Most of the women are very young. Almost all the venereally affected.

Some come because they are childless, begging for either medicine or an operation to give them the one thing that buys an Indian wife a place in the sun. "Among such," says the British surgeon-superintedent, "we continually find that the patient has had one child, often dead, and that then she has been infected with gonorrhea, which has utterly destroyed the pelvic organs. The number of young girls that come here, so destroyed in their first years of married life, is appalling. Ninety per cent of the pelvic inflammation is of gonorrheal origin.

"Here," she continues, as we stop at the bedside of a young girl who looks up at us with the eyes of a hungry animal, "here is a new patient. She has had several children, all stillborn. This time, because her husband will no longer keep her unless she bears him a living child, she has come to us for confinement. As usual, it is a venereal case. But I hope we can help her."

"And what about this one?" I ask, pausing by another cot in inward revolt against the death-stricken look on the young face before us.

"That," answers the doctor, "is the wife of a Hindu official. He brought her to us three days ago, in the very onset of her second confinement, because, by the first, she had failed to give him a living child. Also she is suffering from heart-disease, asthma and a broken leg! I had to set her leg and confine her at practically one and the same time. It was a forceps case. Dead twins. She, too, is an internal wreck, from infection, and can never give birth again. But that she does not yet know; I think it would kill her if she heart it now.

"Her age? Thirteen and a few months."

"Now what can be wrong here?" I inquire, catching the smile of a wan-faced child whose bird's-claw hands are clasped around a paper toy.

"Ah!" says the doctor, "this one was a pupil in a Government primary school, a merry wee thing, and so bright that she had just won a prize for scholarship. During the holiday five months ago her brother sent her home to the man to whom they had married her. That man is fifty years old. From their point of view he is a Hindu gentleman beyond reproach. From our point of view he is a beast. ... What happened, this mite was too terrified to tell. For weeks she grew worse and worse. At last she went completely off her head. Then her sister, an old patient of ours, stole her away and dragged her here.

"I have never seen a creature so fouled. Her internal wounds were alive with maggots. For days after she got here, she lay speechless on her bed. Not a sound did she utter— only stared, with half blank, half terror-sticken eyes. Then one day it chanced that a child with a fractured arm was brought in and put in a bed near hers. And I, going through the ward, began playing with that child. This little one, watching, evidently began to think that here, perhaps, we were not all cruel monsters. Next day as I passed, she smiled. The day after that she put her arms around my neck, in a sort of maudlin fashion. That was the turning point in her mind. Now her mental balance is mending, though her body is still sick. Her memory, fortunately, has not recovered the immediate past. She lies there with her toys, wondering at them, feebly playing with them, or with her big eyes following our movements about the room. She is pitifully content.

"Meantime her husband is suing her to recover his marital rights and force her back into his possession.

She is not yet thirteen years old."

Such instances of mental derangement are common enough. Where should child-fabric, even though its inheritance had been the best instead of the weakest, find strength to withstand the strain? The case last cited was of well-to-do, educated, city-dwelling stock. But it differed in no essential from that of a younger child whom I saw in a village some three hundred miles distant. Married as a baby, sent to her husband at ten, the shock of incessant use was too much for her brain. It went. After that, beat her as he would, all that she could do was to crouch in the corner, a little twisted heap, panting. Not worth the keep. And so at last, in despair and rage over his bad bargain, he slung her small body over his shoulder, carried her out to the edge of the jungle, cast her in among the scrub thicket, and left her there to die.

This she must have done, but that an Indian witness to the deed carried the tale to an English lady who herself went out into the jungle, found the child, and brought her in. Her mind, they said, was slow in emerging from its stupor. But under the influence of peace and gentleness and the handling proper to a child, she began at last to blossom into normal intelligence. When I first saw her, a year and four months after her abandonment, she was racing about a pleasant old garden, romping with other happy little children, and contentedly hugging a doll. Her English protectors will keep her as long as they can. After that, what?

Except well to the north, the general condition thus indicated is found in most sections of India. Bombay Presidency has an outstanding number of educated and progressive women, but the status of the vast majority in that province, as in the rest, would more fairly be inferred from the other extreme—from, for example, the wife whom I saw, mother at nine and a half, by Cæsarean operation, of a boy weighing one and three quarter pounds.

Strike off across the peninsula, a thousand miles east of Bombay, and you have the same story. "What can be hoped from these infant wives?" says the superintendent of a hospital here—a most competent and devoted British lady doctor. "Their whole small stock of vitality is exhausted in the first pregnancy. Thence they go on, repeating the strain with no chance whatever of building up strength to give to the children that come so fast. A five-pound baby is large. In the neighborhood of four is the usual weight. Many are born dead; and all, because of their low vitality, are predisposed to any and every infection that may come along. My patients, here, are largely the wives of University students. Practically every one is venereally infected. When I first came out to India, I tried going to the parents of each such case to tell them of their daughter's state, in the hope that they would act in her behalf. But when I found that they had known the husband's diseased condition before giving their daughter in marriage, and could still see neither shame nor harm therein, I gave up the attempt. They do not look on it as an inconvenience, nor will they give weight to the fact that they are passing on a vile thing to the children.

"Now my question is, whether, in view of the chronic inadequacy of our hospital funds, I am right in giving the cure to these patients. It costs about twenty rupees ($6.66), and the woman is reinfected the day she returns to her own home. I could do so many other things with those precious twenty rupees! And yet—"

Again, in the great Madras Presidency, east or west, the tale is no better. "For the vast majority of women here," says a widely experienced surgeon, "marriage is a physical tragedy. The girl may bring to birth one or two sound children, but is by that time herself ruined and crippled, either from infection or cruel handling. In the thousands of gynecological cases that I have treated and am still treating, I have never found one woman who had not some form of venereal disease."

In other provinces of India, other medical men and women, European and western-educated Indian alike, gave me ample corroborative statements as to the effects of child motherhood. On the mother's part, increased predisposition to tuberculosis; displacement of organs; softening of immature bones, due to weight on spine and pelvis, presently causing disastrous obstructions to birth; hysteria and pathological mental derangements; stunting of mental and physical growth.

"A very small percentage of Indian women seem to me to be well and strong," adds a woman physician of wide present-day Indian experience. "This state I believe to be accounted for by a morbid and unawakened mentality, by venereal infection, and by sexual exhaustion. They commonly experience marital use two and three times a day."[†]

Thirty-six years ago, when the Age of Consent bill was being argued in the Indian Legislature, all the women doctors then working in India united to lay before the Viceroy a memorial and petition for the relief of those to whose help their own lives were dedicated. Affirming that they instanced only ordinary cases—cases taken from the common personal practice of one or another of their own number—they give as follows the conditions in which certain patients first came into their hands:[2]

A.—Aged 9. Day after marriage. Left femur dislocated, pelvis crushed out of shape. Flesh hanging in shreds.
B.—Aged 10. Unable to stand, bleeding profusely, flesh much lacerated.
C.—Aged 9. So completely ravished as to be almost beyond surgical repair. Her husband had two other living wives and spoke very fine English.
I.—Aged about 7. Living with husband. Died in great agony after three days.
M.—Aged about 10. Crawled to hospital on her hands and knees. Has never been able to stand erect since her marriage.

The original list is longer than here given. It will be found in the appendix of this book.[3]

This was in 1891. In 1922, the subject being again before the Indian Legislature, this same petition of the women surgeons was once more brought forward as equally applicable after the lapse of years. No one disputed, no one can yet dispute, its continued force. The Englishman who now introduced it into the debate could not bring himself to read its text aloud. But, referring to the bill raising the Age of Consent then under discussion, he concluded his speech thus:

A number of persons ... have said that this Bill is likely to give rise to agitation. No one dislikes agitation more than I do. I am sick of agitation. But

[2]*Legislative Assembly Debates*, 1922, Vol. III, Part I, pp. 881–3, and Appendix, p. 919.
[3]See Appendix I.
[†]Mayo is quoting from Miss Simon, Secretary of the Lady Chelmsford League in Punjab, who shared Mayo's views about the bleakness of the Indian situation without British help; see Folder no. 180, *Katherine Mayo Papers*, Series 4, Box 34.

when, Sir, it is a case of the lives of women and children, I can only say, in the words of the Duke of Wellington: "Agitate and be damned!"

In a recent issue of his weekly paper, *Young India*,[4] Mr. Gandhi printed an article over his own name entitled "Curse of Child Marriage." Said Mr. Gandhi:

It is sapping the vitality of thousands of our promising boys and girls on whom the future of our society entirely rests.

It is bringing into existence every year thousands of weaklings—both boys and girls—who are born of immature parenthood.

It is a very fruitful source of appalling child-mortality and still-births that now prevail in our society.

It is a very important cause of the gradual and steady decline of Hindu society in point of (1) numbers, (2) physical strength and courage, and (3) morality.

Not less interesting than the article itself is the reply that it quickly elicits from an Indian correspondent whom Mr. Gandhi himself vouches for as "a man occupying a high position in society." This correspondent writes:[5]

I am very much pained to read your article on "Curse of Child Marriage." ...

I fail to understand why you could not take a charitable view of those whose opinion differs from you. ... I think it improper to say that those who insist on child marriage are "steeped in vice." ...

The practice of early marriage is not confined to any province or class of society, but is practically a universal custom in India. ...

The chief objection to early marriage is that it weakens the health of the girl and her children. But this objection is not very convincing for the following reasons. The age of marriage is not rising among the Hindus, but the race is becoming weaker. Fifty or a hundred years ago the men and women were generally stronger, healthier and more long-lived than now. But early marriage was then more in vogue. ... From these facts it appears probable that early marriage does not cause as much physical deterioration as some people believe. ...

The type of logic employed in the paragraph last quoted is so essentially Indian that its character should not be passed by without particular note. The writer sees no connection between the practice of the grand-parents and the condition of

[4]*Young India*, August 26, 1926, p. 302.

[5] *Young India*, Sept. 9, 1926, p. 318.

the grandchildren, even though he sets both down in black and white on the paper before him.

A voice in the wilderness, Mr. Gandhi continues the attack, printing still further correspondence drawn forth by his original article. He gives the letter of a Bengali Hindu lady, who writes:[6]

I don't know how to thank you for your speaking on behalf of the poor girl-wives of our Hindu society. ... Our women always bear their burden of sorrow, in silence, with meekness. They have no power left in them to fight against any evil whatever.

To this Mr. Gandhi rejoins by adducing from his own knowledge instances in support, such as that of a sixty-year-old educationalist, who, without loss of public respect, has taken home a wife of nine years. But he ends on a rare new note, arraigning India's western-taught women who spend their energies in politics, publicity-seeking, and empty talk, to the utter neglect of the crucial work for India that only they can do:[7]

May women always throw the blame on men and salve their consciences? ... They may fight, if they like, for votes for women. It costs neither time nor trouble. It provides them with innocent recreation. But where are the brave women who work among the girl-wives and girl-widows, and who would take no rest and leave none for men, till girl-marriage became an impossibility?

It has been the habit, in approaching these matters, to draw a veil before their nakedness and pass quickly by. Searching missionaries' reports for light out of their long experience, one finds neat rows of dots, marking the silent tombs of the indecorous. For the missionary is thinking, first, of the dovecotes at home whence his money comes, and on whose sitting-room tables his report will be laid; and, second, of the super-sensitive Indians on whose sufferance he depends for whatever measure of success he may attain. Again, laymen who know the facts have written around rather than about them, swathing the spot in euphemisms, partly to avoid the

[6]*Ibid.*, Oct. 7, 1926, p. 349.
[7]*Ibid.*

Indian's resentment at being held up to a disapproval whose grounds he can neither feel nor understand, partly out of respect to the occidental reader's taste.

Yet, to suppress or to veil the bare truth is, in cases such as this, to belie it. For few western readers, without plain telling, spade by spade, will imagine the conditions that exist.

Given, then, a constructive desire really to understand India's problems, it is merely what Mr. Gandhi calls "self-deception, the worst of sins," to beg off from facing the facts in these fundamental aspects of Indian life. And if any one is inclined to bolt the task, let him stop to consider whether he has a right so to humor himself, a right to find it too hard even to speak or to hear of things that millions of little children, and of women scarcely more than children, are this very day enduring in their tormented flesh.

PART II

Interlude

THE GRAND TRUNK ROAD

The Grand Trunk Road, at the Khyber. Black, barren, jagged hills scowl into the chasm that cleaves them. Tribesmen's villages on either side—each house in itself a fortalice, its high fighting towers surrounded by high, blind walls loop-holed for rifles.

"What is your calling?" you ask the master. "What but the calling of my people?" says he. "We are raiders."

They may not shoot across the road, it being the highway of the King-Emperor. But on either side they shoot as they please, the country being their country. Their whole life is war, clan on clan, house on house, man on man, yet, for utter joy, Muslim on Hindu. Hills are bare, food is scarce, and the delight of life is stalking human prey, excelling its cunning.

Two miles of camels, majestic, tail to nose, nose to tail, bearing salt, cotton and sugar from India to Asia, swinging gloriously past two miles of camels, nose to tail, tail to nose, bearing the wares of Asia into India. Armed escorts of Afridi soldiers. Armed posts. Frequent roadside emplacements for three or four sharp-shooters with rifles. Barbed wire entanglements. Tribesmen afoot, hawk-nosed, hawk-eyed, carrying two rifles apiece, taking the lay of the land on the off-chance. Tramp—tramp—a marching detachment of the 2nd Battalion Royal Fusiliers—open-faced, bright-skinned English lads, smart and keen—an incredible sight in that setting. Yet because of them and them only may the Hindu today venture the Khyber. Until the Pax Britannica reached so far, few Hindus came through alive, unless mounted and clad as women.

The Grand Trunk Road rolls South and South—a broad, smooth river of peace whose waves are unthinking humanity. Monkeys of many sorts play along its sides. Peacocks. Deer. Herds of camels shepherded by little naked boys entirely competent. Dust of traffic. White bullocks, almond-eyed, string upon string of sky-blue beads twisted around their necks and horns, pulling wains heaped high with cotton for Japan. Villages—villages—villages—true homes of India, scattered, miles apart, across the open country. Each just a handful of mud-walled huts clustered beside the hole they took the mud from, now half full of stagnant water in which they wash and bathe and quench their thirst. In villages such as these live nine-tenths of all the peoples of India. Hindu or Muhammadan alike—hard-working cultivators of the soil, simple, illiterate, peaceful, kindly, save when men steal amongst them carrying fire.

Sunset. The ghost of a ghost—a thin long veil of blue, floating twice a man's height above the earth. Softly it widens, deepens, till all the air is blue and the tall tree-trunks and the stars themselves show blue behind it. Now comes its breath—a biting tang of smoke—the smoke of all the hearth-fires in all the villages. And this is the hour, this the incense, this the invocation of Mother India, walking among the tree-trunks in the twilight, veiled in the smoke of the heart-fires of her children, her hands outstretched in entreaty, blue stars shining in her hair.

For the rest, the Grand Trunk is just *Kim*. Read it again, for all of it is true. Zam Zammah still stands in Lahore. Mahbub Ali died three years ago, but his two boys are in England at school. And the old Lady still travels in her bullock-cart, scolding shrilly through her curtains into the clouds of dust.

Chapter VI

THE EARTHLY GOD

A beautiful Rolls-Royce of His Highness's sending was whirling us along the road from the Guest House to the Palace. My escort, one of the chief officials of the Prince's household, a high-caste orthodox Brahman scholar easily at home in his European dress, had already shown readiness to converse and to explain.

"Let us suppose," I now asked him, "that you have an infant daughter. At what age will you marry her?"

"At five—at seven—but I must surely marry her," he replied in his excellent English, "before she completes her ninth year."

"And if you do not, what is the penalty, and upon whom does it fall?"

"It falls upon me; I am outcasted by my caste. None of them will eat with me or give me water to drink or admit me to any ceremony. None will give me his daughter to marry my son, so that I can have no son's son of right birth. I shall have, in fact, no further social existence. No fellow caste-man will even lend his shoulder to carry my body to the burning-ghat. And my penance in the next life will be heavier still than this."

"Then as to the child herself, what would befall her?"

"The child? Ah, yes. According to our law I must turn her out of my house and send her into the forest alone. There I must leave her with empty hands. Thenceforth I may not notice her in any way. Nor may any Hindu give her food or help from the wild beasts, on penalty of sharing the curse."

"And would you really do that thing?"

"No; for the reason that occasion would not arise. I could not conceivably commit the sin whose consequence it is."

It was noticeable that in this picture the speaker saw no suffering figure save his own.

A girl child, in the Hindu scheme, is usually a heavy and unwelcome cash liability. Her birth elicits the formal con- dolences of family friends. But not always would one find so ingenuous a witness as that prosperous old Hindu landowner who said to me: "I have had twelve children. Ten girls, which, naturally, did not live. Who, indeed, could have borne that burden! The two boys, of course, I preserved."

Yet Sir Michael O'Dwyer records a similar instance of open speech from his own days of service as Settlement Commis- sioner in Bharatpur:[1]

The sister of the Maharaja was to be married to a great Punjab Sirdar. The family pressed [the Maharaja being a minor] for the lavish expenditure usual on those occasions—£30,000 to £40,000—and the local members of the State Council supported their view. The Political Agent—the State being then under British supervision—and I strongly protested against such ex- travagance in a year of severe scarcity and distress. Finally, the matter was discussed in full Council. I asked the oldest member of the Council to quote precedents—how much had been sanctioned on similar marriages of the daughter or sister of a Maharaja in the past. He shook his head and said their was no precedent. I said, "How can that be?—the State has been in existence over two hundred years, and there have been eleven successions without adoption, from father to son; do you mean to tell me that there were never any daughters?" The old man hesitated a little, and then said, "Sahib, you know our customs, surely you know the reason. There were daughters born, but till this generation they were not allowed to grow up." And it was so.

But it is fair to remember that infanticide has been common not with primitive races only but with Greece, with Rome, with nearly all peoples known to history save those who have been affected by Christian or Muhammadan culture. Forbid- den in India by Imperial law, the ancient practice, so easily followed in secret, seems still to persist in many parts of the country.[2]

Statistical proof in such matters is practically unattainable, as will be realized later in this chapter. But the statement of the Superintendent of the United Provinces Census regarding

[1]*India As I Knew It*, Sir Michael O'Dwyer, Constable & Co., Ltd., London, 1925, p. 102.

[2]See *Census of India*, Vol. I, Part I, 1921, Appendix VI. See also *The Punjab Peasant in Prosperity and Debt*, M.L. Darling, Oxford 1925, pp. 58–9.

girl children of older growth is cautious enough to avoid all pitfalls:[3]

I very much doubt whether there is any active dislike of girl babies. ... But if there is no active dislike, there is unquestionably passive neglect. "The parents look after the son, and God looks after the daughter." The daughter is less warmly clad, she receives less attention when ill, and less and worse food when well. This is not due to cruelty, or even to indifference; it is due simply to the fact that the son is preferred to the daughter and all the care, attention and dainties are lavished on him, whilst the daughter must be content with the remnants of all three. ... The result is that [the female] death-rate between one and five is almost invariably somewhat higher than the male death-rate.

This attitude toward the unwanted was illustrated in an incident that I myself chanced upon in a hospital in Bengal. The patient, a girl of five or six years, had fallen down a well and sustained a bad cut across her head. The mother, with the bleeding and unconscious child in her arms, had rushed to the hospital for help. In a day or two tetanus developed. Now the child lay at death's door, in agony terrible to see. The crisis was on, and the mother, crouching beside her, a figure of grief and fear, muttered prayers to the gods while the English doctor worked. Suddenly, there at the bedside, stood a man—a Bengali *babu*—some sort of small official or clerk.

"Miss Sahib," he said, addressing the doctor, "I have come for my wife."

"Your wife!" exclaimed the doctor, sternly. "Look at your wife. Look at your child. What do you mean!"

"I mean," he went on, "that I have come to fetch my wife home, at once, for my proper marital use."

"But your child will die if her mother leaves her now. You cannot separate them—see!" and the child, who had somehow understood the threat even through her mortal pain, clung to her mother, wailing.

The woman threw herself prostrate upon the floor, clutched his knees, imploring, kissed his feet, and with her two hands, Indian fashion, took the dust from his feet and put

[3]*Census of India*, 1911, Vol. XV, p. 190.

it upon her head. "My lord, my lord," she wept, "be merciful!"

"Come away," said he. "I have need of you, I say. You have
left me long enough."

"My lord—the child—the little child—my Master!"

He gave the suppliant figure a thrust with his foot. "I have
spoken"—and with never another word or look, turning on
the threshold, he walked away into the world of sun.

The woman rose. The child screamed.

"Will you obey?" exclaimed the doctor, incredulous for all
her years of seeing.

"I dare not disobey," sobbed the woman—and, pulling her
veil across her stricken face, she ran after her man—crouching, like a small, weak animal.

The girl, going to her husband by her ninth or twelfth year,
or earlier, has little time and less chance to learn from books.
But two things she surely will have learned—her duty toward
her husband and her duty toward those gods and devils that
concern her.

Her duty toward her husband, as of old laid down in the
Padmapurana,[4] is thus translated:[5]

There is no other god on earth for a woman than her husband. The most
excellent of all the good works that she can do is to seek to please him by
manifesting perfect obedience to him. Therein should lie her sole rule of life.

Be her husband deformed, aged, infirm, offensive in his manners; let him
also be choleric, debauched, immoral, a drunkard, a gambler; let him frequent places of ill-repute, live in open sin with other women, have no affection whatever for his home; let him rave like a lunatic; let him live without
honour; let him be blind, deaf, dumb or crippled, in a word, let his defects be
what they may, let his wickedness be what it may, a wife should always look
upon him as her god, should lavish on him all her attention and care, paying
no heed whatsoever to his character and giving him no cause whatsoever for
displeasure. ...

A wife must eat only after her husband has had his fill. If the latter fasts,
she shall fast, too; if he touch not food, she also shall not touch it; if he be in
affliction, she shall be so, too; if he be cheerful she shall share his joy. ... She

---

[4]The *Puranas*, ancient religious poems, are the Bible of the Hindu
peoples.

[5]*Hindu Manners, Customs, and Ceremonies*, pp. 344–9.

must, on the death of her husband, allow herself to be burnt alive on the same funeral pyre; then everybody will praise her virtue. ...

If he sing she must be in ecstasy; if he dance she must look at him with delight; if he speak of learned things she must listen to him with admiration. In his presence, indeed, she ought always to be cheerful, and never show signs of sadness or discontent.

Let her carefully avoid creating domestic squabbles on the subject of her parents, or on account of another woman whom her husband may wish to keep, or on account of any unpleasant remark which may have been addressed to her. To leave the house for reasons such as these would expose her to public ridicule, and would give cause for much evil speaking.

If her husband flies into a passion, threatens her, abuses her grossly, even beats her unjustly, she shall answer him meekly, shall lay hold of his hands, kiss them, and beg his pardon, instead of uttering loud cries and running away from the house. ...

Let all her words and actions give public proof that she looks upon her husband as her god. Honoured by everybody, she shall thus enjoy the reputation of a faithful and virtuous spouse.

The Abbé Dubois found this ancient law still the code of nineteenth-century Hinduism, and weighed its aspect with philosophic care.[†] His comment ran:[6]

A real union with sincere and mutual affection, or even peace, is very rare in Hindu households. The moral gulf which exists in this country between the sexes is so great that in the eyes of a native the woman is simply a passive object who must be abjectly submissive to her husband's will and fancy. She is never looked upon as a companion who can share her husband's thoughts and be the first object of his care and affection. The Hindu wife finds in her husband only a proud and overbearing master who regards her as a fortunate woman to be allowed the honour of sharing his bed and board.

In the handling of this point by the modern [writer], Rabindranath Tagore, appears another useful hint as to the caution we might well observe in accepting, at their face value

---

[6]*Hindu Manners, Customs, and Ceremonies*, p. 231.

[†]Mayo's extensive quotations from Abbé J.A. Dubois's early nineteenth-century text on Hindu customs was criticised by Mayo's Indian critics. Mr. Walter F. Guthrie, Manager of the Standard Oil Company in Calcutta, had assured Mayo during her visit to India that all the nineteenth-century Frenchman had to say about India was still valid today. See Notes, Folder 189, *Katherine Mayo Papers*, Series 4 Box 35.

to us, the expressions of Hindu speakers and writers. Says Tagore, presenting the Hindu theory:[7]

For the purpose of marriage, spontaneous love is unreliable; its proper cultivation should yield the best results ... and this cultivation should begin before marriage. Therefore from their earliest years, the husband as an idea is held up before our girls, in verse and story, through ceremonial and worship. When at length they get this husband, he is to them not a person but a principle, like loyalty, patriotism, or such other abstractions. ...

As to the theory of the matter, let that be what it may. As to the actual practice of the times, material will be recalled from the previous pages of this book bearing upon the likeness of the Hindu husband, as such, to "loyalty," "patriotism," or any impersonal abstraction.

Mr. Gandhi tirelessly denounces the dominance of the old teaching. "By sheer force of a vicious custom," he repeats, "even the most ignorant and worthless men have been enjoying a superiority over women which they do not deserve and ought not to have."[8]

But a creed through tens of centuries bred into weak, ignorant, and fanatical peoples is not to be uprooted in one or two hundred years; neither can it be shaken by the wrath of a single prophet, however reverenced. The general body of the ancient law relating to the status and conduct of women yet reigns practically supreme among the great Hindu majority.

In the Puranic code great stress is laid upon the duty of the wife to her mother-in-law. Upon this foundation rests a tremendous factor in every woman's life. A Hindu marriage does not betoken the setting up of a new homestead; the little bride, on the contrary, is simply added to the household of the groom's parents, as that household already exists. There she becomes at once the acknowledged servant of the mother-in-law, at whose beck and call she lives. The father-in-law, the sister-in-law, demand what they like of her, and, bred as she is, it lies not in her to rebel. The very idea that she possibly could rebel or acquire any degree of freedom has neither root

[7]*The Book of Marriage* Keyserling, pp. 112–13.
[8]Quoted in *The Indian Social Reformer*, Oct. 29, 1922, p. 135.

nor ground in her mind. She exists to serve. The mother-in-law is often hard, ruling without mercy or affection; and if by chance the child is slow to bear children, or if her children be daughters, then, too frequently, the elder woman's tongue is a flail, her hand heavy in blows, her revengeful spirit set on clouding her victim's life with threats of the new wife who, according to the Hindu code, may supplant and enslave her.

Not infrequently, in pursuing my inquiry in the rural districts, I came upon the record of suicides of women between the ages of fourteen and nineteen. The commonest cause assigned by the Indian police recorder was "colic pains, and a quarrel with the mother-in-law."

As to the direct relation of wife to husband, as understood in high-class Hindu families today, it has thus been described by that most eminent of Indian ladies, whose knowledge of her sisters of all ranks and creeds is wide, deep, and kind, Miss Cornelia Sorabji:[9]

Chief priestess of her husband, whom to serve is her religion and her delight ... moving on a plane far below him for all purposes religious, mental and social; gentle and adoring, but incapable of participation in the larger interests of his life. ... To please his mother, whose chief handmaiden she is, and to bring him a son, these are her two ambitions. ... The whole idea of marriage in the east revolves simply on the conception of life; a community of interests, companionship, these never enter into the general calculation. She waits upon her husband when he feeds, silent in his presence, with downcast eyes. To look him in the face were bold indeed.

Then says Miss Sorabji, continuing her picture:[10]

When she is the mother of a son, greater respect is hers from the other women in the zenana ... she has been successful, has justified her existence. The self-respect it gives the woman herself is most marked. She is still a faithful slave to her husband, but she is an entity, a person, in so far as that is possible in a Hindu zenana; she can lift her head above the women who taunted her, her heart above the fear of a rival.

This general characterization of the wife in the *zenana* of educated, well-to-do, and prominent Hindus finds its faithful

---

[9]*Between the Twilights*, Cornelia Sorabji, Harper Brothers, London, 1908, pp. 125–32.

[10]*Ibid.*, pp. 45–6.

echo in one of many similar incidents that came to my notice in humbler fields. For the orthodox Hindu woman, whoever she be, will obey the law of her ancestors and her gods with a pride and integrity unaffected by her social condition.

The woman, in this case, was the wife of a small landowner in a district not far from Delhi. The man, unusually enlightened, sent her to hospital for her first confinement. But he sent her too late, and, after a severe ordeal, the child was born dead.

Again, the following year, the same story was repeated. The patient was brought late, and even the necessary Cæsarean operation did not save the child. Still a third time the *zemindar* appeared, bringing the wife; but now, taught by experience, he had moved in time. As the woman came out of the ether, the young English nurse bent over her, all aglow with the news.

"Little mother, happy little mother, don't you want to see your baby—don't you want to see your boy?"

The head on the pillow turned away. Faintly, slowly the words came back out of the pit of hopeless night:

"Who wants to see—a dead baby! I have seen—too many—too many—dead—dead—" the voice trailed into silence. The heavy eyelids closed.

Then Sister picked up the baby. Baby squealed.

On that instant the thing was already done—so quickly done that none could measure the time of its doing. The lifeless figure on the bed tautened. The great black eyes flashed wide. The thin arms lifted in a gesture of demand. For the first time in all her life, perhaps, this girl was thinking in the imperative.

"Give me my son!" She spoke as an empress might speak. "Send at once to my village and inform the father of my son that I desire his presence." Utterly changed. Endued with dignity—with self-respect—with importance.

The father came. All the relatives came, heaping like flies into the little family quarters attached, in Indian women's hospitals, to each private room. Ten days they sat there—over a dozen of them, in a space some fifteen by twenty feet square.

And on the tenth, in a triumphant procession, they bore home to their village mother and son.

Rich or poor, high caste or low caste, the mother of a son will idolize the child. She has little knowledge to give him, save knowledge of strange taboos and fears and charms and ceremonies to propitiate a universe of powers unseen. She would never discipline him, even though she knew the meaning of the word. She would never teach him to restrain passion or impulse or appetite. She has not the vaguest conception how to feed him or develop him. Her idea of a sufficient meal is to tie a string around his little brown body and stuff him till the string bursts. And so through all his childhood he grows as grew his father before him, back into the mists of time.

Yet, when the boy himself assumes married life, he will honor his mother above his wife, and show her often a real affection and deference. Then it is that the woman comes into her own, ruling indoors with an iron hand, stoutly maintaining the ancient tradition, and, forgetful of her former misery, visiting upon the slender shoulder of her little daughters-in-law all the burdens and the wrath that fell upon her own young back. But one higher step is perhaps reserved for her. With each grandson laid in her arms she is again exalted. The family line is secure. Her husband's soul is protected. Proud is she among women. Blessed be the gods!

Chapter VII

WAGES OF SIN

The reverse of the picture shows the Hindu widow—the accursed. That so hideous a fate as widowhood should befall a woman can be but for one cause—the enormity of her sins in a former incarnation. From the moment of her husband's decease till the last hour of her own life, she must expiate those sins in shame and suffering and self-immolation, chained in every thought to the service of his soul. Be she a child of three, who knows nothing of the marriage that bound her, or be she a wife in fact, having lived with her husband, her case is the same. By his death she is revealed as a creature of innate guilt and evil portent, herself convinced, when she is old enough to think at all, of the justice of her fate. Miss Sorab-ji thus treats the subject:[1]

The orthodox Hindu widow suffers her lot with the fierce enjoyment of martyrdom ... but nothing can minimize the evils of that lot. ... That she accepts the fact makes it no less of a hardship. For some sin committed in a previous birth, the gods have deprived her of a husband. What is left to her now but to work out his "salvation" and by her prayers and penances to win him a better place in his next genesis? ... for the mother-in-law, what also is left but the obligation to curse? ... But for this luckless one, her son might still be in the land of the living. ... There is no determined animosity in the attitude. The person cursing is as much an instrument of Fate as the person cursed. ... [But] it is all very well to assert no personal animosity toward her whom you hold it a privilege to curse and to burden with every unpleasant duty imaginable. Your practise is apt to mislead.

The widow becomes the menial of every other person in the house of her late husband. All the hardest and ugliest tasks are hers, no comforts, no ease. She may take but one meal a day and that of the meanest. She must perform strict fasts. Her hair must be shaven of. She must take care to absent

[1]*Between the Twilights*, pp. 144–6.

herself from any scene of ceremony or rejoicing, from a marriage, from a religious celebration, from the sight of an expectant mother or of any person whom the curse of her glance might harm. Those who speak to her may speak in terms of contempt and reproach; and she herself is the priestess of her own misery, for its due continuance is her one remaining merit.

The old French traveler, Bernier, states that the pains of widowhood were imposed "as an easy mode of keeping wives in subjection, of securing their attention in times of sickness, and of deterring them from administering poison to their husbands."[2]

But once, however, did I hear this ideal from a Hindu's lips. "We husbands so often make our wives unhappy," said this frank witness, "that we might well fear they would poison us. Therefore did our wise ancestors make the penalty of widowhood so frightful—in order that the woman may not be tempted."

In the female wards of prisons in many parts of India I have seen women under sentence for the murder of their husbands. These are perhaps rare mentalities, perhaps hysteria cases. More characteristic are the still-recurring instances of practical *suttee*, where the newly-widowed wife deliberately pours oil over her garments, sets them afire and burns to death, in a connived-at secrecy. She has seen the fate of other widows. She is about to become a drudge, a slave, starved, tyrannized over, abused—and this is the sacred way out— "following the divine law." Committing a pious and meritorious act, in spite of all foreign-made interdicts, she escapes a present hell and may hope for happier birth in her next incarnation.

Although demanded in the scripture already quoted, the practice of burning the widow upon the husband's funeral pyre is today unlawful. But it must be noted that this change represents an exceptional episode; it represents not a natural

[2]*Travels in the Mogul Empire, A.D. 1956–1668*, François Bernier, Oxford University Press, 1916, pp. 310–11.

advance of public opinion, but one of the rare incursions of the British strong hand into the field of native religions. *Suttee* was forbidden by British Governors[3] some twenty-nine years before the actual taking over by the Crown of direct government.[†] That advanced Indian, Raja Ram Mohan Roy, supported the act. But other influential Bengali gentlemen, vigorously opposing, did not hesitate to push their fight for the preservation of the practice even to the court of last resort—the Privy council in London.

Is it conceivable that, given opportunity, the submerged root of the matter might come again to life and light? In Mr. Gandhi's weekly[4] of November 11, 1926, a Hindu writer declares the impossibility of a widow's remarriage today, without the deathbed permission of the deceased husband. No devout husband will give such permission, the correspondent affirms, and adds: "He will rather fain agree to his wife's becoming *sati* [suttee] if she can."

An inmate of her husband's home at the time of his death, the widow, although she has no legal claim for protection, may be retained there on the terms above described, or she may be turned adrift. Then she must live by charity—or by prostitution, into which she not seldom falls. And her dingy, ragged figure, her bristly, shaven head, even though its stubble be white over the haggard face of unhappy age, is often to be seen in temple crowds or in the streets of pilgrimage cities, where sometimes niggard piety doles her a handful of rice.

As to remarriage, that, in orthodox Hinduism, is impossible. Marriage is not a personal affair, but an eternal sacrament. And it must never be forgotten that the great majority of the Hindus are orthodox to the bone. Whether the widow

[3]Regulation XVII of 1829.

[4]*Young India.*

[†]For a discussion of the abolition of the practice of 'sati' see Lata Mani, "The Production of an Official Discourse on Sati in Early 19th Century Bengal", *Economic and Political Weekly* (26 April 1987): WS32–WS40; and Anand Yang, "The Many Faces of Sati in the Early Nineteenth Century", *Manushi* 42–43 (1987): 26–29.

be an infant and a stranger to the man whose death, she is
told, was caused by her sins, or whether she be twenty and of
his bed and board, orthodoxy forbids her remarriage. Of
recent years, however, the gradual if unrecognized influence
of western teaching has aroused a certain response. In different sections of India, several associations have sprung up,
having the remarriage of virgin widows as one of their chief
purported objects. The movement, however, is almost wholly
restricted to the most advanced element of Hindu society, and
its influence is, as yet, too fractional appreciably to affect
statistics.

The observations on this point made by the Abbé Dubois a
century since still, in general, hold good. He saw that the marriage of a small child to a man of sixty and the forbidding of
her remarriage after his death must often throw the child, as a
widow, into a dissolute life. Yet widow remarriage was unknown.[†] Even were it permitted, says the Abbé, "the strange
preference which Brahmins have for children of very tender
years would make such a permission almost nominal in the
case of their widows."[5]

And one cannot forget, in estimating the effect of the
young widow on the social structure of which she is a part,
that, in her infancy, she lived in the same atmosphere of sexual
stimulus that surrounded the boy child, her brother. If a girl
child so reared in thought and so sharpened in desire be
barred from lawful satisfaction of desire, is it strange if the
desire prove stronger with her than the social law? Her family,

[5]*Hindu Manners, Customs and Ceremonies*, p. 212.

[†]For a discussion of how generalisations from the experience of certain
classes of women to all women in India affected those for whom
widow-remarriage was not prohibited traditionally, see Lucy Carroll,
"Law, Custom, and Statutory Social Reform: The Hindu Widow's
Remarriage Act of 1856", in *Women in Colonial India* (ed.) J. Krishnamurthy
(Delhi: Oxford University Press, 1989), pp. 1–26. See also Rosalind
O'Hanlon, "Issues of Widowhood: Gender and Resistance in Colonial
Western India" in *Contesting Power* (eds.) Douglas Haynes and Gyan
Prakash (Delhi: Oxford University Press, 1991).

the family of the dead husband, will, for their credit's sake, restrain her if they can. And often, perhaps most often, she needs no restraint save her own spirit of sacrifice. But the opposite example is frequently commented upon by Indian speakers. Lala Lajpat Rai, Swarajist politician, laments:[6]

The condition of child-widows is indescribable. God may bless those who are opposed to their remarriage, but their superstition introduces so many abuses and brings about so much moral and physical misery as to cripple society as a whole and handicap it in the struggle for life.

Mr. Gandhi acquiescently cites another Indian writer on child marriage and enforced child widowhood, thus: "It is bringing into existence thousands of girl-widows every year who in their turn are a source of corruption and dangerous infection to society."[7]

Talk there is, resolutions passed, in caste and association conventions, as to changing these things of oppression and of scornings. But a virgin widow's remarriage is still a headline event, even to the reform newspapers, while the remarriage of a Hindu widowed wife is still held to be inconceivable.

And here, curiously enough, the very influence that on the one hand most strongly operates to rescue the woman, on the other more widely enslaves her. While British practice and western education tend, at the top of the ladder, to breed discontent with ancient darkness, British public works, British sanitation and agricultural development, steadily raising the economic condition of the lower classes, as steadily breed aspirants to greater social prestige. Thus the census of 1921 finds restriction in widow remarriage definitely increasing in those low ranks of the social scale that, by their own code, have no such inhibition. Hindu caste rank is entirely independent of worldly wealth; but the first move of the man of little place, suddenly awakening to a new prosperity, security, and peace, is to mimic the manners of those to whom he has

[6]Presidential Speech delivered before the Hindu Mahasabha Conference, in Bombay, December, 1925.

[7]*Young India*, Aug. 26, 1926, p. 302.

looked up. He becomes a social climber, not less in India than in the United States, and assumes the shackles of the elect.

Mr. Mukerjea of Baroda, an Indian official observer, thus writes of attempts to break down the custom of obligatory widowhood:[8]

All such efforts will be powerless as long as authoritative Hindu opinion continues to regard the prohibition of widow remarriage as a badge of respectability. Amongst the lower Hindu castes, the socially affluent sections are discountenancing the practice of widow remarriage as actively as any Brahman.

It was a distinguished Bengali, the Pundit Iswar Chunder Vidyasagar, who, among Indians, started the movement for remarriage of virgin widows and supported Government in the enactment of a law legalizing such remarriages. But over him and the fruit of his work another eminent Indian thus laments:[9]

I well remember the stir and agitation which the movement produced and how orthodox Hindus were up in arms against it. ... The champion of the Hindu widows died a disappointed man, like so many of those who were in advance of their age, leaving his message unfulfilled. ... The progress which the movement has made since his death in 1891 has been slow. A new generation has sprung up, but he has found no successor. The mantle of Elijah has not fallen upon Elisha. The lot of the Hindu widow today remains very much the same that it was fifty years ago. There are few to wipe her tears and to remove the enforced widowhood that is her lot. The group of sentimental sympathisers have perhaps increased—shouting at public meetings on the Vidyasagar anniversary day, but leaving unredeemed the message of the great champion of the Hindu widow.

Mr. Gandhi, always true to his light, himself has said:[10]

To force widowhood upon little girls is a brutal crime for which we Hindus are daily paying dearly. ... There is no warrant in any shastra[11] for such widowhood. Voluntary widowhood consciously adopted by a woman who has felt the affection of a partner adds grace and dignity of life, sanctifies the home and uplifts religions itself. Widowhood imposed by religion or custom

[8]Census of India 1921, Vol. I, Chapter VII, paragraph 134.

[9]A Nation in the Making. Sir Surendranath Banerjea, Oxford University Press, 1925, pp. 8–3.

[10]Young India, August 5, 1926, p. 276.

[11]Hindu book of sacred institutes.

is an unbearable yoke and defiles the home by secret vice and degrades religion. And does not the Hindu widowhood stink in one's nostrils when one thinks of old and diseased men over fifty taking or rather purchasing girl wives, sometimes one on top of another?

But this, again, is a personal opinion, rather than a public force. "We want no more of Gandhi's doctrines," one conspicuous Indian politician told me; "Gandhi is a deluded man."

That distinguished Indian, Sir Ganga Ram, C.I.E., C.V.O., with some help from Government has built and endowed a fine home and school for Hindu widows in the city of Lahore. This establishment, in 1926, had over forty inmates. In Bombay Presidency are five Government-aided institutes for widows and deserted wives, run by philanthropic Indian gentlemen. Other such institutions may exist; but, if they do, their existence has escaped the official recorders. I myself saw, in the pilgrim city of Nawadwip, in Bengal, a refuge for widows maintained by local subscription and pilgrims' gifts. It was fourteen years old and had eight inmates—the extent, it appeared, of its intention and capacity.

The number of widows in India is, according to the latest published official computation, 26, 834, 838.[12]

[12]*Statistical Abstract for British India,* 1914–15 to 1923–24, Government of India Publication, 1925, p. 20.

Chapter VIII

MOTHER INDIA

Row upon row of girl children—little tots all, four, five, six, even seven years old, sitting cross-legged on the floor, facing the brazen goddess. Before each one, laid straight and tidy, certain treasures—a flower, a bead or two, a piece of fruit—precious things brought from their homes as sacrifice offerings. For this is a sort of day-school of piety. These babies are learning texts—"mantrims" to use in worship—learning the rites that belong to the various ceremonies incumbent upon Hindu women. And that is all they are learning; that is all they need to know. Now in unison they pray.

"What are they praying for?" one asks the teacher, a grave-faced Hindu lady.

"What should a woman-child pray for? A husband, if she is not married; or, if she is, then for a better husband at her next re-birth."

Women pray first as to husbands; then, to bear sons. Men must have sons to serve their souls.

Already we have seen some evidence of the general attitude of the Hindu toward this, the greatest of all his concerns, in its prenatal aspect. But another cardinal point that, in any practical survey of Indian competency, can be neither contested nor suppressed, is the manner in which the Hindu of all classes permits his much-coveted son to be ushered into the light of day.

We have spoken of women's hospitals in various parts of India. These are doing excellent work, mostly gynecological. But they are few, relatively to the work to be done, nor could the vast majority of Indian women, in their present state of development, be induced to use a hospital, were it at their very door.

What the typical Indian woman wants in her hour of trial is the thing to which she is historically used—the midwife—the *dhai*.[†] And the *dhai* is a creature that must indeed be seen to be credited.

According to the Hindu code, a woman in child-birth and in convalescence therefrom is ceremonially unclean, contaminating all that she touches. Therefore only those become *dhais* who are themselves of the unclean, "untouchable" class, the class whose filthy habits will be adduced by the orthodox Hindu as his good and sufficient reason for barring them from contact with himself. Again according to the Hindu code, a woman in childbirth, like the new-born child itself, is peculiarly susceptible to the "evil eye." Therefore no woman whose child has died, no one who has had no abortion, may, in many parts of India, serve as *dhai*, because of the malice or jealousy that may secretly inspire her. Neither may any widow so serve, being herself a thing of evil omen. Not all of these disqualifications obtain everywhere. But each holds in large sections.

Further, no sort of training is held necessary for the work. As a calling, it descends in families. At the death of a *dhai*, her daughter or daughter-in-law may adopt it, beginning at once to practice even though she has never seen a confinement in all her life.[1] But other women, outside the line of descent, may also take on the work and, if they are properly beyond the lines of the taboos, will find ready employment without any sort of preparation and for the mere asking.

Therefore, in total, you have the half-blind, the aged, the crippled, the palsied and the diseased, drawn from the dirtiest

[1]Cf. Edris Griffin, Health Visitor, Delhi, in *National Health*, Oct., 1925, p. 125.

[†]For a discussion of attitudes towards the India midwife/*dai*, see Sandhya Shetty, "(Dis) Locating Gender: Space and Medical Discourse in Colonial India", *Genders* 20 (1994): 188–230; and Geraldine Forbes, "Managing Midwifery in India", in *Contesting Colonial Hegemony* (eds.) Dagmar Engels and Shula Marks (London: German Historical Institute, 1994), pp. 515–30.

poor, as sole ministrants to the women of India in the most delicate, the most dangerous and the most important hour of their existence.

The expectant mother makes no preparations for the baby's coming—such as the getting ready of little garments. This would be taking dangerously for granted the favor of the gods. But she may and does toss into a shed or into a small dark chamber whatever soiled and disreputable rags, incapable of further use, fall from the hands of the household during the year.

And it is into this evil-smelling rubbish-hole that the young wife creeps when her hour is come upon her. "Unclean" she is, in her pain—unclean whatever she touches, and fit thereafter only to be destroyed. In the name of thrift, therefore, give her about her only the unclean and the worthless, whether human or inanimate. If there be a broke-legged, ragged string-cot, let her have that to lie upon; it can be saved in that same black chamber for the next to need it. Otherwise, make her a little support of cow-dung or of stones, on the bare earthen floor. And let no one waste effort in sweeping or dusting or washing the place till this occasion be over.[2]

When the pains begin, send for the *dhai*. If the *dhai*, when the call reaches her, chances to be wearing decent clothes, she will stop, whatever the haste, to change into the rags she keeps for the purpose, infected and re-infected from the succession of diseased cases that have come into her practice. And so, at her dirtiest, a bearer of multiple contagions, she shuts herself in with her victim.

If there be an air-hole in the room, she stops it up with straw and refuse; fresh air is bad in confinements—it gives fever. If there be rags sufficient to make curtains, she cobbles them together, strings them across a corner and puts the patient within, against the wall, still farther to keep away the air. Then, to make darkness darker, she lights the tiniest glim—a bit of cord in a bit of oil, or a little kerosene lamp

[2] *National Health*, 1925, p. 70. See also Maggie Ghose in *Victoria Memorial Scholarship Fund Report*, Calcutta, 1918, p. 153.

without a chimney, smoking villainously. Next, she makes a small charcoal fire in a pan beneath the bed or close by the patient's side, whence it joins its poisonous breath to the serried stenches.

The first *dhai* that I saw in action tossed upon this coal-pot, as I entered the room, a handful of some special vile-smelling stuff to ward off the evil eye—my evil eye. The smoke of it rose thick—also a tongue of flame. By that light one saw her Witch-of-Endor face through its vermin-infested elf-locks, her hanging rags, her dirty claws, as she peered with festered and almost sightless eyes out over the stink-cloud she had raised. But it was not she who ran to quench the flame that caught in the bed and went writhing up the body of her unconscious patient. She was too blind—too dull of sense to see or to feel it.

If the delivery is at all delayed, the *dhai* is expected to explore for the reason of the delay. She thrusts her long-un-washed hand, loaded with dirty rings and bracelets and encrusted with untold living contaminations, into the patient's body, pulling and twisting at what she finds there.[3] If the delivery is long delayed and difficult, a second or a third *dhai* may be called in, if the husband of the patient will sanction the expense, and the child may be dragged forth in detached sections—a leg or an arm torn off at a time.[4]

Again to quote from a medical woman:[5]

One often sees in cases of contracted pelvis due to osteomalacia, if there seems no chance of the head passing down [that the *dhai*] attempts to draw on the limbs, and, if possible, breaks them off. She prefers to extract the child *by main force*, and the patient in such cases is badly torn, often into her bladder, with the resulting large vesico-vaginal fistulae so common in Indian women and which causes them so much misery.

[3]*V.M.S.F. Report*, "Improvement of the Conditions of Child-Birth in India," pp. 70 et seq.

[4]Dr. Marion A. Wylie., M.A., M.B., Ch. B., *Ibid.*, p. 85, and *Ibid.*, Appendix V, p. 69.

[5]*Ibid.*, p. 71.

Such labor may last three, four, five, even six days. During all this period the woman is given no nourishment whatever—such is the code—and the *dhai* resorts to all her traditions. She kneads the patient with her fists; stands her against the wall and butts her with her head; props her upright on the bare ground, seizes her hands and shoves against her thighs with gruesome bare feet, until, so the doctors state, the patient's flesh is often torn to ribbons by the *dhai's* long, ragged toe-nails.[6] Or, she lays the woman flat and walks up and down her body, like one treading grapes. Also, she makes balls of strange substances, such as hollyhock roots, or dirty string, or rags full of quince-seeds; or earth, or earth mixed with cloves, butter and marigold flowers; or nuts, or spices—any irritant—and thrusts them into the uterus, to hasten the event. In some parts of the country, goats' hair, scorpions' stings, monkey-skulls, and snake-skins are considered valuable applications.[7]

These insertions and the wounds they occasion commonly result in partial or complete permanent closing of the passage.

If the afterbirth be over five minutes in appearing, again the filthy, ringed and bracelet-loaded hand and wrist are thrust in, and the placenta is ripped loose and dragged away.[8]

No clean clothes are provided for use in the confinement, and no hot water. Fresh cow-dung or goats' droppings, or hot ashes, however, often serve as heating agents' when the patient's body begins to turn cold.[9]

In Benares, sacred among cities, citadel of orthodox Hinduism, the sweepers, all of whom are "Untouchables," are divided into seven grades. From the first come the *dhais*; from the last and lowest come the "cord-cutters." To cut the umbilical cord is considered a task so degrading that in the Holy City even a sweep will not undertake it, unless she be at the bottom of her kind. Therefore the unspeakable *dhai* brings

---

[6]*V.M.S.F. Report*, p. 99, Dr. K.O. Vaughan.

[7]*Ibid.*, pp. 151–2, Mrs. Chowdhri, sub-assistant surgeon.

[8]*V.M.S.F. Report*, p. 86, Dr. M.A. Wylie.

[9]*Ibid.*, p. 152, Miss Vidyabai M. Ram.

with her a still more unspeakable servant to wreak her quality upon the mother and the child in birth.

Sometimes it is a split bamboo that they use; sometimes a bit of all old tin can, or a rusty nail, or a potsherd or a fragment of broken glass. Sometimes, having no tool of their own and having found nothing sharp-edged lying about, they go out to the neighbors to borrow. I shall not soon forget the cry: "Hi, there, inside! Bring me back that knife! I hadn't finished paring my vegetables for dinner."

The end of the cut cord, at best, is left undressed, to take care of itself. In more careful and less happy cases, it is treated with a handful of earth, or with charcoal, or with several other substances, including cow-dung. Needless to add, a heavy per cent of such children as survive the strain of birth, die of lock-jaw[10] or of erysipelas.

As the child is taken from the mother, it is commonly laid upon the bare floor, uncovered and unattended, until the *dhai* is ready to take it up. If it be a girl child, many simple rules have been handed down through the ages for discontinuing the unwelcome life then and there.

In the matter of feeding, practice varies. In the Central Provinces, the first feedings are likely to be of crude sugar mixed with the child's own urine.[11] In Delhi, it may get sugar and spices, or wine, or honey. Or, it may be fed for the first three days on something called *gutli*, a combination of spices in which have been stewed old rust-encrusted lucky coins and charms written out on scraps of paper. These things, differing somewhat in different regions, castes and communities, differ more in detail than in the quality of intelligence displayed.

As to the mother, she, as has already been said, is usually kept without any food or drink for from four to seven days

[10]"Ordinarily half the children born in Bengal die before reaching the age of eight years, and only one-quarter of the population reaches the age of forty years. ... As to the causes influencing infant mortality, 50 per cent of the deaths are due to debility at birth and 11.4 per cent to tetanus." *54th Annual Report of the Director of Public Health of Bengal*, pp. 8–10.

[11]*V.M.S.F. Report*, p. 86, Dr. M.A. Wylie.

from the outset of her confinement; or, if she be fed, she is given only a few dry nuts and dates. The purpose here seems sometimes to be one of thrift—to save the family utensils from pollution. But in any case it enjoys the prestige of an ancient tenet to which the economical spirit of the household lends a spontaneous support.[12]

In some regions or communities the baby is not put to the breast till after the third day[13]—a custom productive of dire results. But in others the mother is expected to feed not only the newly born, but her elder children as well, if she have them. A child three years old will not seldom be sent in to be fed at the mother's breast during the throes of a difficult labor. "It cried—it was hungry. It wouldn't have other food," the women outside will explain.

As a result, first, of their feeble and diseased ancestry; second, of their poor diet; and, third, of their own infant marriage and premature sexual use and infection, a heavy percentage of the women of India are either too small-boned or too internally misshapen and diseased to give normal birth to a child, but require surgical aid. It may safely be said that all these cases die by slow torture, unless they receive the care of a British or American woman doctor, or of an Indian woman, British-trained.[14] Such care, even though it be at hand, is often denied the sufferer, either by the husband or by the elder women of the family, in their devotion to the ancient cults.

[12]Edris Griffin, in *National Health,* Oct., 1925, p. 124.

[13]*V.M.S.F. Report,* p. 86.

[14]For the male medical student in India, instruction in gynecology and midwifery is extremely difficult to get, for the reason that Indian women can rarely be persuaded to come to hospitals open to medical men. With the exception of certain extremely limited opportunities, therefore, the Indian student must get his gynecology from books. Even though he learns it abroad, he has little or no opportunity to practice it. Sometimes, it is true, the western-diplomaed Indian doctor will conduct a labor case by sitting on the far side of a heavy curtain calling out advice based on the statements shouted across by the *dhai* who is handling the patient. But this scarcely constitutes "practice" as the word is generally meant.

Or, even in cases where a delivery is normal, the results, from an Indian point of view, are often more tragic than death. An able woman surgeon, Dr. K.O. Vaughan, of the Zenana Hospital at Srinagar, thus expresses it:[15]

Many women who are childless and permanently disabled are so from the maltreatment received during parturition; many men are without male issue because the child has been killed by ignorance when born, or their wives so mangled by the midwives they are incapable of further childbearing. ...

I [illustrate] my remarks with a few cases typical of the sort of thing every medical woman practising in this country encounters.

A summons comes, and we are told a woman is in labour. On arrival at the house we are taken into a small, dark and dirty room, often with no window. If there is one it is stopped up. Puerperal fever is supposed to be caused by fresh air. The remaining air is vitiated by the presence of a charcoal fire burning in a pan, and on a *charpoy* [cot] or on the floor is the woman. With her are one or two dirty old women, their clothes filthy, their hands begrimed with dirt, their heads alive with vermin. They explain that they are midwives, that the patient has been in labour three days, and they cannot get the child out. They are rubbing their hands on the floor previous to making another effort. On inspection we find the vulva swollen and torn. They tell us, yes, it is a bad case and they have had to use both feet and hands in their effort to deliver her. ... Chloroform is given and the child extracted with forceps. We are sure to find hollyhock roots which have been pushed inside the mother, sometimes string and a dirty rag containing quince-seeds in the uterus itself. ...

Do not think it is the poor only who suffer like this. I can show you the homes of many Indian men with University degrees whose wives are confined on filthy rags and attended by these Bazaar *dhais* because it is the custom, and the course for the B.A. degree does not include a little common sense.

Doctor Vaughan then proceeds to quote further illustrations from her own practice, of which the following is a specimen:[16]

A wealthy Hindu, a graduate of an Indian University and a lecturer himself, a man who is highly educated, calls us to his house, as his wife has been delivered of a child and has fever. ... We find that [the *dhai*] had no disinfectants as they would have cost her about Rs. 3 [one dollar, American], and the fee she will get on the case is only Rs. 1 and a few dirty clothes. The patient is lying on a heap of cast-off and dirty clothes, an old waistcoat, an English

[15]*V.M.S.F. Report*, pp. 98–9.
[16]*V.M.S.F. Report*, pp. 99–100.

railway rug, a piece of water-proof packing from a parcel, half a stained and dirty shirt of her husband's. There are no sheets or clean rags of any kind. As her husband tells me: "We shall give her clean things on the fifth day, but not now; that is our custom."

That woman, in spite of all we could do, died of septicæmia contracted either from the dirty clothing which is saved from one confinement in the family to another [unwashed], or from the *dhai*, who did her best in the absence of either hot water, soap, nail-brush or disinfectants.

Evidence is in hand of educated, traveled and well-born Indians, themselves holders of European university degrees, who permit their wives to undergo this same inheritance of darkness. The case may be cited of an Indian medical man, holding an English University's Ph.D. and M.D. degrees, considered to be exceptionally able and brilliant and now actually in charge of a government center for the training of *dhais* in modern midwifery. His own young wife being recently confined, he yielded to the pressure of the elder women of his family and called in an old-school *dhai*, dirty and ignorant as the rest, to attend her. The wife died of puerperal fever; the child died in the birth. "When we have the spectacle of even educated Indians with English degrees allowing their wives and children to be killed off like flies by ignorant midwives," says Doctor Vaughan again, "we can faintly imagine the sufferings of their humbler sisters."

But the question of station or of worldly goods has small part in the matter. To this the admirable sisterhood of English and American women doctors unites to testify.

Dr. Marion A. Wylie's words are:[17]

These conditions are by no means confined to the poorest or most ignorant classes. I have attended the families of Rajahs, where many of these practices were carried out, and met with strenuous opposition when I introduced ventilation and aseptic measures.

Sweeper-girl or Brahman, outcaste or queen, there is essentially little to choose between their lots, in that fierce moment for which alone they were born. An Indian Christian lady of distinguished position and attainment, whose character has opened to her many doors that remain to others fast closed,

[17]*Ibid.*, p. 86.

gives the following story of her visit of mercy to a child-princess.

The little thing, wife of a ruling prince and just past her tenth year, was already in labor when her visitor entered the room. The *dhais* were busy over her, but the case was obviously serious, and priestly assistance had been called. Outside the door sat its exponent—an old man, reading aloud from the scriptures and from time to time chanting words of direction deciphered from his book.

"Hark, within, there!" he suddenly shouted. "Now it is time to make a fire upon this woman's body. Make and light a fire upon her body, quick!"

Instantly the *dhais* set about to obey.

"And what will the fire do to our little princess?" quietly asked the visitor, too practiced to express alarm.

"Oh," replied the women, listlessly, "if it be her fate to live, she will live, and there will, of course, be a great scar branded upon her. Or, if it be her fate to die, then she will die"—and on they went with their fire-building.

Out to the ministrant squatting at the door flew the quick-witted visitor. "Holy One," she asked, "are you not afraid of the divine jealousies? You are about to make the Fire-sacrifice—but this is a queen, not a common mortal. Will not Mother Ganges see and be jealous that no honor is paid to her?"

The old man looked up, perplexed. "It is true," he said, "it is true the gods are ever jealous and easily provoked to anger—but the Book here surely says—" And his troubled eyes turned to the ancient writ out-spread upon his knees.

"Have you Ganges water here in the house?" interrupted the other.

"Surely. Dare the house live without it!" answered the old one.

"Then here is what I am given to say: Let water of Holy Ganges be put upon bright fire and made thrice hot. Let it then be poured into a marvel-sack that the gods, by my hand, shall provide. And let that sack be laid upon the Maharani's body. So in a united offering—fire and water together—shall the gods be propitiated and their wrath escaped."

"This is wisdom. So be it!" cried the old man. Then quick ran the visitor to fetch her Bond Street hot-water bag.

Superstition, among the Indian peoples, knows few boundary lines of condition or class. Women in general are prone to believe that disease is an evidence of the approach of a god. Medicine and surgery, driving that god away, offend him, and it is ill business to offend the Great Ones; better, therefore, charms and propitiations, with an eye to the long run.

And besides the gods, there are the demons and evil spirits, already as many as the sands of the sea, to whose number more must not be added.

Among the worst of demons are the spirits of women who died in childbirth before the child was born. These walk with their feet turned backward, haunting lonely roads and the family hearth, and are malicious beyond the rest.

Therefore, when a woman is seen to be about to breathe her last, her child yet undelivered—she may have lain for days in labor for a birth against which her starveling bones are locked—the *dhai*, as in duty bound, sets to work upon precautions for the protection of the family.

First she brings pepper and rubs it into the dying eyes, that the soul may be blinded and unable to find its way out. Then she takes two long iron nails, and, stretching out her victim's unresisting arms—for the poor creature knows and accepts her fate—drives a spike straight through each palm fast into the floor. This is done to pinion the soul to the ground, to delay its passing or that it may not rise and wander, vexing the living. And so the woman dies, piteously calling to the gods for pardon for those black sins of a former life for which she now is suffering.

This statement, horrible as it is, rests upon the testimony of many and unimpeachable medical witnesses in widely separated parts of India. All the main statements in this chapter rest upon such testimony and upon my own observation.

It would be unjust to assume, however, that the *dhai*, for all her monstrous deeds, is a blameworthy creature. Every move that she makes is a part of the ancient and accepted ritual of her calling. Did she omit or change any part of it, nothing would be gained; simply the elder women of the households she serves would revile her for incapacity and call in another more faithful to the creed.

Her services include attendance at the time of confinement and for ten days, more or less, thereafter, the approximate interval during which no member of the family will approach the patient because of her uncleanness. During this time the *dhai* does all that is done for the sick woman and the infant. At its end she is expected to clean the defiled room and coat with cow-dung its floor and walls.

She receives her pay in accordance with the sex of the child that was born. These sums vary. A rich man may give her for the entire period of service as much as Rs. 15 (about $5.00) if the child be a son. From the well-to-do the more usual fee is about Rs. 1 ($.33) for a son and eight annas ($.16) for a daughter. The poor pay the *dhai* for her fortnight's work the equivalent of four or five cents for a son and two to three cents for a daughter. Herself the poorest of the poor, she has no means of her own wherewith to buy as much as a cake of soap or a bit of clean cotton. None are anywhere provided for her. And so, the slaughter goes on.[18]

Various funds subscribed by British charity sustain maternal and child-welfare works in many parts of India, whose devoted British doctors and nurses attempt to teach the *dhais*. But the task is extremely difficult. Invariably the *dhais* protest that they have nothing to learn, in which their clients agree with them. One medical woman said in showing me her *dhai* class, an appalling array of decrepit old crones:

"We pay these women, out of a fund from England, for coming to class. We also pay some of them not to practice, a small sum, but just enough to live on. They are too old, too stupid and too generally miserable to be capable of learning. Yet, when we beg them not to take cases because of the harm

[18]*V.M.S.F. Report*, p. 89.

they do, they say: 'How else can we live? This is our only means to earn food.' Which is true."

A characteristic incident, freshly happened when it came to my knowledge, concerned a Public Health instructor stationed, by one of the funds above mentioned, in the north. To visualize the scene, one must think of the instructor as what she is—a conspicuously comely and spirited young lady of the type that under all circumstances looks *chic* and wellgroomed. She had been training a class of *dhais* in Lahore, and had invited her "graduates" when handling a difficult case to call her in for advice.

At three o'clock one cold winter's morning of 1926, a graduate summoned her. The summons led to the house of an outcaste, a little mud hut with an interior perhaps eight by twelve feet square. In the room were ten people, three generations of the family, all save the patient fast asleep. Also, a sheep, two goats, some chickens and a cow, because the owner did not trust his neighbors. No light but a glim in an earthen pot. No heat but that from the bodies of man and beast. No aperture but the door, which was closed.

In a small alcove at the back of the room four cot beds, planted one upon another, all occupied by members of the family. In the cot third from the ground lay a woman in advanced labor.

"*Dhai* went outside," observed Grandmother, stirring sleepily, and turned her face to the wall.

Not a moment to be lost. No time to hunt up the *dhai*. By good luck, the cow lay snug against the cotpile. So our trig little English lady climbs up on the back of the placid and unobjecting cow, and from that vantage point successfully brings into the world a pair of tiny Hindus—a girl and a boy.

Just as the thing is over, back comes the *dhai*, in a rage. She had been out in the yard, quarreling with the husband about the size of the coin that he should lay in her palm, on which to cut the cord—without which coin already in her possession no canny *dhai* will operate.

And this is merely an ordinary experience.

"Our Indian conduct of midwifery undoubtedly should be otherwise than it is," said a group of Indian gentlemen discussing the whole problem as it exists in their own superior circle, "but is it possible, do you think, that enough English ladies will be found to come out and do the work inclusively?"

A fractional percentage of the young wives are now found ready to accept modern medical help. But it is from the elder women of the household that resistance both determined and effective comes.

Says Dr. Agnes C. Scott, M.B., B.S., of the Punjab, one of the most distinguished of the many British medical women today giving their lives to India:[19]

An educated man may desire a better-trained woman to attend on his wife, but he is helpless against the stone wall of ignorance and prejudice built and kept up by the older women of the *zenana* who are the real rulers of the house.

Dr. K.O. Vaughan says upon this point:[20]

The women are their own greatest enemies, and if any one can devise a system of education and enlightenment for grandmother, great-grandmother and great-great-grandmother which will persuade them not to employ the ignorant, dirty Bazaar *dhai*, they will deserve well of the Indian nation. In my opinion that is an impossible task.

And another woman surgeon adds:[21]

Usually a mother-in-law or some ancient dame superintends the confinement, who is herself used to the old traditions and insists on their observance. ... It has been the immemorial custom that the management of a confinement is the province of the leading woman of the house, and the men are powerless to interfere.

Thus arises a curious picture—the picture of the man who has since time immemorial enslaved his wife, and whose most vital need in all life, present and to come, is the getting of a son; and of this man, by means none other than the will of his

[19] *V.M.S.F. Report*, p. 91. Cf. Sir Patrick Hehir, *The Medical Profession in India*, Henry Frowde & Hodder and Stoughton, London, 1923, pp. 125–31.
[20] *Ibid.*, p. 101.
[21] *Ibid.*, p. 71.

willing slave, balked in his heart's desire! He has thought it good that she be kept ignorant; that she forever suppress her natural spirit and inclinations, walking ceremonially, in stiff harness, before him, her "earthly god." She has so walked, obedient from infancy to death, through untold centuries of merciless discipline, while he, from infancy to death, through untold centuries, has given himself no discipline at all. And now their harvests ripen in kind: hers a death-grip on the rock of the old law, making her dead-weight negative to any change, however merciful; his, a weakness of will and purpose, a fatigue of nerve and spirit, that deliver him in his own house, beaten, into the hands of his slave.

Of Indian babies born alive about 2,000,000 die each year. "Available statistics show," says the latest Census of India, "that over forty per cent. Of the deaths of infants occur in the first week after birth, and over sixty per cent, in the first month."[22]

The number of still births is heavy. Syphilis and gonorrhea are among its main causes, to which must be added the sheer inability of the child to bear the strain of coming into the world.

Vital statistics are weak in India, for they must largely depend upon illiterate villagers as collectors. If a baby dies, the mother's wail trails down the darkness of a night or two. But if the village be near a river, the little body may just be tossed into the stream, without waste of a rag for a shroud. Kites and the turtles finish its brief history. And it is more than probable that no one in the village will think it worth while to report either the birth or the death. Statistics as to babies must therefore be taken as at best approximate.

It is probable, however, in view of existing conditions, that the actual figures of infant mortality, were it possible to know them, would surprise the western mind rather by their smallness than by their height. "I used to think," said one of the American medical women, "that a baby was a delicate creature. But experience here is forcing me to believe it the toughest fabric ever made, since it ever survives."

[22]*Census of India*, 1921, Vol. I, Part I, p. 132.

Chapter IX

BEHIND THE VEIL

The chapters preceding have chiefly dealt with the Hindu, who forms, roughly, three-quarters of the population of India. The remaining quarter, the Muhammadans, differ considerably as between the northern element, whose blood contains a substantial strain of the old conquering Persian and Afghan stock, and the southern contingent, who are, for the larger part, descendants of Hindu converts retaining in greater or less degree many of the qualities of Hindu character.

In some respects, Muhammadan women enjoy great advantages over their Hindu sisters. Conspicuous among such advantages is their freedom from infant marriage and from enforced widowhood, with the train of miseries evoked by each. Their consequent better inheritance, supported by a diet greatly superior to that of the Hindu, brings them to the threshold of a maturity sturdier than that of the Hindu type. Upon crossing that threshold the advantage of Muhammadan women of the better class is, however, forfeit. For they pass into practical life-imprisonment within the four walls of the home.

Purdah, as this system of women's seclusion is called, having been introduced by the Muslim conquerors and by them observed, soon came to be regarded by higher caste Hindus as a hall-mark of social prestige.[†] These, therefore, adopted it as a matter of mode. And today, as a consequence of the growing prosperity of the country, this mediaeval custom, like the interdiction of remarriage of virgin widows among the Hindus, seems to be actually on the increase. For

[†]For a discussion of *purdah*, see Hanna Papanek, "Purdah: Separate Worlds and Symbolic Shelter", *Comparative Studies in Society and History* 15 (June 1973): 289–325.

every woman at the top of the scale whom western influence sets free, several humbler but prospering sisters, socially ambitious, deliberately assume the bonds.

That view of women which makes them the proper loot of war was probably the origin of the custom of *purdah*. When a man has his women shut up within his own four walls, he can guard the door. Taking Indian evidence on the question, it appears that in some degree the same necessity exists today. In a part of India where *purdah* but little obtains, I observed the united request of several Hindu ladies of high position that the Amusement Club for English and Indian ladies to which they belong reduce the minimum age required for membership to twelve or, better, to eleven years. This, they frankly said, was because they were afraid to leave their daughters of that age at home, even for one afternoon, without a mother's eye and accessible to the men of the family.

Far down the social scale the same anxiety is found. The Hindu peasant villager's wife will not leave her girl child at home alone for the space of an hour, being practically sure that, if she does so, the child will be ruined. I dare not affirm that this condition everywhere obtains. But I can affirm that it was brought to my attention by Indians and by Occidentals, as regulating daily life in widely separated sections of the country.

No typical Muhammadan will trust another man in his *zenana*, simply because he knows that such liberty would be regarded as opportunity. If there be a handful of Hindus of another persuasion, it is almost or quite invariably because they are reflecting some part of the western attitude toward women; and this they do without abatement of their distrust of their fellowmen. Intercourse between men and women which is both free and innocent is a thing well-nigh incredible to the Indian mind.

In many parts of India the precincts of the *zenana*, among better-class Hindus, are therefore closed and the women cloistered within. And the cloistered Muhammadan women, if they emerge from their seclusion, do so under concealing veils, or in concealing vehicles. The Rolls-Royce of a Hindu reigning prince's wife may sometimes posses dark window-glasses, through which the lady looks out at ease, herself unseen. But the wife of a prosperous Muhammadan cook, if she go out on an errand, will cover herself from the crown of the head downward in a thick cotton shroud, through whose scant three inches of mesh-covered eye-space she peers half-blinded.

I happened to be present at a *"purdah* party"—a party for veiled ladies, attended by ladies only—in a private house in Delhi when tragedy hovered nigh. The Indian ladies had all arrived, stepping heavily swathed from their close-curtained motor cars. Their hostess, wife of a high English official, herself had met them on her threshold; for, out of deference to the custom of the *purdah,* all the men servants had been banished from the house, leaving Lady—— alone to conduct her guests to the dressing room. There they had laid aside their swathings. And now, in all the grace of their native costumes, they were sitting about the room, gently conversing with the English ladies invited to meet them. The senior Indian lady easily dominated her party. She was far advanced in years, they said, and she wore long, light blue velvet trousers, tight from the knee down, golden slippers, a smart little jacket of silk brocade and a beautifully embroidered Kashmir shawl draped over her head.

We went in to tea. And again Lady——, single-handed, except for the help of the English ladies, moved back and forth, from pantry to tea-table, serving her Indian guests.

Suddenly, from the veranda without, arose a sound of incursion—a rushing—men's voices, women's voices, loud, louder, coming close. The hostess with a face of dismay dashed for the door. Within the room panic prevailed. Their great white mantles being out of reach, the Indian ladies ran into the corners, turning their backs, while the English, understanding their plight, stood before them to screen them as best might be.

Meantime, out on the veranda, more fracas had arisen—then a sudden silence and a whir of retreating wheels. Lady——returned, panting, all apologies and relief.

"I am *too* sorry! But it is all over now. Do forgive it! Nothing shall frighten you again," she said to the trembling Indian ladies; and, to the rest of us: "It was the young Roosevelts come to call. They didn't know!"

It was in the talk immediately following that one of the youngest of the Indian ladies exclaimed:

"You find it difficult to like our *purdah*. But we have known nothing else. We lead a quiet, peaceful, protected life within our own homes. And, with men as they are, we should be miserable, terrified, outside."

But one of the ladies of middle age expressed another mind: "I have been with my husband to England," she said, speaking quietly to escape the others' ears. "While we were there he let me leave off *purdah*, for women are respected in England. So I went about freely, in streets and shops and galleries and gardens and to the houses of friends, quite comfortable always. No one frightened or disturbed me and I had much interesting talk with gentlemen as well as ladies. Oh, it was wonderful—a paradise! But here—here there is nothing. I must stay within the *zenana*, keeping strict *purdah*, as becomes our rank, seeing no one but the women, and my husband. We see nothing. We know nothing. We have nothing to say to each other. We quarrel. It is *dull*. But they," nodding surreptitiously toward the oldest woman, "will have it so. It is only because of our hostess that such as she would come here today. More they would never consent to. And they know how to make life horrible for us in each household, if we offer to relax an atom of the *purdah* law."

Then, looking from face to face, one saw the illustration of the talk—the pretty, blank features of the novices; the unutterable listlessness and fatigue of those of the speaker's age; the sharp-eyed, iron-lipped authority of the old.

The report of the Calcutta University Commission says:[1]

[1]Vol. II, Part I, pp. 4–5.

All orthodox Bengali women of the higher classes, whether Hindu or Muslim, pass at an early age behind the *purdah,* and spend the rest of their lives in the complete seclusion of their homes, and under the control of the eldest woman of the household. This seclusion is more strict among the Musalmans than among the Hindus. ... A few westernised women have emancipated themselves, ... [but] they are regarded by most of their countrywomen as denationalised.

Bombay, however, practices but little *purdah,* largely, no doubt, because of the advanced status and liberalizing influence of the Parsi ladies; and in the Province of Madras it is as a rule peculiar only to the Muhammadans and the wealthy Hindus. From two Hindu gentlemen, both trained in England to a scientific profession, I heard that they themselves had insisted that their wives quit *purdah,* and that they were bringing up their little daughters in a European school. But their wives, they added, unhappy in what seemed to them too great exposure, would be only too glad to resume their former sheltered state. And, viewing things as they are, one can scarcely escape the conclusion that much is to be said on that side. One frequently hears, in India and out of it, of the beauty of the sayings of the Hindu masters on the exalted position of women. One finds often quoted such passages as the precept of Manu:

> Where a woman is not honoured
> Vain is sacrificial rite.

But, as Mr. Gandhi tersely sums it up: "What is the teaching worth, if their practice denies it?"[2]

One consequence of *purdah* seclusion is its incubation of tuberculosis. Dr. Arthur Lankester[3] has shown that among the *purdah*-keeping classes the mortality of women from tuberculosis is terribly high. It is also shown that, among persons living in the same locality and of the same habits and means, the men of the *purdah*-keeping classes display a higher in-

[2]Statement to the author, Sabarmati, Ahmedabad, March, 17, 1926.

[3]*Tuberculosis in India,* Arthur Lankester, M.D., Butterworth & Co., London, 1920, p. 140.

cidence of death from tuberculosis than do those whose women are less shut in.

The Health Officer for Calcutta declares in his report for 1917:

In spite of the improvement in the general death-rate of the city, the death-rate amongst females is still more than 40 per cent higher than amongst males. ... Until it is realised that the strict observance of the *purdah* system in a large city, except in the case of the very wealthy who can afford spacious homes standing in their own grounds, necessarily involves the premature death of a large number of women, this standing reproach to the city will never be removed.

Dr. Andrew Balfour, Director of the London School of Hygiene and Tropical Medicine, in pointing out how perfectly the habits of the Indian peoples favor the spread of the disease, speaks of "the system by which big families live together; the *purdah* custom relegating women to the dark and dingy parts of the house; the early marriages, sapping the vitality of thousands of the young; the pernicious habit of indiscriminate spitting."[4] These, added to dirt, bad sanitation, confinement, lack of air and exercise, make a perfect breeding-place for the White Death. Between nine hundred thousand and one million persons, it is estimated, die annually of tuberculosis in India.[5]

It has been further estimated that forty million Indian women, Muhammadan and Hindu, are today in *purdah*.[6] In the opinion, however, of those experienced officers whom I could consult, this estimate, if it is intended to represent the number of women kept so strictly cloistered that they never leave their apartments nor see any male save husband and son, is probably three times too high. Those who never see the outer world, from their marriage day till the day of their death, number by careful estimate of minimum and maximum between 11,250,000 and 17,290,000 persons.

[4]*Health Problems of the Empire*, Dr. Andrew Balfour and Dr. H.H. Scott, Collins, London, 1924, p. 286.

[5]*Ibid.*, p. 285.

[6]*India and Missions*, The Bishop of Dornakal.

As to the mental effect of the *purdah* system upon those who live under it, one may leave its characterization to Indian authorities.

Says Dr. N.N. Parakh, the Indian physician:[7]

Ignorance and the *purdah* system have brought the women of India to the level of animals. They are unable to look after themselves, nor have they any will of their own. They are slaves to their masculine owners.[8]

Said that outstanding Swarajist leader, Lala Lajpat Rai, in his presidential address to the Hindu Mahasabha Conference held in Bombay in December, 1925:

The great feature of present-day Hindu life is passivity. "Let it be so" sums up all their psychology, individual and social. They have got into the habit of taking things lying down. They have imbibed this tendency and this psychology and this habit from their mothers. It seems as if it was in their blood. ... Our women labour under many handicaps. It is not only ignorance and superstition that corrode their intelligence, but even physically they are a poor race. ... Women get very little open air and almost no exercise. How on earth is the race, then, to improve and become efficient? A large number of our women develop consumption and die at an early age. Such of them as are mothers, infect their children also. Segregation of cases affected by tuberculosis is almost impossible. ... There is nothing so hateful as a quarrelsome, unnecessarily assertive, impudent, ill-mannered woman, but even if that were the only road which the Hindu woman must traverse in order to be an efficient, courageous, independent and physically fit mother, I would prefer it to the existing state of things.

At this point, the practical experience of a school-mistress, the English principal of a Calcutta girls' college, may be cited. Dated eight years later than the Report of the Calcutta Health Officer already quoted, it concerns the daughters of the most progressive and liberal of Bengal's families.[9]

They dislike exercise and take it only under compulsion. They will not go into the fresh air if they can avoid doing so. The average student is very weak. She needs good food, exercise, and often remedial gymnastics. The chest is contracted, and the spine often curved. She has no desire for games.

[7]*Legislative Assembly Debates*, Vol. III, Part I, p. 881.

[8]Cf., however, *ante*, pp. 77, 80, 109, 116, etc.

[9]Sister Mary Victoria, Principal of the Diocesan College for Girls, *Fifth Quinquennial Review of the Progress of Education in Bengal*, paragraphs 521–4.

... We want the authority ... to compel the student to take those remedies which will help her to grow into a woman.

But the introduction of physical training as a help to the bankrupt physiques of Hindu girls is thus far only a dream of the occidental intruder. Old orthodoxy will not have it so.

The Hindu father is prone to complain that he does not want his daughter turned into a *nautch* girl. She has to be married into one of a limited number of families; and there is always a chance of one of the old ladies exclaiming, "This girl has been taught to kick her legs about in public. Surely such a shameless one is not to be brought into our hosue!"[10]

"It is, indeed, only among the orthodox," says the authority quoting this testimony, "that this kind of objection is taken. But the orthodox are the majority."[11]

Under the caption, "Thou Shalt Do No Murder," the Oxford Mission of Calcutta printed, in its weekly journal of February 20, 1926, an editorial beginning as follows:

A few years ago we published an article with the above heading in which was vividly described by a woman writer the appalling destruction of life and health which was going on in Bengal behind the *purdah* and in *zenanas* amongst the women herded there. We thought that the revelations then made, based on the health officer's reports, would bring to us a stream of indignant letters demanding instant reform. The effect amongst men folk was entirely *nil*. Apparently not a spark of interest was roused. An article condemning the silly credulity of the use of the charms and talismans at once evokes criticism, and the absurdities of superstition are vigorously defended even by men who are graduates. But not a voice was raised in horror at the fact that for every male who dies of tuberculosis in Calcutta five females die.

Yet among young western-educated men a certain abstract uneasiness begins to appear concerning things as they are. After they have driven the Occident out of India, many of them say, they must surely take up this matter of women. Not often, however, does one find impatience such as that of Abani Mohan Das Gupta, of Calcutta, expressed in the journal just quoted.

[10]The Inspectress for Eastern Bengal, *Calcutta University Commission Report*, Vol. II, Part I, p. 23.

[11]*Ibid.*, p. 24.

I shudder to think about the condition of our mothers and sister in the "harem." ... From early morn till late at night they are working out the same routine throughout the whole of their lives without a murmur, as if they are patience incarnate. There are many instances where a woman has entered the house of her husband at the time of the marriage and did not leave it until death had carried her away. They are always in harness as if they have no will or woe but only to suffer—suffer without any protest. ... I appeal to young Indians to unfurl their flag for the freedom of women. Allow them their right. ... Am I crying in the wilderness?

Bengal is the seat of bitterest political unrest—the producer of India's main crop of anarchists, bomb-throwers and assassins. Bengal is also among the most sexually exaggerated regions of India; and medical and police authorities in any country observe the link between that quality and "queer" criminal minds—the exhaustion of normal avenues of excitement creating a thirst and a search in the abnormal for gratification. But Bengal is also the stronghold of strict *purdah*, and one cannot but speculate as to how many explosions of eccentric crime in which the young politicals of Bengal have indulged were given the detonating touch by the unspeakable flatness of their *purdah*-deadened home lives, made the more irksome by their own half-digested dose of foreign doctrines.

Chapter X

WOMAN THE SPINSTER

Less than 2 per cent of the women of British India are literate in the sense of being able to write a letter of a few simple phrases, and read its answer, in any one language or dialect. To be exact, such literates numbered, in 1921, eighteen to the thousand.[1] But in the year 1911 they numbered only ten to the thousand. And, in order to estimate the significance of that increase, two points should be considered: first, that a century ago literate women, save for a few rare stars, were practically unknown in India; and, second, that the great body of the peoples, always heavily opposed to female education, still so opposes it, and on religio-social grounds.[†]

Writing in the beginning of the nineteenth century, the Abbé Dubois said:[2]

The social condition of the wives of the Brahmins differs very little from that of the women of other castes. ... They are considered incapable of developing any of those higher mental qualities which would make them more worthy of consideration and also more capable of playing a useful part in life. ... As a natural consequence of these views, female education is altogether neglected. A young girl's mind remains totally uncultivated, though many of them have good abilities. ... It would be thought a disgrace to a respectable woman to learn to read; and even if she had learnt she would be ashamed to own it.

[1]*India in 1924–25*, L.F. Rushbrook Williams, C.B.E., p. 276.

[2]*Hindu Manners, Customs and Ceremonies*, pp. 336–7.

[†]For discussion of female education, see Karuna Chanana (ed.) *Socialisation, Education and Women: Explorations in Gender Identity* (New Delhi: Orient Lòngman, 1988); and Gail Minault, "Purdah's Progress: The Beginnings of School Education for Indian Muslim Women", in *Individuals and Ideals in Modern India* (ed.) J.P. Sharma (Calcutta: Firma K.P. Mukhopadhyaya, 1982).

This was written of the Hindu. But Islam in India has also disapproved of the education of women, which, therefore, has been held by the vast majority of both creeds to be unnecessary, unorthodox, and dangerous.

In the year 1917, the Governor-General of India in Council appointed a commission to inquire and recommend as to the status of the University of Calcutta and of tributary educational conditions in Bengal. This commission comprised eminent British educators from the faculties of the Universities of Leeds, Glasgow, Manchester, and London, allied with eminent Indian professionals. Bengal, the field of inquiry, has long stood distinguished among all other provinces of British India for its thirst for learning. The testimonies accumulated by the Commission during its three years' work may consequently be taken as not unkindly reflecting the wider Indian horizon.

With regard to the education of women, it is therefore of interest to find Mr. Brajalal Chakravarti, Secretary of the Hindu Academy at Daulatpur, affirming:[3]

It is strictly enjoined in the religious books of the Hindus that females should not be allowed to come under any influence outside that of the family. For this reason, no system of school and college education can be made to suit their requirements. ... Women get sufficient moral and practical training in the household and that is far more important than the type of education schools can give.

Another of the Commission's witnesses, Mr. Haridas Goswamy, Head Master of the High School at Asansol, amplified the thought, saying:[4]

It is not wise to implant in [girls] by means of education tastes which they would not have an opportunity to gratify in their after life, and thus sow the seeds of future discontent and discord.

And Mr. Rabindra Mohan Dutta,[5] member of the faculty of the University itself, even while deploring that "darkness of ignorance and superstition" which, he asserts, puts the

[3]*Calcutta University Commission Report*, Vol. XII, p. 414.
[4]*Ibid.*, p. 426.
[5]*Ibid.*, p. 422.

women of India "in continual conflict and disagreement with their educated husbands, brothers or sons," would yet follow the orthodox multitude, genuinely fearful of importing into the Indian home, from the distaff side,

the spirit of revolutionary and rationalistic iconoclasm condemning all our ancient institutions that are the outcome of a long past and are part of our flesh and blood as it were.

When, however, the topic of women's education comes up for discussion in Indian political bodies, speakers arise on the side of change. In the Delhi Legislative Assembly, Dr. Hari Singh Gour[6] denounces the sequestration and suppression of women. And Munshi Iswar Saran,[7] member for the cities of the United Provinces, points out, in a spirit of ridicule, that it is

... the sin of this *Kali Yuga* [Age of Destruction] that youngsters receive education and then decline to be ordered about by their elders. ... Such is our foolhardiness that we have started giving education to our girls. ... If this is going on, I ask whether you believe that you will be able to dictate to your daughters?

I recall the heat with which a wealthy young Hindu of my acquaintance, but just returned from an English university, asserted that he would never, never take an Indian bride, because he would not tie himself to "a wife of the tenth century." And among western-educated Indians in the higher walks of life, the desire for similarly educated wives sometimes rises even to a willingness to accept such brides with dowries smaller than would otherwise be exacted.

But this factor, though recognizable, is as yet small. Bombay, perhaps, gives its women more latitude than does any other province. Yet its Education Report asserts:[8]

Educated men desire educated wives for their sons and presumably educate their daughters with the same object in view, but they generally withdraw

[6]*Legislative Assembly Debates*, 1921, Vol. I, Part I, p. 363.

[7]*Ibid.*, 1922, Vol. II, Part II, p. 1631.

[8]Quoted in *Progress of Education in India*, 1917–22, Eighth Quin-quennial Review, pp. 129–30.

them from school on any manifestation of a desire to ... push education to any length which might interfere with or delay marriage.

The Report of the Central Provinces affirms:*

Even those parents who are not averse to their daughters' being literate consider that the primary course is sufficient, and that after its completion girls are too old to be away from their homes.

And Assam adds:*

[Parents] send their girls to school in order to enable themselves to marry them better and occasionally on easier terms. But as soon as a suitable bridegroom is available the girl is at once placed in the seclusion of the *purdah.*

Certainly the great weight of sentiment remains intact in its loyalty to ancient conditions. To disturb them were to risk the mould of manhood. The metaphor of Dr. Brajendranath Seal, M.A., Ph.D., Professor of Mental and Moral Science in Calcutta University, implies the dreaded risk: "Man," writes this Hindu philosopher, "is a home-brew in the vat of woman the brewster, or, as the Indian would put it, a home-spun in the loom of woman the spinster."[9]

On such general grounds, says the Calcutta University Commission,[10] is the feeling against women's education "very commonly supported by the men, even by those who have passed through the whole course of western education." If the child be sent to school at all, it is more often to put her in a safe place out of the family's way, rather than to give her instruction for which is felt so faint a need and so great a distrust.

To use the words of Mr. B. Mukherjee, M.A., F.R.E.S.:[11]

The strict social system which makes the marriage of a girl religiously compulsory at the age of twelve or so also puts an end to all hope of continuing the education of the ordinary Hindu girl beyond the [marriageable] age.

Ibid.
[9]*Calcutta University Commission Report*, Vol. XII, p. 62.
[10]*Ibid.,* Vol. II, Part I, p. 5.
[11]*Calcutta University Commission Report*, Vol. XII, p. 440.

It is estimated that over 73 per cent of the total number of girls at school are withdrawn before they achieve literacy, and in the year 1922, in the great Bengal Presidency, out of every hundred girls under instruction but one was studying above the primary stage.[12]

Such small advance as has been achieved, in the desperately up-hill attempt to bestow literacy upon the women of India, represents, first and foremost, a steady and patient effort of persuasion on the part of the British Government; second, the toil of British and American missionaries; and, third, the ability of the most progressive Indians to conceive and effect the transmission of thought into deed. But it is estimated that, without a radical change in performance on the part of the Indians themselves, ninety-five more years of such combined effort will be required to wrest from hostility and inertia the privilege of primary education for as much as 12 per cent of the female population.[13]

The Seva Sadan Society, pioneer Indian women's organization to provide poor women and girls with training in primary teaching and useful work, was started in 1908, in Poona, near Bombay. By the latest report at hand, it has about a thousand pupils. This society's success shows what the happier women of India could do for the rest, were they so minded. But its work is confined wholly to Bombay Presidency; and unfortunately, it has no counterpart, says the official report, in any other part of India.

In 1921–2, British India possessed 23,778 girls' schools, inclusive of all grades, from primary schools to arts and professional colleges. These schools contained in the primary stage 1,297,643 pupils, only 24,555 in the Middle Schools and a still smaller number 5,818—in the High Schools.[14]

[12]*Progress of Education in Bengal,* J.W. Holme, M.A., Sixth Quinquennial Review.

[13]*Cf. Village Schools in India,* Mason Olcott, Associated Press, Calcutta, 1926, p. 90.

[14]The figures in this paragraph are drawn from *Progress of Education in India,* 1917–22, Vol. II.

"Although," says the report, "the number of girls who proceed beyond the primary stage is still lamentably small—30,000 in all India out of a possible school-going population of fifteen millions—still it shows an increase of thirty per cent over the attendance in 1917."[15]

In Bombay Presidency, in 1924–5 only 2.14 per cent of the female population was under instruction of any kind,[16] while in all India, in 1919, .9 per cent of the Hindu female population, and 1.1 per cent of the Muhammadan females, were in school.[17]

"It would be perfectly easy to multiply schools in which little girls would amuse themselves in preparatory classes, and from which they would drift away gradually during the lower primary stage. The statistical result would be impressive, but the educational effect would be *nil* and public money would be indefensibly wasted."[18]

But, in the fight for conserving female illiteracy, as in those for maintaining the ancient midwifery and for continuing the cloistering of women, the great constant factor on the side of Things-As-They-Were will be found in the elder women themselves. Out of sheer loyalty to their gods of heaven and their gods of earth they would die to keep their daughters like themselves.

As that blunt old Sikh farmer-soldier, Captain Hira Singh Brar, once said, speaking from his seat in the Legislative Assembly on a measure of reform:[19]

So many Lalas and Pandits get up on the platforms and say, "Now the time has come for this reform and that." But what happens? When they go home and when we meet them next morning they say, "What can we do? We are helpless When we went back home, our ladies would not allow us to do

---

[15]*Progress of Education in India*, Vol. I, p. 135.

[16]*Bombay*, 1924–25, Government Central Press, Bombay, 1926, pp. XV–XVI.

[17]*Progress of Education in India*, 1917–22, Vol. I, p. 126.

[18]*Ibid.*, pp. 138–9.

[19]*Legislative Assembly Debates*, 1925, Vol. V, Part III, p. 2830.

what we wanted to do. They say they do not care what we talk, but they would not allow us to act accordingly."

Abreast of these priestesses of ancient custom in preserving the illiteracy of women, stands another mighty influence—that of economic self-interest; a man must marry his daughter or incur an earthly and eternal penalty that few will face. He can rarely marry her without paying a dowry so large that it strains his resources; to which must be added the costs of the wedding—costs so excessive that, as a rule, they plunge him deep into debt. This heavy tax he commonly incurs before his daughter reaches her teens. Why, then, should he spend still more money on her, to educate her; or why, if he be poor and can use her labor, should he go without her help and send her to school, since she is so early to pass forever into another man's service? The idea has been expressed by Rai Harinath Ghosh, Bahadur,[20] fellow of Calcutta University:

People naturally prefer to educate their boys, well knowing that in future they will make them happy and comfortable in their old age, and glorify their family, whilst the girls, after marriage, will be at the mercy of others.

To the average Indian father, of whatever estate, this range of reasoning appears conclusive. And so the momentous opportunities of the motherhood of India continue to be intrusted to the wisdom and judgment of illiterate babies.

Given such a public sentiment toward even rudimentary schooling for girl children, the facts, as to more advanced learning may be easily surmised. Mr. Mohini Mohan Bhattacharjee, of the Calcutta University faculty, expressed it in these words:[21]

The higher education of Indian women ... may almost be said to be beyond the scope of practical reform. No Hindu or Muhammadan woman of an orthodox type has ever joined a college or even read up to the higher classes in a school. The girls who receive university education are either Brahmo[22] or Christian. ... The time is far distant when the University will be called upon

[20]*Calcutta University Commission Report*, Vol. XII, p. 425.

[21]*Calcutta University Commission Report*, Vol. XII, p. 411.

[22]The Brahmo or Brahmo Samaj is a sect numbering 6,388 persons, as shown in the *Census of India* of 1921, p. 119.

to make arrangements for the higher education of any large or even a decent number of girls in Bengal.

By the latest available report, the women students in arts and professional colleges, in all British India, numbered only 961. But a more representative tone than that of Mr. Bhattacharjee's rather deprecatory words is heard in the frank statement of Rai Satis Chandra Sen, Bahadur:

Amongst advanced communities in the West, where women are almost on a footing of equality with men and where every woman cannot expect to enter upon married life, high education may be a necessity to them. But ... the western system ... is not only unsuitable, but also demoralising to the women of India ... and breaks down the ideals and instincts of Indian womanhood.[23]

There remains, then, the question of education after marriage. Under present conditions of Indian thought, this may be dismissed with a word—"impracticable."[24] Directly she enters her husband's home, the little wife, whatever her rank, is at once heavily burdened with services to her husband, to her mother-in-law and to the household gods. Child-bearing quickly overwhelms her and she has neither strength nor leave for other activities. Further, she must be taught by women, if taught at all, since women, only, may have access to her. And so you come to the snake that has swallowed his tail.

For, as we have just seen, the ban that forbids literacy to the women of India thereby discourages the training of women teachers who might break the ban. Those who have such training barely and feebly suffice for the schools that already exist. *Zenana* teaching has thus far languished, an anaemic exotic—a failure, in an undeserving soil.

Returning to the conviction of the uselessness of spending good money on a daughter's education, this should not be supposed a class matter. Nobles and rich men share the sentiment with their lesser compatriots.

[23]*Calcutta University Commission Report*, Vol. XII, p. 449.

[24]The Seva Sadan Society in Bombay has among its pupils a certain percentage of married women of the laboring class who come for two or three hours' instruction daily.

The point is illustrated in Queen Mary's College in Lahore. This institution was founded years ago by two English ladies who saw that the fractional percentage of Indian girls then receiving education came chiefly if not wholly from the low castes, whilst the daughters of princes, the wives and mothers of princes to come, the future regents, perhaps, for minor sons, were left in untouched darkness. The undertaking that the two ladies began enlisted the approval of Government. The reigning princes, spurred on by the visit of Queen Mary to India, subscribed a certain sum. This sum Government tripled. Suitable buildings were erected and equipped, and there the liberality of the princes practically ceased.

For, as will be found in every direction in which the trait can be expressed the raising of a building as a monument to his name, be it school, hospital, or what not, interests the wealthy Indian; but for its maintenance in service he can rarely if ever be induced to give one penny. In this case it was necessary, in order to combat initial indifference, to present schooling practically free. Today, the charges have ben advanced to stand approximately thus: day scholars, junior, $1.50 per month; senior, $3.00 per month; boarding scholars, $10 to $20 per month, inclusive of all tuition, board, laundry, and ordinary medical treatment.

These terms contemplate payment only for the time actually spent at college. And still some of the fathers are both slow and disputatious over the settlement of accounts. "You send a bill of two rupees [$.66] for stationery, all used up in your school by my two daughters in only two months. I consider this bill excessive. They should not be allowed to use so much costly material; it is not right. It should not be paid," protests one personage; and the representative of another conducts a three weeks' correspondence of inquiry, remonstrance, and reproach over a charge for two yards of ribbon to tie up a little girl's bonnie black locks.

Partly because of the original policy of nominal charges adopted by Government to secure an entering wedge, partly because of their traditional dissociation of women and letters, the rich men of India as a whole remain today still convinced at heart that, if indeed their daughters are to be schooled at all, then Government should give them schooling free of charge.

Queen Mary's College, a charming place, with classrooms, dormitories, common rooms and gardens suitably and attractively designed, is staffed by British ladies of university training. The curriculum is planned to suit the needs of the students. Instruction is given in the several languages of the pupils—Arabic, Urdu, Hindi etc., and, against the girls' pleas, native dress is firmly required—lest the elders at home take fright of a contagion of western ideas. Throughout the school's varied activities, the continuous effort is to teach cleanliness of habit; and marks are given not only on scholarship but on helpfulness, tidiness, truthfulness, and the sporting spirit.

Outdoor games in the gardens are encouraged to the utmost possible degree, and a prettier sight would be hard to find than a score or so of these really lovely little gazelle-eyed maidens playing about in their floating gauzes of blue and rose and every rainbow hue.

"They have not ginger enough for good tennis," one of the teachers admits, "but then, they have just emerged from the hands of grandmothers who think it improper for little girls even to walk fast. Do you see that lively small thing in pink and gold? When she first came, two terms ago, she truly maintained that her 'legs wouldn't run.' Now she is one of the best at games.

"But what a pity it is," the teacher continues, "to think of the life of dead passivity to which, in a year or two at best, they will all have relapsed!"

"Will they carry into that after-life much of what they have learned here?" I ask.

"Think of the huge pervading influence that will encompass them! The old palace *Zenana*, crowded with women bowed under traditions as fixed as death itself! Where would these delicate children find strength to hold their own alone, through year upon year of that ancient, changeless, smothering domination? Our best hope is that they may, somehow, transmit a little of tonic thought to their children; that they may send their daughters to us; and that so, each generation adding its bit, the end may justify our work."

Queen Mary's is the only school in all India instituted especially for ladies of rank. Not unnaturally, therefore, some of the new Indian officials, themselves without rank other than that which office gives, covet the social prestige of enrolling their daughters in Queen Mary's. The question of enrollment rests as yet with an English Commissioner, and the Commissioner lets the young climbers in. With the result that the princes, displeased, are sending fewer of their children than of yore.

"Shall our daughters be subjected to the presence of daughters of *babus*—of upstart Bengali politicians!" they exclaim, leaving no doubt as to the reply.

And some of the resident faculty, mindful of the original purpose of the school, anxiously question:

"Is it wise to drive away the young princesses? Their future influence is potentially so much further-reaching than that of other women, however intelligent. Should we not strain all points to get and to hold them?"

But to this question, when asked direct, the Commissioner himself replied:

"In British India we are trying to build a democracy. As for the Native States, undoubtedly it would be well to educate the future *Maharanis*; I say to their fathers, the Princes: 'If you want to keep for your daughters a school for their own rank, it can easily be done—but not on Government funds. You must pay for the school yourselves.' But this, invisible as the cost would be to men of their fortunes, they are not apt to do."

Another center of interest in Lahore is the Victoria Schools, occupying the palace of a grandson of the famous Ranjit Singh, in the heart of the old city, just off the bazaar. The head of this institution is an extremely able Indian lady, Miss K.M. Bose, of the third generation of an Indian Christian family. Miss Bose's firm and powerful character, her liberal and genial spirit, her strong influence and fine mind, indicate the possibilities of Indian womanhood set free.

In Victoria school are five hundred girl pupils. "Some are rich, some poor," says Miss Bose, "but all are of good caste, and all are daughters of the leading men of the city.[†] If we took lower caste children here, it would increase expense to an impossible degree. The others would neither sit nor eat with them. Separate classes would have to be maintained, an almost double teaching staff employed, and so on through innumerable embarrassments.

"'The tuition fees?' Merely nominal; we Indians will not pay for the education of our daughters. In days but just gone by, the richest refused to pay even for lesson books. Books, teaching, and all, had at first to be given free, or we should have got no pupils. This school is maintained by Government grant and by private subscriptions from England."

Many rooms on many floors honeycomb the old barren rabbit-warren of a palace, each chamber filled with children, from mites of four or five in Montessori classes up to big, hearty Muhammadan girls of fifteen or sixteen, not yet given in marriage. Like Queen Mary's, this is a strict *purdah* school. The eye of man may not gaze upon it. When it is necessary to introduce some learned pundit to teach his pundit's specialty, he is separated from the class he teaches by a long, deep, thick, and wholly competent curtain. And he is chosen, not only for learning, but also for tottering age.

"I am responsible for these schools," says the Commissioner, smiling ruefully, "and yet, being a man, I may never inspect them!"

Work, in Victoria School, is done in six languages—Urdu, Persian, Hindi, Punjabi, and Sanskrit, with optional English.

"We give no books to the children until they can really read," says Miss Bose. "Otherwise they merely memorize, learning nothing."[25] And the whole aim and hope of the

[25]The Muslim Indian boy may be letter-perfect in long sections of the Arabic Koran without understanding one word that he speaks; similarly

[†]Mona Bose quckly distanced herself from Mayo, and denied having made the comments attributed to her by Mayo; see Rev. H.A. Popley, *The Indian Witness* (Lucknow), 7 Sept. 1927.

scheme is to implant in the girls' minds something so definitely applicable to their future life in the *zenana* that some part of
it may endure alive through the years of dark and narrow
things so soon to come.

Reading, writing, arithmetic enough to keep simple
household accounts; a little history; sewing—which art, by the
way, is almost unknown to most of the women of India; a little
drawing and music; habits of cleanliness and sanitary observance—both subjects of incredible difficulty; first aid, to save
themselves and their future babies as far as may be from the
barbarities of the domestic code—these are the main studies in
this practical institution. Added to them is simple cooking,
especially cooking for infants and invalids, using always the
native type of stove and utensils; and the handling and serving of food, with particular emphasis on keeping it clean and
off the floor.

"Their cooking, in later life, they would never by nature do
with their own hands, but would leave entirely to filthy servants, whence come much sickness and death," says the in-
structress. "Our effort here is to give them a conviction of the
use and beauty of cleanliness and order in all things."

Miss L. Sorabji, the Indian lady-principal of the Eden High
School for girls at Dacca, thus discreetly suggests the nature of
the teacher's struggle:[26]

Undesirable home influences are a great hindrance to progress. Un-
punctuality, sloth, untidiness, carelessness regarding the laws of health and
sanitation, untruthfulness, irresponsibility, absence of any code of honour,
lack of home discipline, are some of the difficulties we have to contend with
in our schools. Character-building is what is most needed.

And—the patient upbuilding of a public opinion that,
eventually, may create and sustain a genuine and practical
Indian movement toward self-help.

---

the young Hindu, so both English and Indian teachers testify, easily learns
by rote whole chapters of text whose words are mere meaningless sounds
to his mind.

[26]*Calcutta University Commission Report*, Vol. XII, p. 453.

At present one beholds a curious spectacle: the daughters of rich landlords; of haughty Brahman plutocrats; of militant nationalist politicians, ferocious denouncers of the white man and all his works, fed and lodged by the dimes and sixpences of dear old ladies in Illinois and Derbyshire, and taught the a-b-c of responsible living by despised Christians and outcaste apostates.

PART III

Interlude

THE BRAHMAN

Rattling south by rail, out of Bengal into Madras. Square masses of elephant-colored rock piled up to build rectangular hills, sitting one upon another in segments, like elephant Gods on pedestals.—Miles and more miles of it.

Madras, citadel of Brahmanic Hinduism. Citadel also of the remnant of the ancient folk, the dark-skinned Dravidians. Brahmanic Hinduism broke them, cast them down and tramped upon them, commanded them in their multi-millions to be pariahs, outcasts, ignorant and poor. Then came the Briton, for whatever reason, establishing peace, order, and such measure of democracy as could survive in the soil.

Gradually the Dravidian raised his eyes, and then, most timidly, his head. With him, also, the multitudes of the low castes of the Brahman's world. And now all these, become an Anti-Brahman party, had developed strength enough, for the time at least, to snatch from the Brahman his political majority in the Legislative council of Madras Presidency.[1] Which, in itself, constituted an epoch in Indian history.[†]

With one of these low-caste men become rich, respected and politically powerful, I sat in private conference, in the city of Madras. A little, vivacious person he was, full of heat and free of tongue. "Will you draw me your picture of the Brahman?" I asked. He answered—and these are his actual words, written down at the moment:

"Once upon a time, when all men lived according to their choice, the Brahman was the only fellow who applied himself

[1] In the fall elections of 1926, the Brahmans regained the majority in the Legislative Council of Madras Presidency.

[†] For a discussion of anti-Brahman politics in the Madras Presidency, see R.L. Hardgrave Jr., *The Dravidian Movement* (Bombay: Popular Prakashan, 1965); and Eugene F. Irschick, *Politics and Social Conflict in South India* (Berkeley: Univ. of California Press, 1969).

to learning. Then, having become learned, and being by nature subtle-minded, he secretly laid hold upon the sacred books, and secretly wrote into those books false texts that declared him, the Brahman, to be lord over all the people. Ages passed. And gradually, because the Brahman only could read and because he gave out his false texts that forbade learning to others, the people grew to believe him the Earthly God he called himself and to obey him accordingly. So in all Hindu India he ruled the spirit of man, and none dared dispute him, not till England came with schools for all.

"Now, here in this Province, Madras, we fight the Brahman. But still he is very strong, because the might of thousands of years breaks slowly, and he is as shrewd as a host of demons. He owns the press, he sways the bench, he holds eighty per cent of the public offices, and he terrorizes the people, especially the women. For we are all superstitious and mostly illiterate. The 'Earthly God' has seen to that. Also, he hates the British, because they keep him from strangling us. He makes much 'patriotic' outcry, demanding that the British go. And we—we know that if they go now, before we have had time to steady ourselves, he will strangle us again and India will be what it used to be, a cruel despotism wielded by fat priests against a mass of slaves, because our imaginations are not yet free from him. Listen:

"Each Hindu in India pays to the Brahman many times more than he pays to the State. From the day of his birth to the day of his death, a man must be feeding the Earthly God. When a child is born, the Brahman must be paid; otherwise, the child will not prosper. Sixteen days afterward, to be cleansed of 'birth pollution,' the Brahman must be paid. A little later, the child must be named; and the Brahman must be paid. In the third month, the baby's hair must be clipped; and the Brahman must be paid. In the sixth month, we begin to feed the child solids; and the Brahman must be paid. When the child begins to walk, the Brahman must be paid. At the completion of the first year comes the birthday ceremony and the Brahman must be paid. At the end of the seventh year the boy's education begins and the Brahman must be paid well. In well-to-do families he performs the ceremony by guiding golden writing-sticks placed in the boy's hand; and the sticks also go to the Brahman.

"When a girl reaches her first birthday, her seventh, or her ninth, or when a boy is one and a half, or two years old, or anywhere up to sixteen, comes the betrothal, and big pay to the Brahman. Then, when puberty comes, or earlier, if the marriage is consummated earlier, rich pay to the Brahman. At an eclipse, the Brahman must be paid heavily. And so it goes on. When a man dies, the corpse can be removed only after receiving the blessing of the Brahman, for which he is paid. At the cremation, again a lot of money must be paid to many Brahmans. After cremation, every month for a year, the dead man's son must hold a feast for Brahmans—as great a feast as he can—and give them clothes, ornaments, food and whatever would be dear to the dead. For whatever a Brahman eats, drinks or uses is enjoyed by the dead. Thereafter, once a year, during the son's life, he must repeat this observance.

"All such ceremonies and many more the Brahman calls his 'vested rights,' made so by religious law. Whoever neglects them goes to eternal damnation. During the performance of each rite we must wash the Brahman's feet with water and then we must drink some of that water from the palm of our hand. The Brahman is indolent, produces, nothing, and takes to no calling but that of lawyer or government official. In this Province he numbers one and a half million and the rest of us, over forty-one millions, feed him.

"Now do you understand that, until we others are able to hold our own in India, we prefer a distant King beyond the sea, who gives us peace, justice, something back for our money and a chance to become free men, to a million and a half masters, here, who eat us up yet say our very touch would pollute them?"

Chapter XI

LESS THAN MEN

The conundrums of India have a way of answering themselves, when one looks close.

Long and easily we have accepted the catchword "mysterious India." But "mystery," as far as matters concrete are concerned, remains such only as long as one persists in seeking a mysterious cause for the phenomena. Look for a practical cause, as you would do in any bread-and-butter country not labeled "inscrutable," and your mystery vanishes in smoke.

"Why, after so many years of British rule, do we remain 92 per cent illiterate?" reiterates the Hindu politician, implying that the blame must be laid at the ruler's door.

But in naming his figure, he does not call to your attention a fact which, left to yourself, you would be slow to guess: he does not tell you that of the 247,000,000 inhabitants of British India, about 25 per cent—60,000,000—have from time immemorial been specially condemned to illiteracy, even to sub-humanity, by their brother Indians. Surely, if there be a mystery in India, it lies here—it lies in the Hindu's ability anywhere, under any circumstances, to accuse any man, any society, any nation, of "race prejudice," so long as he can be reminded of the existence in India of sixty million fellow Indians to whom he violently denies the common rights of man.[1]

[1] Indian politicians have for some time been directing a loud and continuous fire upon the British Home Government for not finding means to coerce the Government of the Union of South Africa into a complaisant attitude toward British Indian immigrants in that country. It is worthy of note that of the original 130,000 British Indian immigrants to South Africa, one-third were "Untouchables," mostly from Madras Presidency, whose condition in India is indicated in this chapter, and who would find themselves again in such status, were they to return to Hindu India. The British

In the beginning, it is explained, when the light-skinned ancestors of the present Hindus first came to India, they found there a darker, thicker-featured native race, the Dravidians, builders of the great temples of the South. And the priests of the newcomers desired that the blood of their people be not mixed with the native stock, but be kept of one strain. So they declared Dravidians to be unclean, "untouchable."

Then the old lawmakers, gradually devising the caste system, placed themselves at the head thereof, under the title of "earthly gods"—Brahmans. Next beneath them they put the Kshattryas, or fighting men; after the fighters, the Vaisyas, or cultivators, upon whom the two above look down; and finally, the fourth division, or Sudra caste, born solely to be servants to the other three. Of these four divisions, themselves today much subdivided, was built the frame of Hindu society. Outside and below all caste, in a limbo of scorn earned by their sins of former existences, must forever grovel the Untouchables.

A quotation from the rule by which the unfortunates were nailed to their fate will suffice to show its nature; the *Bhagavata*,[2] treating of the murder of a Brahman, decrees:

Whoever is guilty of it will be condemned at his death to take the form of one of those insects which feed on filth. Being reborn long afterwards a Pariah [Untouchable], he will belong to this caste, and will be blind for more than four times as many years as there are hairs on the body of a cow. He can, nevertheless, expiate his crime by feeding forty thousand Brahmins.

Thus, at one sweep, is explained the Untouchable's existence as such; are justified the indignities heaped upon him; is emphasized his unspeakable degradation; and is safeguarded

---

Indians in South Africa in 1922 numbered, as shown in the official Year-Book, a little over 161,000. This figure includes a later immigration of 10,000 traders, and the natural increase of the combined body.

[2]Chief of the eighteen *Puranas*, sacred books of India. The translation here given is that of the Abbé Dubois, *Hindu Manners, Customs and Ceremonies*, p. 558.

the oppressor from the wrath of him oppressed. Even as the Hindu husband, by the horrors imposed upon widowhood, is safeguarded from a maddened wife's revolt.

If a Brahmin kills a Sudra,[3] it will suffice to efface the sin altogether if he recites the *gayatri* [a prayer] a hundred times,

continues the scripture, by opposites driving home its point.

Leaving the ancient roots of things, and coming down to the year 1926 A.D., we find the orthodox Hindu rule as to Untouchables to be roughly this:

Regarded as if sub-human, the tasks held basest are reserved for them; dishonor is associated with their name. Some are permitted to serve only as scavengers and removers of night soil; some, through the ignorance to which they are condemned, are loathsome in their habits; and to all of them the privilege of any sort of teaching is sternly denied. They may neither possess nor read the Hindu scriptures. No Brahman priest will minister to them; and, except in rarest instances, they may not enter a Hindu temple to worship or pray. Their children may not come to the public schools. They may not draw water from the public wells; and if their habitation be in a region where water is scarce and sources far apart, his means, for them, not greater consideration from others, but greater suffering and greater toil.

They may not enter a court of justice; they may not enter a dispensary to get help for their sick; they may stop at no inn. In some provinces they may not even use the public road, and as laborers or agriculturists, they are continually losers, in that they may not enter the shops or even pass through the streets where shops are, but must trust to a haphazard chain of hungry go-betweens to buy or sell their meager wares. Some, in the abyss of their degradation, are permitted no work at all. These may sell nothing, not even their own labor. They may only beg. And even for that purpose they dare not use the road, but must stand far off, unseen, and cry out for alms from those who pass. If alms be given, it must be tossed on the

---

[3]A member of the fourth division, lowest Hindu caste, yet far above the Untouchable.

ground, well away from the road, and when the giver is out of sight and the roads empty then, and not till then, the watcher may creep up, snatch, and run.

[...] Today almost all that can be accomplished by civil law for the Untouchable has been secured. Government has freely opened their way, as far as Government can determine, to every educational advantage and to high offices. And Government's various land-development and coöperative schemes, steadily increasing, have provided tremendous redeeming agencies and avenues of escape.

But for Provincial Governments to pass legislation asserting the rights of every citizen to enjoy public facilities, such as public schools, is one thing; to enforce that legislation over enormous countrysides and through multitudinous small villages without the co-operation and against the will of the people, is another. Witness that paragraph in the Madras Government Order of March 17, 1919, reading:

Children of Panchamas [Untouchables] are admitted only into 609 schools out of 8,157 in the Presidency, although the regulations state that no boy is to be refused admission merely on the ground of caste.

Yet, rightly read, the announcement proclaims a signal advantage won. Six hundred and nine schools in a most orthodox province admitting outcastes, as against only twelve times that number who refuse!

In the Bombay Legislative council, one day in August, 1926, they were discussing a resolution to coerce local boards to permit Untouchables to send their children to schools, to draw water from public wells, and to enjoy other common rights of citizenship. Most of the Hindu members approved in principle. "But if the resolution is put into effect we would be faced with a storm of opposition," demurred one member, representative of many others. "Orthodox opinion is too strong, and while I sympathize with the resolution I think that … given effect, it may have disastrous effect."[4] And he submits that the path of wisdom, for friends of the Untouchables,

[4]*Bombay Legislative Council Debates*, 1926, Vol. XVIII, Part IX, 717.

is not to ask for action, but, instead, to content themselves with verbal expressions of sympathy, such as his own.

A second Hindu member, with characteristic nimbleness, pitchforks the load toward shoulders broad enough to bear it:[5]

I think the British Government have followed a very timid policy in this presidency. They have refused to take part in any social legislation. Probably, being an alien Government, they were afraid that they would be accused of tampering with the religion of the various communities. In spite of the Proclamation of Queen Victoria about equality between the different classes and communities, Government have not given practical effect to it.

It remains, however, to a Muhammadan, Mr. Noor Mahomed, of Sind, to strike the practical note:[6]

I think the day will not be distant when the people who are placed by the tyranny of the higher classes into the lower grade of society ... will find themselves driven to other religious folds. There will then be no reason at all for the Hindu society to complain that Mahomedan or Christian missionaries are inducing members of depressed classes to change the religion of their birth. ... If the Hindu society refuses to allow other human beings, fellow creatures at that, to attend public schools, and if ... the president of a local board representing so many lakhs[7] of people in this House refuses to allow his fellows and brothers the bare elementary human right of having water to drink, what right have they to ask for more rights from the bureaucracy? ... Before we accuse people coming from other lands, we should see how we ourselves behave toward our own people. ... How can [we] ask for greater political rights when [we ourselves] deny elementary rights of human beings?

[...] Thus, the "depressed classes" have begun holding annual conferences of delegates to air their wrongs and to advance their rights. Their special representatives now appointed to legislatures and to local bodies, grow more and more assertive. Their economic situation, under Government's steady effort, is, in some communities, looking up. With it their sense of manhood is developing in the shape of resentment of the degradation to which until now they have bowed. Among

[5]*Ibid.*, p. 728.
[6]*Ibid.*, August 5, p. 721.
[7]A lakh is one hundred thousand.

them a few men of power and parts are beginning to stand out.

Finally, their women, as Christian converts, furnish the main body of Indian teachers for the girls of India of all castes, and of trained nurses for the hospitals; both callings despised and rejected by the superior castes, both necessitating education, and both carrying the possibility of increasing influence.

The first time that I, personally, approached a realizing sense of what the doctrine of Untouchability means, in terms of man's inhumanity to man, was during a visit to a child-welfare centre in a northerly Indian city.

The place was crowded with Indian women who had brought their babies to be examined by the English professional in charge, a trained public health nurse. Toward her their attitude was that of children toward a wise and loving mother—confiding, affectionate, trusting. And their needs were inclusive. All morning I had been watching babies washed and weighed and examined, simple remedies handed out, questions answered, advice and friendly cautions given, encouragement and praise. Just now I happened to be looking at a matronly high-caste woman with an intelligent, clean-cut face. She was loaded with heavy gold and silver jewelry and wore a silken mantle. She sat down on the floor to show her baby, unrolling him from the torn fragement of an old quilt, his only garment. This revealed his whole little body caked in a mass of dry and half-dry excreta.

"She appears unconcerned," I remarked to the Sister. The Sister replied:

"We try to get such women to have napkins for their babies, but they won't buy them, they won't wash them themselves, and they won't pay washers to wash them, although they are quite able to do so. This woman is well born. Her husband is well educated—a technical man—and enjoys a good salary. Sometime it may please her to hang that bit of quilt out in the sun in her courtyard, and, when it is dry, to brush off what will come off. That's all. This, incidentally, helps explain why infantile diarrhæa spreads through the families in a district. They will make no attempt whatever to keep things clean."

As the Sister spoke, a figure appeared before the open doorway—a young woman so graceful and with a face so sweet and appealing as to rivet attention at once. She carried an ailing baby on her arm, but came no farther—just stood still beyond the doorway, wistfully smiling. The Sister, looking up, smiled back.

"Why does she not come in?" I asked.

"She dare not. If she did, all these others would go. She is an untouchable—an outcaste. She herself would feel it wicked to set her foot upon that sill."

"She looks at least as decent as they," I remarked.

"Untouchables many be as intelligent as anyone else—and you see for yourself that they couldn't be dirtier," said the Sister. "But such is the custom of India. Since we can't alter it, we just plod on, trying to help them all, as best we can."

And so the gentle suppliant waited outside, among a crowd of others of her kind, till Sister could go to them, bringing to this one ointment for baby's eyes, to that one a mixture for baby's cough, and hearing the story of another.

But they might not bring their little ones in, to the mercy of the warm bath, as the other women were doing at will. They might not come to the sewing class. They might not defile the scales by laying their babies in its basket, to see what the milk-dole was doing. For they were all horrible sinners in aeons past, deserving now neither help nor sympathy while they worked out their curse.

Chapter XII

BEHOLD, A LIGHT!

[...] So much, thus far, Britain, greatly aided by the Christian Missions, has accomplished for the outcaste, by patient, up-hill work, teaching, persuading, encouraging, on either side of the social gulf. And the last few years have seen the rise of new portents in the sky.

One of these is the tendency, in the National Social Conference and in Hindu political conventions, to declare openly against the oppression of the outcaste. But these declarations, though eloquent, have as yet borne little fruit other than words. A second phenomenon is the appearance of Indian volunteer associations partially pledged against Untouchability. These include the Servants of India,[1] avowedly political; Lord Sinha's society for the help of the outcastes of Bengal and Assam; the Brahmo Samaj, and others. Their work, useful where it touches, is sporadic, and infinitesimal compared to the need, but notable in comparison with the nothingness that went before.

For no such conception is native to India. "All our Indian social work of today," the most distinguished of the Brahmo Samaj leaders said to me, "is frankly an imitation of the English and an outgrowth of their influence in the land." Again and again I heard the gist of that statement from the lips of thoughtful Indians, in frank acknowledgement of the source of the budding change.

"The curse of Untouchability prevails to this day in all parts of India," said Sir Narayan Chandravarkar,[2] adding,

---

[1] *A Brief Account of the Work of the Servants of India Society*, Aryabhushan Press, Poona, 1924, pp. 60–1.

[2] Hindu reformer, Judge of the High Court of Bombay, quoted in *India in 1920*, p. 155.

"with the liberalizing forces of the British Government, the problem is leaping into full light. Thanks to that Government, it has become ... an all-India problem."

Mr. Gandhi has been less ready to acknowledge beneficent influence from such a source—has, in fact, described the whole administrative system in India as "vile beyond description." But for the last five years his own warfare on Untouchability has not flagged even though his one unfaltering co-worker therein has been the British Government, aided preëminently by the Salvation Army. In its course he reprinted from the Indian vernacular press a learned Brahman pundit's recent statement on the subject, including this passage:[3]

Untouchability is a necessity for man's growth.

Man has magnetic powers about him. This *sakti*[4] is like milk. It will be damaged by improper contacts. If one can keep musk and onion together, one may mix Brahmans and Untouchables.

It should be enough that Untouchables are not denied the privileges of the other world.

Says Mr. Gandhi, in comment on the pundit's creed:[5]

If it was possible to deny them the privileges of the other world, it is highly likely that the defenders of the monster would isolate them even in the other world.

"Among living Indians," says Professor Rushbrook Williams,[6] Mr. Gandhi has done most to impress upon his fellow countrymen the necessity for elevating the depressed classes. ... When he was at the height of his reputation, the more orthodox sections of opinion did not dare to challenge his schemes."

But today the defenders of Untouchability are myriad, and, though Mr. Gandhi lives his faith, but few of his supporters have at any time cared to follow him so far.

[3]*Young India*, July 29, 1926, p. 268. Mr. Gandhi's phrase quoted a few lines above will be found in *Gandhi's Letters on Indian Affairs*, Madras, V. Narayanah and Co., p. 121.

[4]Energy, or the power of the Supreme personified.

[5]*Young India*, July 29, 1926.

[6]*India in 1924–25*, p. 264.

On January 5, 1926, a mass meeting of Hindus was held in Bombay to protest against Mr. Gandhi's "heresy" in attacking Untouchability. The presiding officer, Mr. Manmohandas Ramji, explained that Untouchability rests on a plane with the segregation of persons afflicted with contagious diseases. Later he interpreted the speaker who pointedly suggested lynching for "heretics" who "threaten the disruption of Hindu society," to mean only that Hindus are "prepared to sacrifice their lives for the Hindu religion in order to preserve its ancient purity." The meeting closed after appointing a committee specially to undermine Mr. Gandhi's propaganda.

[...] Meantime another and a curious development has come to the Untouchables' aid. With the rapid Indianization of Government services, with the rapid concessions in Indian autonomy that have characterized British administration since the World War, an intense jealousy has arisen between the Hindu three-quarters and the Muhammadan fourth of the population. This subject will be treated elsewhere. Here it will suffice merely to name it as the reason why the Untouchables, simply because of numbers, have suddenly become an object of solicitude to the Hindu world.

[...] In the autumn of 1917, the then Secretary of State for India, Mr. Montagu, chief advocate of the speedy Indianization of the Government, sat in Delhi receiving deputations from such elements of the Indian peoples as were moved to address him on that subject. All sorts and conditions of men appeared, all sorts of documentary petitions were submitted, all sorts of angles and interests. Among these, not meanly represented, loomed an element new on the Indian political stage—the Untouchables, awake and assertive, in many organized groups entreating the Secretary's attention.

Without one divergent voice they deprecated the thought of Home Rule for India. To quote them at length would be repetition. Their tenor may be sufficiently gathered from two excerpts.

The Panchama Kalvi Abivirthi-Abimana Sanga, a Madras Presidency outcastes' association,[7] "deprecates political change and desires only to be saved from the Brahmin, whose motive in seeking a greater share in the Government is ... that of the cobra seeking the charge of a young frog."

The Madras Adi Dravida Jana Sabha, organized to represent six million Dravidian aborigines of Madras Presidency, said:[8]

The caste system of the Hindus stigmatises us as untouchables. ... Caste Hindus could not, however, get on without our assistance. We supplied labour and they enjoyed the fruit, giving us a mere pittance in return. Our improvement in the social and economic scale began with and is due to the British Government. The Britishers in India—Government officers, merchants, and last, but not least, Christian missionaries—love us, and we love them in return. Though the general condition of the community is still very low, there are some educated men amongst us. But these are not allowed to rise in society on account of the general stigma attached by the Hindus to the community. The very names by which these people refer to us breathe contempt.

We need not say that we are strongly opposed to Home Rule. We shall fight to the last drop of our blood any attempt to transfer the seat of authority in this country from British hands to so-called high caste Hindus who have ill-treated us in the past and would do so again but for the protection of British laws. Even as it is, our claims, nay, our very existence, is ignored by the Hindus; and how will they promote our interests if the control of the administration passes into their hands?

"We love them," said these spokesmen of the outcaste— and the expression strikes home with a certain shock. But one is forced to remember that the sorrows of these particular under-dogs have never before, in all their dim centuries of history, elicited from any creature a thought or a helping hand.

[...] When the Prince of Wales sailed to India, late in 1921, Mr. Gandhi, then at the height of his popularity, proclaimed to the

---

[7] *Addresses Presented in India to His Excellency the Viceroy and the Right Honourable the Secretary of State for India,* London, 1918, p. 87.

[8] *Ibid.,* pp. 60–1.

Hindu world that the coming visit was "an insult added to injury," and called for a general boycott.[9]

Political workers obediently snatched up the torch, rushing it through their organizations, and the Prince's landing in Bombay became thereby the signal for murderous riot and destruction. No outbreak occurred among the responsible part of the population, nor along the line of progress, which was, of course, well guarded. But in the remoter areas of the city, hooliganism ran on for several days, with some fifty killings and four hundred woundings, Indian attacking Indian, while arson and loot played their ruinous part.

Meanwhile the Prince, seemingly unmoved by the first unfriendly reception of all his life, proceeded to carry out his officially arranged programme in and about the city. On the evening of November 22 it was scheduled that he should depart for the North.

As he left Government House on the three-or four-mile drive to the Bombay railway station, his automobile ran unguarded save for the pilot police car that went before. Where it entered the city, however, a cordon of police lined the streets on both sides. And behind that cordon pressed the people— the common poor people of the countryside in their uncountable thousands; pressed and pushed until, with the railway station yet half a mile away, the police line bent and broke beneath the strain.

Instantly the crowd surged in, closing around the car, shouting, fighting each other to work nearer—nearer still. What would they do? What was their temper? God knew! Gandhi's hot words had spread among them, and God alone, now, could help. Some reached the running-boards and clung. Others shoved them off, for one instant to take their places, the next themselves to be dragged away. And what was this they shouted? At first nothing could be made of it, in the bedlam of voices, though those charged with the safety of the progress strained their ears to catch the cries.

[9]*Gandhi's Letters on Indian Affairs*, pp. 96–7.

Then words stood out, continuously chanted, and the words were these:

"*Yuvaraj Maharaj ki jai!*" "Hail to the Prince!" And: "Let me see my Prince! Let me see my Prince! Let me only see my Prince just once before I die!"

[...] So the Prince of Wales moved northward. And as he moved, much of his wholesome influence was lost, through the active hostility of the Indian political leader.

But if Gandhi's exhortations traveled, so did the news of the Prince's aspect—traveled far and fast, as such things do amongst primitive peoples.[†]

And when he turned back from his transit of the Great North Gate—the Khyber Pass itself—a strange thing awaited him. A swarm of Untouchables, emboldened by news that had reached them, clustered at the roadside to do him reverence.

"Government *ki jai!*" "Hail to the Government!" they shouted, with cheers that echoed from the barren hills.

And when the Prince slowed down his car to return their greetings, they leapt and danced in their excitement.

For nowhere in all their store of memory or of legend had they any history of an Indian magnate who had noticed an Untouchable except to scorn him. And here was a greater than all India contained—the son of the Supreme Power, to them almost divine, who deigned not only to receive but even to thank them for their homage! Small wonder that their spirits soared, that their eyes saw visions, that their tongues laid hold upon mystic words.

"Look! Look!" they cried to one another. "Behold, the Light! the Light!"

[†]The veracity of Mayo's description of the visit of the Prince of Wales to India was challenged by several of her Indian critics. Even Cornelia Sorabji, a friend and sympathiser of Mayo's, advised her to drop this chapter from subsequent editions of *Mother India*. Letter from C. Sorabji to Mayo, 6 Oct. 1927, Folder no. 39, *Katherine Mayo Papers*, Series 1 Box 5.

And such was their exaltation that many of them somehow worked through to Delhi to add themselves to the twenty-five thousand of their kind who there awaited the Prince's coming. The village people from round about flocked in to join them— the simple people of the soil who know nothing of politics but much of friendship as shown in works. And all together haunted the roadside, waiting and hoping for a glimpse of his face.

At last he came, down the Grand Trunk Road, toward the Delhi Gate. And in the center of the hosts of the Untouchables, one, standing higher than the rest, unfurled a flag.

"Yuvaraj Maharaj ki jai! Raja ke Bete ki jai!" "Hail to the Prince! Hail to the King's Son!" they all shouted together, to burst their throats. And the Prince, while the high-caste Indian spectators wondered and revolted within themselves at his lack of princely pride, ordered his car stopped.

Then a spokesman ventured forward, to offer in a humble little speech the love and fealty of the sixty millions of the Unclean and to beg the heir to the throne to intercede for them with his father the King Emperor, never to abandon them into the hands of those who despised them and would keep them slaves.

The Prince heard him through. Then—whether he realized the magnitude of what he did, or whether he acted merely on the impulse of his natural friendly courtesy toward all the world—he did an unheard—of thing. He stood up—stood up, for them, the "worse than dogs," spoke a few words of kindness, looked them all over, slowly, and so, with a radiant smile, gave them his salute.

No sun that had risen in India had witnessed such a sight. As the car started on, moving slowly not to crush them, they went almost mad. And again their eastern tongues clothed their thought. "Brother—that word was truth that our brothers brought us. Behold, the Light is there indeed! The Light—the Glory—on his face!"

Chapter XIII

GIVE ME OFFICE OR GIVE ME DEATH

Education, some Indian politicians affirm, should be driven into the Indian masses by compulsory measures. "England," they say, "introduced compulsory education at home long ago. Why does she not do so here? Because, clearly, it suits her purpose to leave the people ignorant."

To this I took down a hot reply from the lips of the Raja of Panagal, then anti-Brahman leader of Madras Presidency.

"Rubbish!" he exclaimed. "What did the Brahmans do for our education in the five thousand years before Britain came? I remind you: They asserted their right to pour hot lead into the ears of the low-caste man who should dare to study books. All learning belonged to them, they said. When the Muhammadans swarmed in and took us, even that was an improvement on the old Hindu régime. But only in Britain's day did education become the right of all, with state schools, colleges, and universities accessible to all·castes, communities, and peoples."

[...] In the thirty years following 1857, five universities were established—in Calcutta, Bombay, Madras, Lahore, and Allahabad. Aside from literacy courses, instruction in practical, non-literary branches was urged upon the attention of all minded to learn.

But the difficulty then as now was that commerce, scientific agriculture, forestry, engineering, teaching, none of these avenues for service smiled to Indian ambition. India as a national entity was ever an unknown concept to the Indian. And thought for the country at large holds little or no part in native ethical equipment.

This last-named fact, damaging as it is from our viewpoint, should be thoughtfully taken as a fact and not as an accusation. It is the logical fruit of the honestly held doctrines of fate and transmigration and of the consequent egocentric attitude.

For present purposes, the history of modern India's educational progress may be passed over, to reach statistics of today.

In 1923–4 thirteen universities of British India put forth a total of 11,222 graduates. Of these, 7,822 took their degrees in arts and sciences, 2,046 in law, 446 in medicine, 140 in engineering, 546 in education, 136 in commerce, and 86 in agriculture. At the same time, the universities showed an enrollment of 68,530 under-graduates, not dissimilarly apportioned.[1] The high figures consistently stand opposite the arts and law courses, while such vital subjects as agriculture, hygiene and sanitation, surgery, obstetrics, veterinary science and commerce, under whatever aegis offered, still attract few disciples.

For example, the agricultural school maintained by the American Presbyterian Mission near Allahabad, although equipped to receive two hundred scholars, had in 1926 only fifty men in residence.

"We don't care to be coolies," the majority say, turning away in disgust when they find that the study of agriculture demands familiarity with soil and crops.

"If," says the director, "we could guarantee our graduates a Government office, we should be crowded."

I heard of few technical schools, anywhere in India, that are pressed for room.

The representative Indian desires a university Arts degree, yet not for learning's sake,[2] but solely as a means to public office. To attain this vantage-ground he will grind cruelly hard, driven by the whip and spur of his own and his family's ambition, and will often finally wreck the poor little body that he and his forebears have already so mercilessly maltreated.

---

[1] *Statistical Abstract for British India*, 1914–15 to 1923–24, p. 279.

[2] Cf. Mr. Thyagarajaiyer (Indian), Census Superintendent of Mysore *Census of India*, Vol. I, p. 182: "The pursuit of letters purely as a means for intellectual growth is mostly a figment of the theorists."

Previous chapters have indicated the nature of this maltreatment. One of its consequences is to be seen in the sudden mental drooping and failure—the "fading," as it has come to be called, that so frequently develops in the brilliant Indian student shortly after his university years.

Meantime, if, when he stands panting and exhausted, degree in hand, his chosen reward is not forthcoming, the whole family's disappointment is bitter, their sense of injury and injustice great.

Then it is that the young man's poverty of alternatives stands most in his light and in that of Mother India. A land rich in opportunities for usefulness pleads for the service of his brain and his hands, but tradition and "pride" make him blind, deaf and callous to the call.

As Sir Gooroo Dass Banerjee mildly states it:[3]

The caste system ... has created in the higher castes a prejudice against agricultural, technological, and even commercial pursuits.

The university graduate in these latter days may not be a high-caste man. But if he is not, all the more is he hungry to assume high-caste customs, since education's dearest prize is its promise of increased *izzat*—prestige. Whatever their birth, men disappointed of office are therefore apt flatly to refuse to turn their energies in other directions where their superior knowledge and training would make them infinitely useful to their less favored brothers. Rather than take employment which they consider below their newly acquired dignity, they will sponge forever, idle and unashamed, on the family to which they belong.

"I am a Bachelor of Arts," said a typical youth, simply; "I have not been able to secure a suitable post since my graduation two years ago, so my brother is supporting me. He, having no B.A., can afford to work for one-third the wages that my position compels me to expect."

Nor had the speaker the faintest suspicion that he might be presenting himself in an unflattering light. Even the attempt to capture a degree is held to confer distinction. A man may

[3]*Calcutta University Commission Report*, Vol. III, p. 161.

and does write after his name, "B.A. Plucked" or "B.A. Failed," without exciting the mirth of his public.[4]

[...] Sanskrit scholars of a century ago or B.A.'s of today, whether plucked or feathered, the principle remains the same, though the spirit has mounted from mild complaint to bitterness.

All over India, among politicians and intelligentsia, Government is hotly assailed for its failure to provide offices for the yearly output of university graduates. With rancor and seeming conviction, Indian gentlemen of the highest political leadership hurl charges from this ground.

"Government," they repeat, "sustains the university. Government is responsible for its existence. What does it mean by accepting our fees for educating us and then not giving us the only thing we want education for? Cursed be the Government! Come, let us drive it out and make places for ourselves and our friends."

Nor is there anywhere that saving humor of public opinion whose Homeric laugh would greet the American lad, just out of Yale or Harvard or Leland Stanford, who should present his shining sheepskin as a draft on the Treasury Department, and who should tragically refuse any form of work save anti-government agitation if the draft were not promptly cashed.

---

[4]The terms are actually used in common parlance as if in themselves a title, like M.A. or Ph.D.—as: "The school ... is now under an enthusiastic B.A. plucked teacher." *Fifteenth Annual Report of the Society for the Improvement of the Backward Classes. Bengal & Assam*, Calcutta, 1925, p. 12.

Chapter XIV

WE BOTH MEANT WELL

Between the years 1918 and 1920, compulsory education laws for primary grades were, indeed, enacted in the seven major provinces of India. This was largely the effect of an Indian political opinion which saw, in principle, at least, the need of a literate electorate in a future democracy.

The laws, however, although operative in some few localities, are permissive in character and have since remained largely inactive[1]—a result partly due to the fact that the period of their passage was the period of the "Reforms." "Dyarchy" came in, with its increased Indianization of Government. Education itself, as a function of Government, became a "transferred subject" passing into the hands of Indian provincial ministers responsible to elected legislative councils. The responsibility, and with it the unpopularity to be incurred by enforcement of unpopular measures, had now changed sides. The Indian ministers, the Indian municipal boards, found it less easy to shoulder the burden than it had been to blame their predecessors in burden-bearing. No elected officer, anywhere, wanted either to sponsor the run-

[1]For example: "The Bengal Legislature ... passed an Act introducing the principle of compulsory primary education in May, 1919; but it does not appear that a single local authority in the province has availed itself of the option for which the Act provides"—"Primary Education in Bengal," London *Times*, Educational Supplement, Nov. 13, 1926, p. 484.

A recent official report prepared by Mr. Govindbhai H. Desai, Naib Dewan of Baroda, by order of the reigning prince, shows that although that state has had compulsory education for twenty years, its proportion of literacy is less than that of the adjoining British districts where education began much earlier than in Baroda, but where compulsion scarcely exists.

ning up of budgets or to dragoon the children of a resentful public into schools undesired.

[...] Schools and universities ... in India, have continued to pour the phrases of western political-social history into Asiatic minds. Asiatic memories have caught and held the phrases, supplying strange meanings from their alien inheritance. The result in each case has been identical. "All the teaching we have received ... has made us clerks or platform orators," said Mr. Gandhi.[2]

[...] A little while ago a certain American Mission Board, being well replenished in means from home and about to embark on a new period of work, convened a number of such Indian gentlemen as were strongest in citizenship and asked their advice as to future efforts. The Indian gentlemen, having consulted together, proposed that all higher education (which is city work), and also the administration of all funds, be at once turned over to them, the Indians.

"Does that, then, mean that you see no more use for Americans in India?"

"By no means! You Americans, of course, will look after the villages."

"To you, perhaps, it sounds dubious," said a British Civil Servant of thirty years' experience, to whom I submitted my doubts, "but we who have spent our lives in the work know that the answer is this: We must just plod along, giving the people more and yet more education, as fast as we can get them to take it, until education becomes too general to arrogate to itself, as it does today, a distinction by rights due only to ability and character."

[2]Statement to the author, Ahmedabad, March, 1926.

Chapter XV

"WHY IS LIGHT DENIED?"

The illiteracy of India is sometimes attributed to her poverty—a theory as elusive as the famous priority dispute between the hen and the egg. But Indian political critics are wont to charge the high illiteracy rate to the inefficiency, even to the deliberate purpose, of the sovereign power. Thus, Lala Lajpat Rai, the Swaraj political leader, refers to the Viceregal Government as having "so far refused even elementary instruction in the three R's to our masses,"[1] And Mr. Mahomed Ali Jinnah[2] accusingly asks, "Why is light denied?"

But, before subscribing to the views of either of these legislative leaders, before accepting either India's poverty or Britain's greed as determining the people's darkness, it may be well to remember the two points recently examined, and to record a third.

First, of British India's population of two hundred and forty-seven million persons, about 50 per cent are women. The people of India, as has been shown, have steadfastly opposed the education of women. And the combined efforts of the British Government, the few other-minded Indians, and the Christian missions, have thus far succeeded in conferring literacy upon less than 2 per cent of the womankind. Performing the arithmetical calculation herein suggested, one arrives

---

[1] In 1923–24, India's total expenditure of public funds on education, including municipal, local, Provincial and Central Government contributions, reached 19.9 crores of rupees, or $66,333,300. This sum is much too small for the work to be done. Nevertheless, when taken in relation to the total revenue of British India it compares not unfavorably with the educational allotments of other countries. See *India in 1924–25*, p. 278; and *Statistical Abstract for British India*, p. 262.

[2] Leader of the Nationalist party in the Legislature of 1925–26.

at an approximate figure of 121,000,000, representing British India's illiterate women.

Secondly, reckoned in with the population of British India[3] are sixty million human beings called "Untouchables." To the education of this element the great Hindu majority has ever been and still is strongly, actively and effectively opposed. Subtracting from the Untouchables' total their female half, as having already been dealt with in the comprehensive figure, and assuming, in the absence of authoritative figures, 5 per cent of literacy among its males, we arrive at another 28,500,000, representing another lot of Indians condemned to illiteracy by direct action of the majority will.

Now, neither with the inhibition of the women nor with the inhibition of the Untouchables has poverty anything whatever to do. As to the action of Government, it has displayed from the first, both as to women and as to outcastes, a steadfast effort in behalf of the inhibited against the dictum of their own people.

[...] Apart from these two factors appears, however, a third of significance as great, to appreciate whose weight one must keep in mind that the total population of British India is 90 per cent rural—village folk.

As long, therefore, as the villages remain untaught, the all-India percentage of literacy, no matter what else happens, must continue practically where it is today—hugging the world's low-record line.

But to give primary education to one-eighth of the human race, scattered over an area of 1,094,300 square miles, in five hundred thousand little villages, obviously demands an army of teachers.

Now, consider the problem of recruiting that army when no native women are available for the job. For the village school ma'am, in the India of today, does not and cannot exist.

[3]*Census of India 1921*, Vol. I, Part I, p. 225.

[...] As for the reason why India's women cannot teach India's children, that may be re-stated in few words. Indian women of child-bearing age cannot safely venture, without special protection, within reach of Indian men.

It would thus appear clear that if Indian self-government were established tomorrow, and if wealth tomorrow rushed in, succeeding poverty in the land, India, unless she reversed her own views as to her "Untouchables" and as to her women, must still continue in the front line of the earth's illiterates.

[...] "I should not have thought of telling you about it," said an Indian gentleman of high position, a strong nationalist, a life-long social reformer. "It is so apparent to us that we give it no thought. Our attitude toward women does not permit a woman of character and of marriageable age to leave the protection of her family. Those who have ventured to go out to the villages to teach—and they are usually Christians—lead a hard life, until or unless they submit to the incessant importunities of their male superiors; and their whole career, success and comfort are determined by the manner in which they receive such importunities. The same would apply to women nurses. An appeal to departmental chiefs, since those also are now Indians, would, as a rule, merely transfer the seat of trouble. The fact is, we Indians do not credit the possibility of free and honest women. To us it is against nature. The two terms cancel each other."

The Calcutta University Commission, made up, as will be recalled, of British, Muhammadan, and Hindu professional men, the latter distinguished representatives of their respective communities, expressed the point as follows:[4]

The fact has to be faced that until Bengali men generally learn the rudiments of respect and chivalry toward women who are not living in *zenanas*, anything like a service of women teachers will be impossible.

If the localizing adjective "Bengali" were withdrawn, the Commission's statement would, it seems, as fairly apply to all

[4]*Report*, Vol. II, Part I, p. 9.

India. Mason Olcott[5] is referring to the whole field when he says:

On account of social obstacles and dangers, it is practically impossible for women to teach in the villages, unless they are accompanied by their husbands.

Treating of the "almost desperate condition" of mass education in rural parts, for lack of women teachers, the late Director of Public Instruction of the Central Provinces says:[6]

The general conditions of *mofussil* [rural] life and the Indian attitude toward professional unmarried women are such that life for such as are available is usually intolerable.

"No Indian girl can go alone to teach in rural districts. If she does, she is ruined," the head of a large American Mission college in northern India affirmed. The speaker was a widely experienced woman of the world, characterized by as matter-of-fact a freedom from ignorance as from prejudice. "It is disheartening to know," she went on, "that not one of the young women that you see running about this campus, between classroom and classroom, can be used on the great job of educating India. Not one will go out into the villages to answer the abysmal need of the country. Not one dare risk what awaits her there, for it is not risk, but a certainty. And yet these people cry out to be given *self-government!*"[7]

"Unless women teachers in the *mofussil* are provided with protected residences, and enabled to have elderly and near relatives living with them, it is more than useless, it is almost cruel, to encourage women to become teachers," concludes the Calcutta University Commission after its prolonged survey.[8]

[5]*Village Schools in India*, p. 196.

[6]*The Education of India*, Arthur Mayhew, London, Faber and Gwyer, 1926, p. 268.

[7]Statement to the author, February, 1926.

[8]*Calcutta University Report*, Vol. II, Part I, p. 9.

And the authors of an inquiry covering British India, one of whom is the Indian head of the Y.M.C.A., Mr. Kanakarayan T. Paul, report:[9]

The social difficulties which so militate against an adequate supply of women teachers are well known, and are immensely serious for the welfare of the country. All the primary school work in the villages is preëminently women's work, and yet the social conditions are such that no single woman can undertake it. ... The lack of women teachers seems to be all but insuperable, except as the result of a great social change.

That a social stigma should attach to the woman who, under such circumstances, chooses to become a teacher, is perhaps inevitable. One long and closely familiar with Indian conditions writes:[10]

It is said that there is a feeling that the calling cannot be pursued by modest women. *Prima facie*, it is difficult to see how such a feeling could arise, but the Indian argument to support it would take, probably, some such form as this: "The life's object of woman is marriage; if she is married her household duties prevent her teaching. If she teaches, she can have no household duties or else she neglects them. If she has no household duties she must be unmarried, and the only unmarried women are no better than they should be.[11] If she neglects her household duties, she is ... no better than she should be.

This argument might seem to leave room for the deployment of a rescue contingent drafted from India's 26,800,000 widows calling them out of their dismal cloister and into happy constructive work. The possibility of such a move is, indeed, discussed; some efforts are afoot in that direction, and

[9]*Village Education in India, the Report of a Commission of Inquiry*, Oxford University Press, 1922, p. 98.

[10]*Census of India*, E.A.H. Blunt, C.I.E., O.B.E., I.C.S., 1911, Vol. XV, pp. 260–1.

[11]*Census of India*, 1911, Vol. XV, p. 229. "It is safe to say that after the age of seventeen or eighteen no females are unmarried who are not prostitutes or persons suffering from some bodily affliction such as leprosy or blindness; the number of genuine spinsters over twenty is exceedingly small and an old maid is the rarest of phenomena." These age figures are set high in order to include the Muhammadan women and the small Christian and Brahmo Samaj element, all of whom marry later than the Hindu majority.

a certain number of widows have been trained. Their usefulness, however, is almost prohibitively handicapped, in the great school-shy orthodox field, by the deep-seated religious conviction that bad luck and the evil eye are the widow's birthright.

[...] Thus is reached the almost complete ban which today brands teaching as socially degrading, and which, as an Indian writer puts it,[12] "condemns women to be economically dependent upon men, and makes it impossible for them to engage in any profession other than that of a housewife."

The rule has, however, its exceptions. In the year 1922, out of British India's 123,500,000 women, 4,391 were studying in teachers' training schools. But of that 4,391, nearly half—2,050—came from the Indian Christian community,[13] although this body forms but 1.5 per cent of the total population. And exceedingly few of the few who are trained serve their country's greatest need.

[...] Now it chanced, in my own case, that I had seen a good deal of Indian village life before opportunity arose to visit the women's training schools. When that opportunity came, I met it, therefore, with rural conditions fresh in mind and with a strong sense of the overwhelming importance of rural needs in any scheme for serving the body politic.

"What are you training for?" I asked the students.

"To be teachers," they generally replied.

"Will you teach in the villages?"

"Oh, no!" as though the question were curiously unintelligent.

"Then who is to teach the village children?"

"Oh—Government must see to that."

"And can Government teach without teachers?"

"We cannot tell. Government should arrange."

[12]*Reconstructing India*, Sir M. Visvesvaraya, London, P.S. King and Sons, 1920, p. 243.

[13]*Progress of Education in India*, 1917–22, Vol. II, pp. 14–15.

They apparently felt neither duty nor impulse urging them to go out among their people. Such sentiments, indeed, would have no history in their mental inheritance; whereas the human instinct of self-protection would subconsciously bar the notion of an independent life from crossing their field of thought.

It would seem, then, taking the several elements of the case into consideration, that utterances such as Mr. Jinnah's and Lala Lajpat Rai's[14] must be classified, at best, as relating to the twig-tips, rather than to the root and trunk, of their "deadly upas tree."

[...]

[14]See *ante*, p. 200.

Chapter XVI

A COUNSEL OF PERFECTION

It was one of the most eminent of living Indians who gave me this elucidation of the attitude of a respected Hindu nobleman toward his own "home town."

"Disease, dirt and ignorance are the characteristics of my country," he said in his perfect English, sitting in his city-house library where his long rows of law-books stand marshaled along the walls. "Take my own village, where for centuries the head of my family has been chief. When I, who am now head, left it seventeen years ago, it contained some eighteen hundred inhabitants. When I revisited it, which I did for the first time a few weeks since, I found that the population had dwindled to fewer than six hundred persons. I was horrified.

"In the school were seventy or eighty boys apparently five or six years old. 'Why are you teaching these little children such advanced subjects?' I asked.

"'But they are not as young as you think,' the schoolteacher replied.

"They were stunted—that is all; stunted for lack of intelligent care, for lack of proper food, and from malaria, which, say what you like about mosquitoes, comes because people are hungry. Such children, such men and women, will be found all over western Bengal. They have no life, no energy.

"My question, therefore, is plain: *What have the British been doing in the last hundred years that my village should be like this?* It is true that they have turned the Punjab from a desert to a garden, that they have given food in abundance to millions there. But what satisfaction is that to me when they let my people sit in a corner and strave? The British say: 'We had to establish peace and order before we could take other matters up'; also, 'this is a vast country, we have to build bridges and roads and irrigation canals.' But surely, surely, they could have done more, and faster. And they let my people starve!"

Now this gentleman's village whose decadence he so deplored, lies not over four hours by railroad from the city in which he lives. He is understood to be a man of large wealth, and himself informed me that his law practice was highly lucrative, naming an income that would be envied by an eminent lawyer in New York. Yet he, the one great man of his village, had left that village without help, advice, leadership, or even a friendly look-in, for seventeen years, though it lay but a comfortable afternoon's ride away from his home. And when at last he visited it and found its decay, he could see no one to blame but a Government that has 500,000 such villages to care for, and which can but work through human hands and human intelligence.

Also, he entirely neglected to mention, in accounting for the present depopulation of his birthplace, that a large industrial plant lately erected near it had drawn away a heavy percentage of the villagers by its opportunities of gain.

It would be a graceless requital of courtesy to name the gentleman just quoted.[†] But perhaps I may without offense name another, Sirdar Mohammed Nawaz Khan, lord of twenty-six villages in Attock District, northern Punjab.

This young Muslim went for his early education to the College for Punjab Chiefs, at Lahore, and thence to the royal Military College at Sandhurst, to earn a commission in the Indian Army. During his stay in England, being from time to time a guest in English country houses, his attention was caught and fixed by the attitude of large English landlords toward their tenants.

[†]The reference was to Lord Sinha, the only Indian to be appointed Governor of a province, who at the time was a Member of the Judicial Committee of the Privy Council. Sir Charles Teggart, the Chief Commissioner of Police in Calcutta, provided Mayo with arguments to discredit the views expressed by Sinha during her appointment with him; see Notes on 'Mother India', Folder no. 189, *Katherine Mayo Papers*, Series 4, Box 35.

Coming as a living illustration of the novel principles of landlord's duties laid down by the English headmaster of his college in Lahore, the thing struck root in his mind and soon possessed him. Dashing young soldier that he made, after eighteen months' service with a Hussar regiment, popular with officers and men, he resigned his commission and returned to his estates. "For I see where my place is now," he said.

There he spends his time, riding from village to village, working out better conditions, better farming methods, better sanitation, anything that will improve the status of his people. Twenty-seven years old and with an annual income of some four lakhs of rupees, he is an enthusiastic dynamo of citizenship, a living force for good, and the sworn ally of the equally enthusiastic and hard-working English Deputy Commissioner.

Curiously enough, he strongly objects to Government's new policy of rapid Indianization of the public services, takes no interest in Swaraj politics, and less than none in criticism of Government's efforts to clean up, educate, and enrich the people. His whole time goes to vigorous coöperation with Government betterment schemes, and to vigorous original effort.

If the good of the people is the object of government, then multiplication of the type of Sirdar Mohammed Nawaz Khan, rather than of the talkers, would produce the strongest argument for more rapid transfer of responsibility into Indian hands.

[...] "There is in rural India very little public opinion in favour of the education of the common folk," says the Commission of Inquiry, and "the wealthy land-owner or even the well-to-do farmer has by no means discovered yet that it is to his interest to educate the agricultural labourer."

[...] [Yet] the villagers are dignified, interesting, enlisting people, commanding affection and regard and well worthy the service that for the last sixty-odd years they have enjoyed—good men's best effort. Without their active and intelligent partnership, no native Government better than an oligarchy can ever exist in India.

But it is only to the Briton that the Indian villager of today can look for steady, sympathetic and practical interest and steady, reliable help in his multitudinous necessities. It is the British Deputy Commissioner, none other, who is "his father and his mother," and upon the mind of that Deputy Commissioner the villagers' troubles and the villagers' interests sit day and night.

In my own experience, it was an outstanding fact that in every one of the scores of villages I visited, from one end of India to the other, I got from the people a friendly, confiding, happy reception. King George and the young god Krishna, looking down from the walls of many a mud cottage, seemed to link the sources of benefit. All attempts to explain myself as an American proving futile, since a white face meant only England to them, an "American" nothing at all—I let it go at that, accepting the welcome that the work of generations had prepared.

Yet there are so few Britons in India—fewer than 200,000 counting every head, man, woman and child—and there are 500,000 British Indian villages!

"Would not your educated and brilliant young men of India," I once asked Mr. Gandhi, "be doing better service to India, if, instead of fighting for political advantage, social place and, in general, the limelight, they were to efface themselves, go to the villages, and give their lives to the people?"

"Ah, yes," Mr. Gandhi replied, "but that is a counsel of perfection."

To four interesting young Indian political leaders in Calcutta, men well considered in the city, I put the same question: "Would not you and all like you best serve your beloved Mother India by the sacrifice to her of your personal and political ambitions—by losing yourselves in your villages, to work there for the people, just as so many British, both men and women, are doing today? In twenty years' time, might not your accomplishment be so great that those political

powers you now vainly and angrily demand would fall into
your hands simply because you had proved yourselves their
fit custodians?"

"Perhaps," said the three [sic]. "But talk, also, is work. Talk
is now the only work. Nothing else can be done till we push
the alien out of India."

[...]

PART IV

Interlude

MR. GANDHI

A small stone house, such as would pass unremarked in any small town in America. A wicket gate, a sun-baked garden, a bare and clean room flooded with light from a broadside of windows. In the room, sitting on a floor cushion with his back to a blank wall, a man. To his right two younger men, near a slant-topped desk perhaps eighteen inches high. To his left, a backless wooden bench for the use of western visitors. If there are other objects in the room, one does not see them for interest in the man with his back to the wall.

His head is close-shaven, and such hair as he has is turning gray. His eyes, small and dark, have a look of weariness, almost of renunciation, as of one who, having vainly striven, now withdraws from striving, unconvinced. Yet from time to time, as he talks, his eyes flash. His ears are large and conspicuously protruding. His costume, being merely a loincloth, exposes his hairy body, his thin, wiry arms, and his bare, thin, interlaced legs, upon which he sits like Buddha with the soles of his feet turned up. His hands are busy with a little wooden spinning-wheel planted on the ground before him. The right hand twirls the wheel while the left evolves a cotton thread.

"'What is my message to America?'" he repeated in his light, dispassionate, even voice. "My message to America is the hum of this spinning-wheel."[†] [...]

[†]Gandhi, like several other Indians quoted in the book, felt that his words had been taken out of context and used mischievously; see *Nidhi-Sabarmati Gandhi Papers:* "Correspondence with Katherine Mayo". Mayo remained one of the strongest critics of Gandhi in the U.S.; see her articles "Gandhi's Inconsistencies", *Current History* (Aug. 1930): 864–70; "Gandhi's March Past", *Atlantic Monthly* Sept. 1930): 327–33; and "Is Gandhi Sincere?" *Nash's and Cosmopolitan* (Feb. 1932).

Chapter XVII

THE SIN OF THE SALVATION ARMY

"Why, after so many years of British rule, is India still so poor?" the Indian agitator tirelessly repeats.

If he could but take his eyes from the far horizon and direct them to things under his feet, he would find an answer on every side, crying aloud for honest thought and labor.

For example, the cattle question, by itself alone, might determine India's poverty.

India is being eaten up by its own cattle. And even at that the cattle are starving.

[...] One of Mr. Gandhi's Indian writers, Mr. Desai, sees the matter in this way:[1]

In ancient times and even during the Musalman period, cattle enjoyed the benefit of common pastures and had also the free run of the forests. The maintenance of the cattle cost their owners practically nothing. But the British Government cast a greedy eye upon this time-honoured property of the cattle, which could not speak for themselves and which had none else to speak on their behalf, and confiscated it, sometimes with an increase in the land-revenue in view, and at other times in order to oblige their friends, such as the missionaries.

This writer then supports his last-quoted phrase by the statement that the Salvation Army was once allowed by Government to take up 560 acres of public grazing-ground in Gujarat for farm purposes. He continues:

The result of this encroachment upon grazing areas has been that at the present day in India the proportion of grazing grounds to the total area is the smallest of all countries. ... It is not therefore a matter for surprise that our cattle should have rapidly deteriorated under British rule.

[1]*Young India*, June 3, 1926, V.G. Desai, p. 200.

[...] Still pursuing the question of India's cattle, Mr. Gandhi invoked the counsel of an Italian-trained specialist, domiciled in India. From him came the impatient reply of the practical man who sees small beauty in the spared rod where childish folly is wasting precious substance. If the Indian were not so callous, and so unintelligent as to the needs of his cattle—if he were only compelled to rotate crops and to grow fodder as Italians do in circumstances no better than the Indians', his troubles were done, says this witness.

[...] Mr. Gandhi's correspondent has shown us in the cow's hunger one of the evil effects of British rule. And British rule is indeed largely responsible for the present disastrous condition.

Up to the advent of the British in India, raids great and small, thieving, banditry and endless internal broils and warfares kept the country in chronic distress; and a sure butt of every such activity was the cattle of the attacked. Consequently, with a spasmodic regularity whose beneficent effect is more easily appreciated today than can well have been possible at the time, the cattle of any given area were killed off or driven away, the grazing-grounds of that area, such as they were, got an interval of rest, and, for the moment, inbreeding stopped. For new animals had to be slowly accumulated.

Upon this order broke the British with their self-elected commitment, first of all, to stop banditry, warfare and destruction and to establish peace. The task was precisely the same that America set for herself in the Philippines. As we achieved it in the Philippines, so did the British achieve it in India—in a greater interval of time commensurate with the greater area and population to be pacified. About fifty years ago Britain's work in this respect, until then all-absorbing, stood at last almost accomplished. Life and property under her controlling hand had now become as nearly safe as is, perhaps, possible. Epidemics, also, were checked and famine largely forestalled. So that, shielded from enemies that had before kept down their numbers, men and cattle alike multiplied. And men must be fed. Therefore, Government leased them land[2] in quantity according to their necessities, that they might raise food for themselves and not die.

They have raised food for themselves, but they will not raise food for their mother the cow. So the cow starves. And the fault—is the greed of Britain or of the Salvation Army.[3]

[2]By ancient law all land ownership is vested in Government.

[3]Government has largely entrusted to the Salvation Army, because of its conspicuous success therewith, the reformation of the criminal tribes, nomads, whose first need is domestication in a fixed habitat where they may be trained to earn an honest and sufficient livelihood by agriculture, cattle-raising, and handiwork. For this purpose and to further its excellent work for the Untouchables in general, the Salvation Army has received from Government the use of certain small and scattered tracts of uncultivated land in Gujarat and elsewhere. It is to this step that Mr. Gandhi's organ objects. See *ante*, p. 216. See further, *Muktifauj*, by Commissioner Booth-Tucker, Salvationist Publishing and Supplies, London.

Chapter XVIII

THE SACRED COW

Turning from the people and the cattle within their gates to Government's experimental work on Government farms, we find one world-contribution. They have solved a main domestic problem of low latitudes—how to get milk for the babies.

[...] All the fine animals produced at Lucknow, Pusa, Bangalore and the other Government plants, are conscientiously watched over by British breeders. In point of general competence, of cleanliness and order, and of simple practicality, the plants stand inspection. But all such matters are utterly foreign to the minds of the Indian peasant, and for those who might best and quickest teach the peasant—the Indian aris-. tocrat, the Indian intelligentsia—rarely do peasant or cattle carry any appeal.

With the exception of certain princes of Indian states who have learned from England to take pride in their herds, and again with the exception of a mere handful of estate-holders scattered over the country, cattle breeding is left entirely to a generally illiterate class known as *gvalas*, who lack enterprise, capital and intelligence to carry on the work.

[...] We of the West are continually in danger of misunderstanding the Indian through supposing that the mental picture produced by a given word or idea is the same in weight and significance to him and to us. His facility in English helps us to this error. We assume that his thought is like his tongue. He says, for example, that he venerates all life and is filled with tenderness for all animals. Lecturing in America, he speaks of the Hindu's sensitive refinement in this direction and of his shrinking from our gross unspirituality, our incomprehension of the sacred unity of the vital spark.

[...] It is one of the puzzles of India that a man whose bullock is his best asset will deliberately overload his animal, and then, half starved as it is, will drive it till it drops dead. The steep hillsides of Madras are a Calvary of draft bullocks. One sees them, branded from head to tail, almost raw from brands and blows, forced up-hill until they fall and die. If a British official sees this or any other deed of cruelty, he acts. But the British are few in the land. Yet far fewer are the Indians whose sensibilities are touched by the sufferings of dumb beasts, or whose wrath is aroused by pain and abuse inflicted upon defenseless creatures.

But if you suppose, from these seemingly plain words, that the average Hindu in India shows what we would call common humaneness toward animal life, you go far astray.

[...]

Chapter XIX

THE QUALITY OF MERCY

[...] Legislation for the prevention of cruelty to animals was enacted in the early years of Crown rule in India. But such legislation, anywhere, must rest for effectiveness on public opinion, and the opinion of Mr. Gandhi's paper is, in this matter, as a voice crying in the wilderness, awakening but the faintest of echoes. If the people feel no compassion; if the police, themselves drawn from the people, privately consider the law a silly, perhaps an irreligious law, whose greatest virtue lies in the chance it gives them to fill their pockets; and if little or no leaven of another sentiment exists in the higher classes, Government's purpose, as far as it means immediate relief, is handicapped indeed.

[...] Laws in India for the prevention of cruelty to animals have uniformly originated as Government bills. Whether of the Central or of the Provincial Administrations, measures for the protection of animals from cruelty have been passed over the indifference, if not over the pronounced hostility, of the Indian representation.

[...] Britain, by example and by teaching, has been working for nearly three-quarters of a century to implant her own ideas of mercy on an alien soil. In this and in uncounted other directions she might perhaps have produced more visible results, in her areas of direct contact, by the use of force. But her administrative theory has been that small constructive value lies in the use of force to bring about surface compliance where the underlying principle is not yet grasped. And, given a people still barbarian in their handling of their own women, it is scarcely to be expected that they should yet have taken on a mentality responsive to the appeal of dumb creatures.

Unhappily for the helpless animal world, Prevention of Cruelty to Animals is, under the current Indianization movement, a "transferred subject" of Government. That is to say: in each province working the "Reforms" the administration of this branches has been transferred by the British Parliament into the hands of an Indian minister. Dumb creation pays with its body the costs of the experiment.

Chapter XX

IN THE HOUSE OF HER FRIENDS

"This country is the cruelest in the world, to animals," said an old veterinarian, long practicing in India. It would perhaps be fairer to repeat that the people of India follow their religions, which, save with the small sect called Jains, produce no mercy either to man or to beast, in the sense that we of the West know mercy.

Mr. Gandhi himself writes:

In a country where the cow is an object of worship there should be no cattle problems at all. But our cow-worship has resolved itself into an ignorant fanaticism. The fact that we have more cattle than we can support is a matter for urgent treatment. I have already suggested the taking over of the question by cow protection societies.

Cow Protection Societies maintain *gaushalas*, or cow asylums. These asylums, like the *pinjrapoles*, or asylums for all animals, are maintained by gifts, and have access, through rich Hindu merchants, to almost unlimited funds.

[...] Having personally visited a number of *gaushalas* and *pinjrapoles*, I cannot but wonder whether those who support them so lavishly, those who commit animals to their care, and those who, like Mr. Gandhi, so strongly advocate their maintenance and increase, ever look inside their gates.

[...] In the heart of the city of Ahmedabad, within a few miles of Mr. Gandhi's pleasant and comfortable home in which he writes his earnest pleas for the support of cow shelters and *pinjrapoles*, I visited a large *pinjrapole* whose description, after that has already been said, need not be inflicted upon the reader's sensibilities. I hope that every animal that I saw in it is safely dead.

[...]

Chapter XXI

HOME OF STARK WANT

One hears a great deal from the new Indian intelligentsia about the glories of the "Golden Age"—a period in the shadowy past when the land smiled with health and plenty, wisdom, beauty and peace and when all went well with India. This happy natural condition was done to death, one is given to understand, by the mephitic influence of the present Government.

[...] A human enterprise covering two centuries of human progress, the name of the East India Company was sometimes dimmed by mistaken judgement or by unfit agents. Some of these were overbearing, some tactless, some wavering, one or two were base and a few succumbed to the temptation to graft. Of their defects, however, not a little nonsense is spun.

[...] Its inclusive achievement was courageous, arduous and essential towards the redemption of the country. Whatever its faults, it cleared and broke the ground for progress. And it lighted the first ray of hope that had ever dawned for the wretched masses of the Indian peoples.

The abolition of ancient indigenous horrors, such as the flourishing trade of the professional strangler tribes, the Thugs; the burning alive of widows; the burying alive of lepers, lie to the credit of the Company.

[...] And no briefest summary of the epoch-making elements of its concerns could be forgiven a failure to cite the gist of Section 87 of the Parliamentary Act of 1784, which reads:

No native of the said territories, nor any natural-born subject of His Majesty resident therein, shall, by reason only of his religion, place of birth, descent, colour, or any of them, be disabled from holding any place, office or employment under the Company.

A bomb, indeed, to drop into caste-fettered, feud-filled, tyrant-crushed India! Nor was this shock of free western ideas without its definitely unsettling influence. The Sikh Rebellion in 1845, the Indian Mutiny in 1857, were in no small degree direct fruits of that influence. And with the conclusion of the latter England felt that the time had come to do away with the awkward Company-Parliament form of government, to end the control of a great territory by commercial interest, however safeguarded, and to bring the administration of India directly under the Crown.

In the year, 1858, this step was taken. Shabby, threadbare, sick and poor, old Mother India stood at last on the brink of another world and turned blind eyes toward the strange new flag above her head. It carried then, as it carries today, a pledge that is, to her, incredible. How can she, the victim and slave of all recorded time, either hope or believe that her latest master brings her the gift of constructive service, democracy and the weal of the common people?

Chapter XXII

THE REFORMS

The roots of the form of government now gradually working out in British India ramify into past centuries and are visible through continuous growth. For the purpose of this book they may be passed over, to reach the briefest outline of the present evolutionary phase.

[...] The effort to decentralize—to magnify the responsibilities of provincial governments for the purpose of training and stimulating Indians to handle their own affairs, stands out preëminent in the present scheme. In part and as applied to the nine major divisions, this makes of the provincial government a two-branched machine operated from the office of the Governor. The Governor and his Executive Council, all Crown appointees, form one branch. Council membership is commonly divided between British and Indians. The Governor and his Ministers of Departments form the second branch. These are appointed by the Governor from the elected members of the legislature and are themselves responsible to that body. All ministers are Indian. Between the two branches the various functions of government formerly handled by a single arm are now divided, under the heads of "reserved" and "transferred" subjects.

Reserved subjects, save for the ultimate power of the Central Government, lie in the hands of the Provincial Governor in Council. Transferred subjects are assigned to the provincial legislatures, and are operated by the Ministers.

The list of transferred subjects represents authority resigned by the British people in favor of the peoples of India. the intention of the plan is, if the experiment succeeds, to enlarge the list of subjects transferred. On the other hand, where the Ministerial machine fails to work, Governors-in-

Council may resume control of a subject already transferred. Transferred subjects at present comprise Education, Public Health, Management of Public Works other than irrigation and railways, Development of Industries, Excise, Agriculture, Local Self-government and others. Reserved subjects include Maintenance of Law and Order, Defense of India, Finance, the Land Revenue system, etc.

[...] Commonly known as "Dyarchy," or "The Reforms," it is in essence no new thing, but merely an accelerated unfolding of the original British theme whose *motif* is the drawing of Indians into responsible participation in Government.

[...] The scheme in its shape of today has not the stability of the slow-growing oak, root for branch, balanced and anchored. Rather, it is a hothouse exotic, weedy, a stranger in its soil, forced forward beyond its inherent strength by the heat of a generous and hasty emotion. An outsider sitting today through sessions of Indian legislatures, Central or Provincial, somehow comes to feel like one observing a roomful of small and rather mischievous children who by accident have got hold of a magnificent watch. They fight and scramble to thrust their fingers into it, to pull off a wheel or two, to play with the mainspring; to pick out the jewels. They have no apparent understanding of the worth of the mechanism, still less of the value of time. And when the teacher tries to explain to them how to wind their toy up, they shriek and grimace in fretful impatience and stuff their butterscotch into the works.

As to the relation of these people to their supposed job, its most conspicuous quality, today, is its artificiality. Adepts in the phraseology of democratic representation, they are, in fact, profoundly innocent of the thought behind the phrase. Despotisms induce no growth of civic spirit, and the peoples of India, up to the coming the Britain, had known no rule but that of despots. Britain, by her educational effort, has gradually raised up an element before unknown in India—a middle class. But this middle class—these lawyers and professional men—are in the main as much dominated today as were their ancestors five hundred years ago by the law of caste and of transmigration—completest denial of democracy. They talk of "the people" simply because the word bulks large in the vocabulary of that western-born representative government which they now essay.

A village headman knows and feels infinitely more than do these elected "representatives" as to the duties and responsibilities of government. An Indian prince has the inherited habit of ruling, and, whatever his failings, whatever his purpose, keeps his people somewhere in mind. And an American unconscious of his own civic debt to his spiritual or blood-lineal ancestors, from Plymouth Rock to Runnymede, may be brought to a wholesome state of humility by a few days' watching of the anchorless legislators of India.

Off and on, during the winter session of 1926, in Delhi, I listened to Assembly debates. Hour after hour, day after day, the Swarajist bench spent their energies in sterile, obstructionist tactics, while for the most part the rest of the House sat apathetic save for an occasional expression of weary contempt from some plain fighting man out of the north. Little or nothing constructive emanated from party benches. The simplest piece of essential legislation proposed by Government evoked from the Swarajist orators fantastic interpretations as to sinister intent.

[...] The history of British administration of India shows that reactionary disorders follows attempts at speeded progress. The East resents being hustled, even in reforms. It was perhaps specially unfortunate for "Dyarchy" that its birthday should fall in the season of Mr. Gandhi's ill-starred adventure into politics, when he could turn upon it the full fire of his non-coöperative guns. His influence in Bengal and the Central Provinces was enough at the time to stop the experiment completely, and although that influence has now everywhere lapsed into negligibility as a political factor, its crippling and embittering after-effects still drag upon the wheels of progress.

Without presuming to offer a criticism of the Reforms Act, it would seem that its chief obstacle lies deeper in the roots of things than any enmity can reach. The whole structure of the Reforms is planned to rest on the foundation of a general electorate which, through its directly elected legislators, controls in each province the Ministers who handle the people's affairs. And the difficulty is that while the structure hangs waiting in midair, the foundation designed to sustain it yet lingers in the blue-print stage—does not in fact exist. India has no electorate, in any workable sense of the word, nor can have on the present basis for many generations to come. And of this statement the natural complement is also true: India's elected representatives are as yet profoundly unaware of the nature of the duties incumbent upon their office.

[...] This illiterate peasantry, these illiterate landholders, have no access to and no interest in the political game, nor in any horizon beyond that which daily meets their physical eyes. The town politician, the legislator actual or aspirant, rarely comes near them unless it be at election time or, as in the period of the "non-violence" agitations, to stir them with some report of evil to rise in blind revolt. When, recently, Swarajist members of the legislative councils decided to try to block the wheels of government by walking out, not one of them, as far as I was able to learn, took the previous step of consulting his constituents. The constituency is as yet too gauzy a figment, too abstract a theory, too non-oriental a conception, to figure as an influence in their minds.

[...] With the Hindu comes, first, the ancient religious law of the family-clan; because of this system the public office-holder who fails to feather the nest of his kin will be branded by all his world not only a fool but a renegade, and will find neither peace at home nor honor abroad. No public opinion sustains him.

Second, beyond the family line comes the circle of caste. The Hindu office-holder who should forget his caste's interests for interests lying outside that circle would bring down upon his head the opprobrium, perhaps the discipline, of his orthodox fellow caste men. And this, be it remembered, means not only temporal discomfort, but also dire penalties inflicted upon his soul, determining the miseries of future incarnations.

Third, the political struggle between Hindu and Muslim, as will be seen in later chapters, brings tremendous pressure to bear upon the official from either camp, practically compelling him to dispense such patronage as he enjoys among his co-religionists only.

With these points in mind, one views with more charity and understanding the breakdown of allegiance to western ideals that generally occurs in even the staunchest of Indian public officials when the British superior officer who has backed him through thick and thin in free work for general good, is replaced by an Indian, himself subject to the ancient code.

It is stiff work to maintain, alone and accursed, an alien standard among one's own people.

Yet with all its increased expense and diminished efficiency, the new constitution is, somehow, turning the wheels. Taking the shorter view, it has improved the position of Indians in the services. It has opened to them the height of office along many lines. It has made Government more directly responsive to the sentiment of vocal India, to such an extent indeed that the onlooker is tempted to wonder whether Government's sense of proportion is not impaired, whether it has not been nervously stifling its conscience to save its ears, whether it is not paying more attention to the spoiled baby's shrieks for the matches than it is to the vital concerns of its whole big, dumb, helpless and infinitely needy family.

A "hard-headed American" long resident in India, himself a person of excellent standing, told me this incident:

One of the principal Swaraj politicians had just delivered himself of a ferocious public diatribe against the Viceroy.

"Now tell me, Pundit," said the American, privately, "how can you shout like that in view of the fact that only a few weeks ago this very Viceroy went far out of his way to be courteous and accommodating to you and to get you what you wanted?"

"How can I shout like that?" laughed the Indian. "Why shouldn't I shout? Of course I shout, when every time I shout he gives me something."

Thus in taking information from the Indian, at home or abroad, a vital preliminary step is to appreciate and keep always in mind the definition and value that he assigns to "truth."

The Indian may be a devoted "seeker after truth" in the sense of metaphysical speculation; he may be of a splendid candor in dealing with most parts of most subjects of which you speak together. And yet he may from time to time embed in the midst of his frank speech statements easily susceptible of proof and totally at variance with the facts.

Having repeatedly come across this trait, I took it up for examination with a distinguished Bengali, one of the most broad-minded of Indian public men. Said he:

"Our *Mahabharata* preaches truth above all. If we have deviated it is because of the adverse circumstances under which we long lived. If we lie it is because we are afraid to face the consequences."

Then I laid it before a great mystic, spiritual teacher of multitudes, who had favored me with a classic and noble metaphysical discourse. His reply was:

"What is truth? Right and wrong are relative terms. You have a certain standard; if things help you, you call them good. It is not a lie to say that which is necessary to produce good. I do not distinguish virtues. Everything is good. Nothing is in itself bad. Not acts, but motives, count."

Finally, I carried the matter to a European long resident in India, and of great sympathy with the Indian mind.

"Why," I asked, "do men of high position make false statements, and then name in support documents which, when I dig them out, either fail to touch the subject at all or else prove the statement to be false?"

"Because," he replied, "to the Hindu nothing is false that he wants to believe. Or, all materiality being nothingness, all statements concerning it are lies. Therefore he may blamelessly choose the lie that serves his purpose. Also, when he presents to you the picture that it suits him to offer, it never occurs to him that you might go to the pains of checking up his words at the source."

In the same line, a well-informed New York journalist, in the winter of 1926–27, asked certain Indians who had been publicly talking in the city: "Why do you make such egregiously false allegations about conditions in India?"

"Because," said one of them, speaking for the rest, "you Americans know nothing of India. And your missionaries, when they come back for more money, tell too much truth, and hurt our pride. So we have to tell lies, to balance up."

As his metaphysics work out, it is no shame to a Hindu to be "caught in a lie." You do not embarrass or annoy him by so catching him. His morality is no more involved in the matter than in a move in a game of chess.

Now, in the name of fair play, it cannot be too strongly emphasized that this characteristic, this point of view, this different evaluation, constitutes not necessarily an inferiority, but certainly a difference, like the color of the skin. Yet as a difference involved in the heart of human intercourse, it must constantly be reckoned with and understood; else that intercourse will often and needlessly crash.

Chapter XXIII

PRINCES OF INDIA

Thus far we have been dealing mainly with British India, as distinct from the Indian Empire composed of British India and the Indian States.

[...] The relation between the British Government and the ruling chiefs is a treaty relation, not that of conqueror and conquered. It leaves the princes free to determine their own types of government, to levy their own taxes, and to wield the power of life and death within their territories. The basis of the relation, on the part of Britain, is (a) non-interference in the states' internal affairs, excepting in cases of grave need, while exercising such progressive influence as may be tactfully possible; and (b) the safeguarding of the interests of the country as a whole, in matters of an Imperial character.

[...] The old normal relation of the prince to the people was the relation of a huge-topped plant to a poor, exhausted, over-taxed root. He squeezed his people dry, giving little or nothing in return. And under such a prince, unless he be too outrageous, the people may today be fairly content.

On the whole, [...] progress is effected when the removal of an unfit ruler leaves the administration of the state in the hands of the Resident, with, it may be, a regent, during the minority of the heir. A measure of comparison is thereby established, favoring the birth of active discontent if a retrograde government follows and tending gradually to force up its quality from below.

As a particular instance, one may cite the case of a certain prince whose minority lasted twenty years. During this period the British Resident administered the state, and, for the first time in its history, its revenues went to the service of the people. Good roads and bridges were built, schools were opened, a modern hospital was established and endowed with a competent staff; order was secured; trade and manufactures were fostered; the exchequer made solvent, the reserve funds built up, justice was put within the reach of all. And, all the years of this pleasant novelty, the people sighed for the day when their prince, not only dearly beloved but also ritualistically half-divine in their eyes, should come home and rule over them as his fathers had done over their fathers.

The day dawned. The boy took over. The wives and the concubines, the court officials, the dancing girls and the ambitious relatives at once laid hold on him, plying him with every soft temptation that could dissolve his energy and will-power, sap his manhood and make him easy to control. In three years' time he had ruined the work of the preceding twenty. The treasury reserves were gone. Taxes shot up. Public services went flat. The excellent doctor, who cost $500 a month, had been replaced by a sixteen-dollar dealer in charms and potions. The competent hospital staff was replaced by useless hangers-on. The hospital itself had turned into a kennel; and so on, through the departments, shabbiness and decay overwhelming them all. No justice was to be had and no appeal could be taken against bought decisions, for there was none who cared to hear, except at a price. Graft did everything, and the people were bled to provide money for their young ruler's extravagances and vices.

At last they came to their old friend, the Resident, pleading:

"We did long to have him come to live among us and rule over us. But we knew not how it would be. We can bear no more. Let the Sahib return and give us peace and justice and the good life we had before."

[...] Here is a story, from the lips of one whose veracity has never, I believe, been questioned. The time was that stormy period in 1920 when the new Reforms Act was casting doubt over the land and giving rise to the persistent rumor that Britain was about to quit India. My informant, an American of

long Indian experience, was visiting one of the most important of the princes—a man of great charm, cultivation and
force, whose work for his state was of the first order. The
prince's Dewan was also present, and the three gentlemen had
been talking at ease, as became the old friends that they were.

"His Highness does not believe," said the Dewan, "that
Britain is going to leave India. But still, under this new régime
in England, they may be so ill-advised. So, His Highness is
getting his troops in shape, accumulating munitions and coin-
ing silver. And if the English do go, three months afterward
not a rupee or a virgin will be left in all Bengal."

To this His Highness, sitting in his capital distant from
Bengal by half the breadth of India, cordially agreed. His ancestors through the ages had been predatory Mahratta chiefs.

The Swarajists, it would appear, forget that, the moment
government were placed in their hands, the princes would
flash into the picture as powers in the land, severally to be
reckoned with exactly as they were a century ago; and that the
Indian Army, if it hung together at all, might be more likely to
follow one of the outstanding princes rather than the com-
mands of a Legislative Assembly composed of a type that
India has never known or obeyed.

The Indian mind is cast in the mould of autocratic aris-
tocracy. A natural war means a princely leader and unlimited
loot. If His Highness above had set out for Bengal, the man-
power of the countrysides, barring Britain's presence, would
surely have romped after him.

But the princes know well that if Britain were to withdraw
from India, they themselves, each for himself, would at once
begin annexing territory; that all would be obliged to live
under arms, each defending his own borders; and that the
present-day politician would in the first onset finally disappear like a whiff of chaff before flame.

The princes, however, want no such issue. They frankly say
that they enjoy the *pax Britannica*, which not only relieves
them from the necessity of sustaining larger military estab-
lishments, but which gives them the enjoyment of public
utilities, as railroads, good highroads, ports, markets, mail,

and wires, while permitting them to develop their properties in peace. Their attitude during the War was wholly loyal, and they contributed munificently of money, men and goods to the Empire's cause. In a word, they are a company of high-spirited, militant aristocrats strongly interested that the British Crown shall remain suzerain in India, but absolutely refusing to carry their complaisance so far as to admit the Indian politician of the Reforms Government as an agent to their courts.

Their supreme contempt of that class is not unmingled with distinct irritation that the Power to which they acknowledge fealty stoops to parley with what seems to them an impudent and ridiculous *canaille*.

"Our treaties are with the Crown of England," one of them said to me, with incisive calm. "The princes of India made no treaty with a Government that included Bengali *babus*. We shall never deal with this new lot of Jacks-in-office. While Britain stays, Britain will send us English gentlemen to speak for the King-Emperor, and all will be as it should be between friends. If Britain leaves, we, the princes, will know how to straighten out India, even as princes should."

Then I recall a little party given in Delhi by an Indian friend in order that I might privately hear the opinions of certain Home Rule politicians. Most of the guests were, like my host, Bengali Hindus belonging to the western-educated professional class. They had spoken at length on the coming expulsion of Britain from India and on the future in which they themselves would rule the land.

"And what," I asked, "is your plan for the princes?"

"We shall wipe them out!" exclaimed one with conviction. And all the rest nodded assent.[†]

[†]Dorothy Roy, wife of K.C. Roy of the Associated Press of India, had hosted this party for Mayo as an opportunity for her to meet with some of the political leaders in India, including M.A. Jinnah. Roy later wrote to Lala Lajpat Rai contradicting Mayo's version of the conversation at the party See Dorothy Roy to Lala Lajpat Rai, 7 Sept. 1927, reprinted in World Citizen [S.G.] Warty], *Sister India: A Critical Examination of and Reasoned Reply to Miss Katherine Mayo's 'Mother India'* (Bombay: Sister India Office, 1928), p. 129.

PART V

Interlude

INTO THE NORTH

[...] In all this world, say the men who, day and night, year in, year out, guard the frontier of India—in all this world are no fighters better than the tribesmen. Also, behind them lies Afghanistan, like a couchant leopard, green eyes fixed on the glittering bait of India. And behind Afghanistan—nay, in Kabul itself, lurks "the Man that walks like a Bear," fingering gold and whispering ceaselessly of the glories of a rush across the border that shall sweep the Crescent through the strong Muslim Punjab, gathering Islam in its train; that shall raise the Muslims of the South and so shall close from both sides, like a tide, forever, over the heads of the Hindus.

"Why not?" asks the Bear. "Are you feebler men than your fathers? What stops you? The English? But look! I worry them on the other flank, stirring up the silly Hindus, North and South, against them. Already these English relax their hand, as the councils of their home-country weaken. And, I, the Bear, am behind you. Look at the loot and the killings! Drive in your wedge! Strike!"

Chapter XXIV

FIREBRANDS TO STRAW

Roughly speaking, three-quarters of the population of British India are Hindus, if the 60,000,000 Untouchables be computed with the Hindus.[1] Roughly speaking, one quarter of the population of British India is Muhammadan. And between the two lies a great gulf whence issues a continuous threatening rumble, with periodic destructive outbursts of sulphur and flame.[†]

This gulf constitutes one of the greatest factors in the present Indian situation.

Its elements formed integral parts of the problem that the British Crown assumed in 1858. And if for the first half-century of Crown rule they remained largely dormant, the reason is not obscure. During that half-century, Government was operated by British officers of the Civil Service, both in the administrative and in the judicial branches. These officers, in the performance of their duties, made no difference between Hindu and Muhammadan, holding the general interest in an equal hand. Therefore, being in the enjoyment of justice and of care, man by man, day by day, and from an outside authority that neither Hindu nor Muhammadan could challenge, neither party was roused to jealousy, and religious communal questions scarcely arose.

[1]The Census of India of 1921 shows about three and a quarter million Sikhs and about one and a sixth million Jains, of both of which sects many members call themselves Hindus. The Buddhists, numbering eleven and a half millions, are largely confined to the Province of Burma, outside the Indian Peninsula.

[†]For a discussion of sectarian Hindu and Muslim politics or "communalism" in late colonial India, see Gyanendra Pandey, *The Construction of Communalism in Colonial North India* (Delhi: Oxford University Press, 1992).

In 1909. however, the wind switched to a stormy quarter. The Minto-Morley scheme was enacted by Parliament as the "Indian Councils Act."

The effect of this measures was instantly to alarm the Muhammadan element, rousing it into self-consciousness as a distinct and separate body, unorganized, but suspicious, militant in spirit and disturbed about its rights. For it saw, clearly enough, that in any elected legislature, and in any advantages thereby to be gained, the Hindu was practically sure to shoulder the Muhammadan out of the path.

[...] As long as British officials administered the affairs of India in town and village, the potentiality of the situation thus created remained obscured. But the first gun of the Minto-Morley "Reforms," rent the curtain, and the startled Islamic chiefs, their hands on the hilt of the sword a-rust in the scabbard, peered forth half-awake upon a world dark with shapes of ill-omen.

And so, greatly at a disadvantage, the Muslims as a political entity reappeared in the field. Yet over the wide country, in the villages and the hamlets, the stir scarcely reached. For there, still, the British official alone represented Government, dealing justice and favor with an even hand, and Muslim and Hindu, side by side, lived at peace.

Then came 1919, the extension of the "Reforms" of 1909, the transfer of much power, place and patronage from British into Indian hands, and the promise, furthermore, of a reviewal of the field at the end of a third ten-year interval, with an eye to still further transfers.

From that moment, except in country districts unreached by agitators, peace between the two elements became a mere name—an artificial appearance maintained wholly by the British presence. And now, as 1929 draws nigh, the tension daily increases, while the two rivals pace around each other in circles, hackles up, looking for first toothhold.

For a time during the political disturbances that followed the War a brief farce of unity was played by the leaders of that day. Mr. Gandhi embraced the Khilafat[2] agitation as embodied in those picturesque freebooters, the Ali brothers, if thereby the Muhammadan weight might be swung with his own to embarrass the British administration. But the Khilafat cause itself died an early death. And a single incident of the Gandhi-Ali alliance may be cited to illustrate the actual depth of the brotherhood it proclaimed.

Up on the mountains overlooking the Malabar coast, among a population of about two million Hindus, live a people known as the Moplahs, descendants of old Arab traders and the women of the country. The Moplahs, who themselves number about a million, live in surprisingly clean and well-kept houses, have often intelligent, rugged faces and, according to my own experience, are an interesting and friendly primitive folk.

But, zealot Muhammadans, they have ever been prone to outbreaks of religious passion in which their one desire is to be sent to Paradise by a bullet or a knife, first having piled up the longest possible list of non-believers dead by their hands.

Among these simple creatures, in the year of disorders 1921, the political combination above indicated sent emissaries preaching a special edition of its doctrines. Government's hand, these proclaimed, was raised against the holy places of Islam. Government was "Satanic," an enemy of the Faith. Government must and would be driven out of India and that right soon. Swaraj must be set up.

From mosque to mosque, from hamlet to hamlet, from cocoanut [sic] grove to cocoanut grove, the fiery words passed. And, whatever meaning they might bear for an abstract philosopher, to the simple Moplah, as, in those miserable years, to so many millions of simple Hindus all over the land, they meant just what they said—War.

But, the point that Mr. Gandhi missed, whatever the humorous Ali brothers may privately have thought about it,

[2]An Islamic movement aiming at the restoration of Turkey to prewar status, including her reconquest of the emancipated Armenians and Arabs, and her recovery of Palestine, Syria, Thrace, and the Dardanelles.

was this: Swaraj, to a Moplah, could only mean the coming of the earthly Kingdom of Islam, in which whatever else happened or failed to happen, no idol-worshiping Hindu could be tolerated alive.

So the Moplahs, secretly and as best they could, made store of weapons—knives, spears, cutlasses. And on August 20, 1921, the thing broke loose. As if by a preliminary gesture of courtesy to the sponsors of the occasion, one European planter was murdered at the start. But without further dissipation of energy the frenzied people then concentrated on the far more congenial task of communal war. First blocking the roads, cutting the telegraph wires and tearing up the railway lines at strategic points, thereby isolating the little police stations scattered through the mountains, they set to work, in earnest and in detail, to establish a Muslim Kingdom and to declare a Swaraj after their own hearts.

Their Hindu neighbors, though outnumbering them two to one, seem to have stood no chance against them. The Hindu women, as a rule, were first circumcised—"forcibly converted," as the process is called—and were then added to Moplah families. The Hindu men were sometimes given the choice of death or "conversion," sometimes flayed alive, sometimes cutlassed at once and thrown down their own wells. In one district, the Ernad Taluk, over nine hundred males were "forcibly converted" and the work spread on through the mountain-slopes.

As rapidly as possible police and troops were thrown into the country, by whose work, after six months of tryng service, the disorders were quelled. But not until some three thousand Moplahs had cast away their lives, without reckoning the Hindus they accounted for, not until much property had been destroyed and many families ruined, and not until a long list of prisoners awaited trial for guilt that certainly belonged on heads higher than theirs.

Meantime, the circumcised male Hindus wandered up and down the land calling upon their brethren to take warning.

A trained American observer, agent of the United States Government, chanced to be in the region at the time. His statement follows:

"I saw them in village after village, through the south and east of Madras Presidency. They had been circumcised by a peculiarly painful method, and now, in many cases, were suffering tortures from blood poisoning. They were proclaiming their misery, and calling on all their gods to curse Swaraj and to keep the British in the land. 'Behold our miserable bodies! We are defiled, outcasted, unclean, and all because of the serpents who crept among us with their poison of Swaraj. Once let the British leave the land and the shame that has befallen us will assuredly befall you also, Hindus, men and women, every one.'

"The terrors of hell were literally upon them.

"And the Brahman priests were asking one hundred to one hundred and fifty rupees a head to perform the purification ceremony which alone could save the poor creatures' souls.

"This ceremony consisted in filling the eyes, ears, mouth and nose with soft cow-dung, which must then be washed out with cow's urine, after which should be administered *ghee* (clarified butter), milk and curds. It sounds simple, but can only be performed by a Brahman, and with proper rites and sacred verses. And the price which the Brahmans now set upon their services was, to most of the needy, prohibitive. Their distress was so desperate that British officials, for once interfering in a religious matter, interceded with the Brahmans and persuaded them, in view of the large number concerned, to accept a wholesale purification fee of not over twelve rupees a head."

I have not verified the final item in this statement. My informant, however, besides having been on the spot at the time, is professionally critical as to evidence.

If there was anything particularly Muhammadan in this outbreak, it was in the feature of "forcible conversion" rather than in the general barbarity educed. Less than six months before the Moplah affair began, occurred the Chauri Chaura incident in the United Provinces, far away from Malabar.

An organization called the "National Volunteers" had lately been formed, more or less under pay, to act as a militia for the enforcement of the decrees of the Working Committee of the Indian National Congress. This "Congress" is a purely political organization, and was, at the time, under the control of Mr. Gandhi.

On February 4, 1921, a body of National Volunteers, followed by a mob whom their anti-government propaganda had inflamed, attacked the little police station at Chauri Chaura, within which were assembled some twenty-one police constables and village watchmen, the common guardians of the rural peace. The peasantry and the "Volunteers," numbering altogether some three thousand men, surrounded the police station, shot a few of its inmates dead, wounded the rest, collected the wounded into a heap, poured oil over them, and fried them alive.[†]

This was as Hindu to Hindu.

Again, in the Punjab during the disorders of 1919, anti-Government workers launched a special propaganda for the violation of foreign women.

Its public declarations took the form of posters such as these: "Blessed the Mahatma Gandhi. We are sons of India. ... Gandhi! We the Indians will fight to death after you;" and "What time are you waiting for now? There are many ladies here to dishonor. Go all around India, clear the country of the ladies," etc., etc.[3]

This was as Indian to white man.

Such language, to such a public could carry neither a figurative nor a second import. Had time been given it to do its work, had a weak hand then held the helm of the Punjab, an unbearable page had been written in the history of India.

---

[3]See *Disorders Inquiry Committee, 1919–20, Report*, Chapter VII, for placards posted in and around Lyallpur, in April, 1919.

[†]For a discussion of the Chauri-Chaura incident, see Shahid Amın, *Event, Metaphor, Memory: Chauri Chaura 1922–1992* (New Delhi: Oxford University Press, 1995).

And if these three instances are here brought forward from among the scores of grim contemporaneous parallels with which they can be diversified and reënforced, it is not for the purpose of shaming the Indian peoples, but rather to point out the wild, primitive and terribly explosive nature of the elements that politicians and theorists take into their hands when they ignite those people's passions.

[...]

Chapter XXV

SONS OF THE PROPHET

In December, 1916, a political body called the All-India Muslim League united with the Indian National Congress already mentioned, in proclaiming the identity of Muhammadan and Hindu interests, and in asserting their common desire for Swaraj.

[...] But in view of the nature of Muhammadan thought, a more ominous weight lay in a simpler pronouncement. The Ulema is the body of official interpreters of the Koran which, on occasion of doubt, delivers decisions that guide the Muslim world. The solemn verdict of the Ulema of Madras, now laid before the British Secretary of State for India, was expressed in three closely similar dicta, one of which follows:[1]

"Verily, Polytheists are unclean." In case the British Government were to hand over the administration, as desired by the Hindus, it would be contrary to the Sacred Law of Musulmans to live under them, Polytheists.

Saiyid Muhi-ud-din
Trustee of the endowments of the
Amir-un-Nisa. Begum Sahiba Mosque
One who is forgiven!

[...] Now, in view of the Militant character developed in any people by the Islamic faith, it appears that British India's Muhammadan factor, even where it is weakest, is strong enough to make trouble. Always an international rather than a nationalist, all over India the Muhammadan is saying today: "We are foreigners, conquerors, fighting men. What if our numbers are small! Is it numbers, or men, that count? When

---

[1]*Addresses Presented in India to His Excellency the Viceroy and the Right Honourable the Secretary of State for India*, pp. 63–64.

the British go, *we* shall rule India. Therefore it behooves us quickly to gain such ground as we can."

The Hindu, on his side wittingly misses no step to consolidate his own position. And so wherever choice rests in Indian hands, every office must be filled, every decision taken, every appropriation spent, on religious communal lines, while the other side fights it, tooth and nail, and the actual merits of the matter concerned disappear from the picture.

Heavily as this condition in all directions handicaps the public service, nowhere is its influence more stultifying than in the judiciary. Always an eager litigant, the Indian finds in his religious quarrels endless occasions for appeal to law. But, if the case must be tried before an Indian judge, one side or the other is in despair. For, though he were, in fact, a miracle of rectitude, he is expected to lean, in his verdict, to the side of his own creed, and nothing can persuade the litigant of the other faith that he will not do so.

The bench of India has been and is graced by some native judges of irreproachable probity. Yet the Indian is traditionally used to the judge who accepts a fee from either side in advance of the trial, feeling that probity is sufficiently served if, after the verdict, the fee of the loser is returned. Bought witnesses are also a matter of course; you may see them today squatting before the court house waiting to be hired. "Theoretically I know it is irregular," said one western-educated barrister of Madras, "but practically I cannot leave that advantage entirely in my opponent's hands it is our custom."

But when the matter of the Hindu-Muslim conflict enters in, all else as a rule gives way. "How shall any judge decide against his gods?" moans the unfortunate. "And does he not hold court in the midst of my enemies? Take me, therefore, before an English judge, who cares naught for these matters but will give me upright judgment, though I be right or wrong."

[...] The Muslim comprises but a bare quarter of the population of British India. But that percentage is growing. His gains indicate both superior fecundity and superior vitality. His brain is not quick, but he has often a gift of horse sense. He is beginning to see that he must go to school. Granted time, opportunity and a sense of security, he may wipe out his handicaps and fit himself for full participation in the administration of the country. Thrown into the arena today, he would see but one recourse—the sword.

And it should never for a moment be forgotten that when the Muslims of India draw the sword, it will not be as an isolated body but as the advance line of an energy now banked up, like the waters of a brimming reservoir, by the Frontier Defense of the Army.

[...] Few Hindu politicians do realize it. "The Afghan has kept off us these many long years. Why should he come through now? Bah! It is a child's bogey!" they say with dull eyes, as unaware of their own life-long protected state and how it is brought about as the oyster on its sea-bed is unaware of the hurricanes that blow.

The North-West Frontier Province, 95 per cent Muhammadan, lies today quiet and contented with its government, a buffer state between, on the one hand, the rich, part-Hindu Punjab and the vast soft Hindu South, and on the other hand, the hungry Muslim fighting hordes whose fingers twitch and whose mouths water to be at them. The contentment of the North-West Frontier Province with things as they are is invaluable to the peace of India.

I talked with many leading men of that province. All seemed·of one mind in the matter. Here, therefore, are the exact words of a single representative—a mountain-bred man of Persian ancestry some generations back—big, lean, hawk-nosed, hawk-eyed, leader of many, sententious until his subject snatched the bridle from his tongue:

"The whole province is satisfied now and desires no change. As for those little folk of the South, we have never called them men. There is far more difference between us and them than between us and the British. If the British withdraw, immediate hell will follow, in the first days of which the Bengali and all his tribe will be removed from the earth. I can account for a few, myself, with much pleasure. Coöperation between the British and us is our one course. They have given us roads, telephones, good water where no water was before, peace, justice, a revenue from trade made possible only by their protection, safety for our families, care for our sick and schools for our children. None of these things did we have till they came. I ask you, is it likely we shall throw them all away because a coward and a sneak and our own inherited enemy calls for 'boycott,' and 'non-coöperation'? Nothing was ever gained and much lost by that stupid 'non-coöperation.' India is a big country and needs all our united strength can do for it. Muslims and British and even Hindus. But without the British no Hindus will remain in India except such as we keep for slaves."

[...] The doctrine of non-coöperation with the established Power led nowhere, as all now see. The mystic doctrine of spiritual war, a war of "soul-force," that uses the language of hate while protesting theories of love, had logically and insistently projected itself upon the material plane in the form of the slaughter of men. The inability of individuals to subordinate personal, family or clan interests and to hold together for team-work, had been demonstrated. And the fact had been driven home to the hilt that neither Hindu nor Muhammadan could think in terms of the whole people.

For the moment, some of them see it. Can they hold the vision? To have seen it at all marks gain.

Chapter XXVI

THE HOLY CITY

[...] Benares is the Sacred City of the Hindu world. Countless temples adorn it, set like tiers of crowns above and among the broad flights of stairs that ascend from the Ganges, Holy River. Chains of yellow marigolds are stretched across that river to welcome Mother Ganges as she comes. And as the worshipers, clad in long robes of tender or brilliant colors, bearing their water-jars upon their heads or shoulders, trail up and down the high gray steps, they seem so like figures in the vision of a prophet of Israel that one almost hears the song they sang as "they went up by the stairs of the city of David, at the going up of the wall."

But my visit to Benares was made in the company of the Municipal Health Officer, a man of whom no artist-soul is apt to think.

This gentleman is an Indian. Before taking up his present duties, he made preparatory studies in America, in the enjoyment of a Rockefeller Foundation Scholarship in Public Health.[†] Without attempting to convey an idea of his whole problem, one may indicate here a few of its points.

The normal stationary population of Benares is about two hundred thousand, of whom some thirty thousand are Brahmans connected with the temples. In addition, two to three hundred thousand pilgrims come yearly for transient stays. And upon special occasions, such as an eclipse, four hundred thousand persons may pour into the city for that day, to depart a few days later as swiftly as they came.

[†]Mayo's close association with several senior Health officials at the Rockefeller Foundation in the U.S. raised a storm of controversy about the Foundation's connections to her project; see B.B. Mundkur, "Miss Mayo and the Rockefeller Foundation", *Nation* (14 Nov. 1928): 127.

To take care of all this humanity the Municipality allows its chief Health Officer an annual sum equal to about ten thousand dollars, which must cover his work in vaccination, registration of births and deaths, and the handling of epidemics and infectious diseases.

Much of his best work lies in watching the pilgrims as they debark from the railroad trains, to catch cholera patients before they disappear into the rabbit-warrens of the town. Let that disappearance once be effected and the case will lie concealed until a burst of epidemic announces the presence of the disease. For, although the municipality pays the higher officials and the foremen of the Public Health Department fairly well, it allows a mere pittance to its menial staff, with the result that, if contagion is reported and disinfection is ordered, the subordinates harass the people for what they can wring from distress.

Benares is an old city. Some of its drains were built in the sixteenth and seventeenth century. No one now knows their course except that, wherever they start, their outlets give into the river. Constructed of stone, their location is sometimes disconcertingly revealed by the caving-in of their masonry beneath a building or a street. Sometimes, silt-choked at the outlet, their mouths have been unwittingly or unthinkingly sealed in the course of river-wall repairs. Not a few still freely discharge their thick[1] stream of house-sewage into the river, anywhere along its humanity-teeming front. But most, having become semi-tight cesspools, await the downpours of the rainy season, when their suddenly swollen contents will push into the city's sub-soil with daily increasing force.

The city stands on a bluff, her streets about seventy-five feet above river level. The face of the bluff, for a distance of three miles or more along the river front, is buttressed by stairs and by high walls of stone. These, because of their continuity, back up the sub-soil water, which, from time to time, bursts the masonry and seeps through into the river, all along its famous templed front. There, among the worshiping

---

[1] "Thick" in particular because of the little water used in Indian houses.

drinkers and bathers, among the high-born pilgrim ladies, the painted holy-men, the ash-pasted *saddhus* and *Yogis*, you may see it oozing and trickling down from those long zigzag cracks that so mellow the beauty of the venerable stones.

Against bitter religious opposition, the British, in 1905, succeeded in getting a partial sewage system and water pipe-line into the city. Its main pumping station is at the south end of the town, not much habitation lying above it. The water is settled in a tank, filtered, and then put into general distribution, the Municipal Health Officer himself doing a weekly chemical and bacteriological analysis from each filter.

But the devout will not drink this filtered water. Instead, they go daily to the river, descend the stairs of some bathing-ghat, scoop up a vesselful in the midst of the bathers under the seepage-cracked wall, and carry it home to quench the thirst of the household. All warnings and protests of the Health Officer they meet with supreme contempt.

"It lies not in the power of man to pollute the Ganges." And "filtering Ganges water takes the holiness out," they reply, firmly.

Now, whoever bathes in the Ganges at Benares and drinks Ganges water there, having at the same time due regard to the needs of the priests, may be cured of the worst disease that flesh is heir to. Consequently upon Benares are deliberately focused all the maladies of the Hindu millions. Again, whoever dies in Benares, goes straight to heaven. Therefore endless sick, hopeless of cure, come here to breathe their last, if possible, on the brink of the river with their feet in the flood.

Many of the incidents connected with this tenet are exquisitely beautiful and exalted in spirit. But the threat to public health needs little emphasis.

[...] Other holy cities exist in India, other centers of pilgrimages. Each, automatically, is a reservoir and a potential distributing point of disease, demanding the utmost vigilance and the utmost tact in handling.

But the public health problem presented by an ordinary Indian city is stiff enough. Take, for example, Lahore. The

European section of the town has something about it of western America—all of one age, new, roomy, airy, with certain of its good modern buildings erected by the public spirit of that fine old Punjabi, Sir Ganga Ram. But Kim's Lahore, the old Indian quarter, where the crowds live and move, and in particular its bazaar, where the crowds adore to congregate, is the danger-point that keeps the Director of Health awake at night.

[...] One must remember that it takes longer to outgrow race thought and habits of life than it does to learn English. The well-dressed man who speaks with an easy Oxford accent may come from a village where, if they desire a new well, they do today what their fathers did a thousand years ago; they choose the site not by the slope of the land but by throwing a bucket of water over a goat. The goat runs away. The people run after. And where the goat first stops and shakes himself, though it be in the middle of the main street, just there the new well is dug.

Chapter XXVII

THE WORLD-MENACE

British India has half a million villages made of mud. Most of them took all their mud from one spot, making thereby a commensurate hole, and built themselves on the edge of the hole.

The hole, at the first rains, filled with water and became the village tank. Thenceforward forever, the village has bathed in its tank, washed its clothes in its tank, washed its pots and its pans in its tank, watered its cattle in its tank, drawn its cooking water from its tank, served the calls of nature by its tank and with the content of its tank has quenched its thirst. Being wholly stagnant, the water breeds mosquitoes and grows steadily thicker in substance as it evaporates between rain and rain. It is sometimes quite beautiful, overgrown with lily-things and shaded by feathered palms. It and its uses pretty generally insure the democratization of any new germs introduced to the village, and its mosquitoes spread malaria with an impartial beak—though not without some aid.

Witness, small Bengali babies put out to lie in the buzzing grass near the tank's edge.

"Why do you mothers plant your babies there to be eaten alive?"

"Because if we protect our babies the gods will be jealous and bring us all bad luck."

[...] Malaria, altogether, is one of the great and costly curses of the land, not alone because of its huge death-rate but even more because of the lowered physical and social conditions that it produces, with their invitation to other forms of disease.

Under present conditions of Indianized control, governmental anti-malarial work, like all other preventive sanitation, is badly crippled. Yet it generally contrives to hold its own, though denied the sinews of progress.

[...] One of the great objectives of the British Sanitary Administration is to put good wells into the villages and to educate the people in their proper use. Now, not infrequently, one finds such *pucca* wells. But, exactly as in the Philippines, the people have a strong hankering for the ancestral type, and, where they can, will usually leave the new and protected water-source for their old accustomed squatting- and gossiping-ground where they all innocently poison each other.

As for pumps, the obvious means to seal the wells and facilitate haulage, some have been installed. But, as a rule, pumps are impractical—for the reason that any bit of machinery is, to the Indian, a thing to consume, not to use and to care for. When the machine drops a nut or a washer, no one puts it back, and thenceforth that machine is junk.

Now, this matter of Indian wells is of more than Indian importance. For cholera is mainly a water-borne disease, and "statistics show that certain provinces in British India are by far the largest and most persistent centers of cholera infection in the world."[1]

The malady is contracted by drinking water infected with the fæces of cholera patients or cholera carriers, or from eating uncooked or insufficiently cooked infected food. It finds its best incubating grounds in a population of low vitality and generally weak and unresisting condition.[2] There is a vaccine for preventive inoculation but, the disease once developed, no cure is known. Outbreaks bring a mortality of from 15 to 90 per cent, usually of about 40 per cent. The area of Lower Bengal and the valley of the Ganges is, in India, the chief cholera center, but "the disease is very generally endemic in some

[1] *The Prevalence of Epidemic Disease ... in the Far East*, Dr. F. Norman White, League of Nations, 1923, p. 24.

[2] Cf. *Philippine Journal of Science*, 1914, Dr. Victor G. Heiser.

degree throughout the greater part of the whole [Indian] peninsula."[3]

Since the year 1817, ten pandemics of cholera have occurred. In 1893, the United States was attacked, and in this explosion the speed of travel from East to West was more rapid than ever before.[4]

In ordinary circumstances, in places where the public water supply is good and under scientific control, cholera is not to be feared. But the great and radical changes of modern times bring about rapid reverses of conditions; such, for example, as the sudden pouring in the year 1920 of hundreds of thousands of disease-sodden refugees out of Russia into Western Europe.

Without fear of the charge of alarmism, international Public Health officers today question whether they can be sure that local controls will always withstand unheralded attacks in force. With that question in mind, they regard India's cholera as a national problem of intense international import.

In estimating the safety of the United States from infection, the element of "carriers" must be considered. Each epidemic produces a crop of "carriers" whose power to spread the disease lasts from one hundred and one days to permanency.[5] Moreover, the existence of healthy carriers is conclusively proved. And India is scarcely a month removed from New York or San Francisco.

"Whenever India's real condition becomes known," said an American Public Health expert now in international service, "all the civilized countries of the world will turn to the League of Nations and demand protection against her."

---

[3]*A Memoranda on the Epidemiology of Cholera*, Major A. J. Russell, Director of Public Health in Madras Presidency, League of Nations, 1925, which see, for the whole topic.

[4]*Recent Research on the Etiology of Cholera*, E.D.W. Grieg, in *The Edinburgh Medical Journal*, July, 1919.

[5]E.D.W. Grieg in *Indian Journal of Medical Research*, 1913, Vol. I, pp. 59–64.

[...] Plague uncontrolled at its source may at any time become an international scourge, a danger to which international health officers are the more alive since latter-day observations continue to show the disease breaking out in regions where its occurrence has been unknown before.

Plague, unlike cholera, is not communicated by man to man, but to man by fleas from the bodies of sick rats. The flea bites the man and leaves a poisonous substance around the bite. Man, scratching the bite, scratches the poison into his skin and the deed is done. When plague breaks out in a village, the effective procedure is to evacuate the village at once and to inoculate the villagers with plague vaccine.

In most countries you simultaneously proceed to real control by killing the rats. But this, in a Hindu land, you cannot effectively do, because of the religion.

The constant obstacle in the Public Health Officer's path is, characteristically, a negative one—the utter apathy of the Indian peoples, based on their fatalistic creed. The intermittent obstacle, acute of latter years, is the political agent who runs here and there among the villages, whispering that an evil Government is bent on working harm. To such a pitch have these persons from time to time wrought their victims, that the latter have murdered the native health agent entrusted with the task of getting them out of an infected site.

[...]

Chapter XXVIII

"QUACKS WHOM WE KNOW"

"It is better to sit than to walk, to lie down than to sit, to sleep than to wake, and death is the best of all," says the Brahman proverb.

Taking into consideration the points with which the preceding chapter is concerned, the question naturally arises as to how the Indian is affected by his own peculiar sanitary habits. That question may be answered in the words of an American scientist now studying in the country:

"From long consumption of diluted sewage they have actually acquired a degree of immunity. Yet all of them are walking menageries of intestinal parasites, which make a heavy drain upon their systems and which inevitably tell when some infection, such as pneumonia or influenza, comes along. Then the people die like flies. They have no resistance."

These conditions, added to infant marriage, sexual recklessness and venereal infections, further let down the bars to physical and mental miseries; and here again one is driven to speculate as to how peoples so living and so bred can have continued to exist.

A reply is thus couched by one of the most eminent of European International Public Health authorities:

"It is a question of adaptation, and of the evolution of a sub-grade of existence on which they now survive. The British are to blame for the world-threat that they constitute. If the British had not protected them, the virile races of the north would have wiped them out."

The superior virility of the northern races—including the Sikhs, and more especially the Pathans and other Muhammadan stocks—is favored by their superior diet. These hardy out-door folk are all large meateaters, and consume much milk and grain. The diet of the southern Hindu has little in it to build or repair tissue. He subsists mainly on sweets and carbo-hydrates, and, to the degree that he is able, he leads a sedentary life. Diabetes is often the incident that brings to its early close the career of the southern Indian public man.[1]

[...] Curiously lucid contributions on this line come from Mr. Gandhi; speaking as of Hindu medical men, he says:[2]

It is worth considering why we take up the profession of medicine. It is certainly not taken up for the purpose of serving humanity. We become doctors so that we may obtain honours and riches.

After which he affirms:

European doctors are the worst of all.

Amplifying his accusation, Mr. Gandhi continues:

These [European] doctors violate our religious instinct. Most of their medical preparations contain either animal fat or spirituous liquors; both of these are tabooed by Hindu and Mahomedans.

And again, more specifically:

I overeat, I have indigestion, I go to a doctor, he gives me medicine. I am cured, I overeat again, and I take his pills again. Had I not taken the pills in the first instance, I would have suffered the punishment deserved by me, and I would not have overeaten again. ... A continuance of a course of medicine must, therefore, result in loss of control over the mind.

"In these circumstances," he concludes, "we are unfit to serve the country." And therefore "to study European medicine is to deepen our slavery."

Whatever may be thought of Mr. Gandhi's judgement, his sincerity is not questioned. Holding such an opinion of the motives and value of western medical men in India, it is scarcely surprising that, in the period of his "non-coöperation" campaign against Government and all its works, not excepting its educational efforts, he should have exhorted medical

---

[1] For an extended exposition of this subject see *The Protein Element in Nutrition*, Major D. McCay, I.M.S., London, Edward Arnold 1912.

[2] Mr.Gandhi's statements quoted in this chapter will be found in his *Indian Home Rule*, Ganesh & Co., Madras, 1924, pp. 61–2.

and public health students to desert their classes and to boycott their schools.

Boy-fashion, they did it—for a time—and at what a cost to India!

The other side of this phase of Indian nationalism is its enthusiasm for the Aruvedic [sic] or ancient Hindu system of medicine under which a large part of the native population is today being treated, more particularly in Bengal and in central and southern India.

[...] The common arguments in favor of the old system are that it is cheaper for the people, that it particularly suits Indian constitutions and that it is of divine sanction and birth. Leaving the last tenet aside, as not in the field of discussion, we find that the cost of running an Aruvedic dispensary is much the same as that of running a dispensary on western lines;[3] and that no material difference has ever been discovered between white man and brown, in the matter of reaction of medicines upon the system.

The Montagu-Chelmsford Reforms, however, have occasioned a great recrudescence of native medicine. Provincial ministers dependent on popular vote are prone to favor spending public money to erect Aruvedic and Unani[4] colleges, hospitals and dispensaries. With the Indian National Congress claiming that Aruvedic medicine is "just as scientific as modern western medicine," with such men as Sir Rabindranath Tagore, the poet, fervently declaring that Aruvedic science surpasses anything the West can offer; and with Swarajists in general pushing it forward on patriotic grounds, you get the melancholy spectacle of the meager appropriations allotted to medicine and public health, in this most disease-stricken of lands, being heavily cut into to prepetuate a "science" on the same level as the "voodoo doctoring" of the West Indian negro.

[3]*The Medical Profession in India*, p. 116.
[4]The ancient Arabic school of medicine.

That the old native systems still exert a strong hold on the imaginations of the masses cannot be questioned. Also, like the voodoo doctors, they teach the use of a few good herbs. These two points enable their practitioners to induce enough "cures" to keep their prestige alive.

But once upon a time it chanced that Mr. Gandhi, having widely and publicly announced that "hospitals are institutions for propagating sin"[5] that "European doctors are the worst of all," and that "quacks whom we know are better than the doctors who put on an air of humaneness,"[6] himself fell suddenly ill of a pain in the side.

As he happened to be in prison at the time, a British surgeon of the Indian Medical Service came straight-way to see him.

"Mr. Gandhi," said the surgeon, as the incident was reported, "I am sorry to have to tell you that you have appendicitis. If you were my patient, I should operate at once. But you will probably prefer to call in your Aruvedic Physician."

Mr. Gandhi proved otherwise minded.

"I should prefer not to operate," pursued the surgeon, "because in case the outcome should be unfortunate, all your friends will lay it as a charge of malicious intent against us whose duty it is to care for you."

"If you will only consent to operate," pleaded Mr. Gandhi, "I will call in my friends, now, and explain to them that you do so at my request."

So, Mr. Gandhi willfully went to an "institution for propagating sin"; was operated upon by one of the "worst of all," an officer of the Indian Medical Service, and was attentively nursed through convalescence by an English Sister whom he is understood to have thought after all rather a useful sort of person.

[5] *Indian Home Rule*, p. 61.
[6] *Ibid.*, p. 62.

Chapter XXIX

PSYCHOLOGICAL GLIMPSES THROUGH THE ECONOMIC LENS

The welfare of any people, we are wont to agree, must finally rest upon economic foundations. In the foregoing pages certain aspects of economic conditions in India have been indicated. To these indications I should like now to add a few more, disclaiming any pretense that they constitute a survey, and offering them merely for what they are worth as scattering observations made in the living field, entirely non-political both in character and in purpose.

The Indian, aside from his grievances earlier described, has other explanations of what he calls his depressed status, in large part covering them with the elastic title of "economic drains" upon the country. Compared with the matters already handled, these considerations seem superficial, serving mainly to befog the issue. The principal drains, as they appear to me, have been shown in the body of this book. But the Indian native politician's category comprises none of them. He speaks, instead, under such headings as cotton, tea, interest on Government bonds, export of grain, army maintenance, and the pay of British Civil Servants in India.

The attempt carefully to examine these or any comparable point with the Indian intelligentsia is likely to end in disappointment and a web of dialectics—for the reason that, as the question grows close, the Indian, as a rule, simply drops it and shifts to another ground where, for the moment, he has more elbow-room.

[...] Now, leaving matters of argument, let us face about and look at indisputable wastages of India's vital resources. The major channels have been shown in earlier pages, but these leave untouched a list of points only second in importance, such as caste marriage costs, the usurer, the hoarding of treasure, and mendicancy.

Caste laws strictly limit the range of possible marriages, sometimes even to the confines of half-a-dozen families, so that, despite his dread of sonlessness, a man may be forced to wait till he is old for the birth of a girl within the circle wherein he may marry,[1] and then may be forced to pay ruinously to secure her. Or again, there is such a scramble for husbands of right caste that, rather than sacrifice their own souls by leaving a girl unmarried, fathers strain their credit to the snapping point to secure eligible matches for their daughters.

In Bengal, of late years, several cases have become public of girls committing suicide at the approach of puberty, to save their fathers the crushing burden of their marriage dowry.[2] And the chorus of praise evoked from Bengal youth by this act has stimulated further self-immolations. Nor do the father's finances greatly affect the case. Though a man prosper and take in much money, marriages in his family still pull him down to ruin, for the reason that pride and custom forever urge him ahead of his means.

Marriage expenses and funeral expenses, love of litigation, thriftlessness and crop failures are among the chief roads that lead the Indian into debt. The Indian money-lender, or *bania*, is the same man as the usurer of the Philippines. And, exactly as in the Philippines, the average Indian having a little money laid by, even though he be not a *bania* by caste and calling, will, if he be minded to lend, lend to his neighbors at 33 per cent and up, rather than to Government at a miserable 3.5 per cent so that Government may build him a railway. Let the silly folk in London do that.

The *bania* is the man who, foreseeing a short crop, corners all the grain in his region, and at sowing-time sells seed-grain to his neighbors at 200 per cent profit, taking the coming crop as security.

---

[1] *Reconstructing India*, Visvesvaraya, p. 241.
[2] *Legislative Assembly Debates, 1922*, Vol. II, Part II, p. 1811.

Once in debt to a *bania*, few escape. Clothing, oxen, and all purchased necessities, are bought of the same wise old spider. Compound interest rolls up in the good old way as the years pass, and posterity limps under the load unto the third and fourth generation.

"The assumption that debt is due to poverty cannot be entertained. Debt is due to credit and credit depends upon prosperity and not poverty," writes Calvert. Credit, in India, is the creation of the British Government by the establishment of peace and security of property, coupled with public works that increase production and the value of land. The *bania* in his fullest glory is therefore a by-product of British rule. In the Punjab, rich among provinces, we find him in his paradise, 40,000 strong, collecting from the people annual interest equaling nearly three times the total sum that they annually pay to Government.

Everywhere, whether openly or covertly, the usurer opposes the education of the people, because a man who can read will not sign the sort of paper by which the *bania* holds his slave, and a man who can figure will know when his debt is cleared. As two Indian members of the profession warmly told me, the *bania* hates "this meddlesome and unsympathetic foreign government that has introduced a system of coöperative credit, which, wherever a Briton directs it, is ruining our good old indigenous banking business. Moreover, not content even with that mischief, it is pushing in night schools and adult-education schemes to upset the people's mind."

Intimately powerful as he is throughout the country, the *bania* exercises a strong undercurrent of influence in the Swarajist party, making it generally hostile to labor interests and currency reforms.

[...] And now we come to a more obscure question, that of the present economic status of the peoples in comparison with their condition in past eras. Mr. Gandhi and his school affirm that the peoples of India have been growing steadily poorer and more miserable, as a result of British rule. To form a close surmise of the facts is difficult indeed. The masses have, as a whole, little ambition to raise or to change actual living conditions. Their minds as a rule do not run to the accumulation of things. They are content with their mud huts. Given windows and chimneys, they stop them up. Given ample space, they crowd in a closet. Rather than keep the house in repair, they let the rains wash it away, building a new one when the old is gone. Rather than work harder for more food, they prefer their ancient measure of leisure and just enough food for the day.[3]

But their margin of safety is indubitably greater, their power of resistance to calamity increased, and, allegations to the contrary notwithstanding, means of enlarging their income lie at all times, now, within their hands. In just such measure as desire for material advance awakens, one sees this demonstrated in individual lives. The question whether or not such desire is good underlies one of the prime differences between eastern and western thought and practice.

Now in assigning value to these factors, one must remember that the soil of India is today supporting the pressure of over 54,000,000 more human beings than it sustained fifty years ago, plus an increase of 20 per cent.[4]

This, again, is a result of freedom from wars and disorders and from killing famines; of the checking of epidemics; and of the multiplied production of food—all elements bound to produce ever greater effect as essential features of an established government. And the prospects it unfolds, of sheer volume of humanity piling up as the decades pass, is staggering. For, deprived of infanticide, of *suttee*, and of her other native escape-valves, yet still clinging to early marriage and unlimited propagation, India stands today at that point of social development where population is controlled by disease, and disease only.[5]

[3]*Census of 1921*, Vol. I, Part I, p. 54.

[4]*Census of India, 1921*, pp. 7. 48. These figures of increase are reached after allowing for the factor of population added by annexation of territory.

[5]*Ibid.*, Vol. I, Part I, p. 49.

Chapter XXX

CONCLUSION

The preceding chapters of this book state living facts of India today. They can easily be denied, but they cannot be disproved or shaken. That there are other facts, other columns of statistics, other angles left untouched by this research I do not contest.

Neither do I wish to imply that some of the most unflattering things were affirmed of India are without counterpart in character and tendency, if not in degree, in certain sections of our western life. But India has carried the principles of egocentricity and of a materialism called spirituality to a further and wider conclusion than has the West. The results, in the individual, the family and the race, are only the more noteworthy. For they cast a spotlight toward the end of that road.

Some few Indians will take plain speech as it is meant—as the faithful wounds of a friend; far more will be hurt at heart. Would that this task of truth-telling might prove so radically performed that all shock of resentment were finally absorbed in it, and that there need be no further waste of life and time for lack of a challenge and a declaration!

Appendix I

MEDICAL EVIDENCE

In the Indian Legislative Assembly of 1922, the following evidence, introduced from the floor of the House as descriptive of the condition of the day, aroused neither question nor opposition from any one of the assembled Indian legislators. The fact that, although thirty-one years old, it still remained beyond challenge, carries a contributing significance. The evidence submitted consists of a list, compiled in 1891 by the western women doctors then practicing in India, and by them laid before the Viceroy, with a petition for intervention on behalf of the children of India. It is made up, they affirm, entirely of instances that have come under the hands of one or another of their own number, and whose like are continually revealed in their ordinary professional experience.

A.—Aged 9. Day after marriage. Left femur dislocated, pelvis crushed out of shape, flesh hanging in shreds.

B.—Aged 10. Unable to stand, bleeding profusely, flesh much lacerated.

C.—Aged 9. So completely ravished as to be almost beyond surgical repair. Her husband had two other living wives and spoke very fine English.

D.—Aged 10. A very small child, and entirely undeveloped physically. This child was bleeding to death from the rectum. Her husband was a man of about forty years of age, weighing not less than eleven stone [154 lbs.]. He had accomplished his desire in an unnatural way.

E.—Aged about 9. Lower limbs completely paralyzed.

F.—Aged about 12. Laceration of the perineum extending through the sphincter ani.

G.—Aged about 10. Very weak from loss of blood. Stated that great violence had been done her, in an unnatural way.

H.—Aged about 12. Pregnant, delivered by craniotomy with great difficulty, on account of the immature state of the pelvis and maternal passage.

I.—Aged about 7. Living with husband. Died in great agony after three days.

K.—Aged about 10. Condition most pitiable. After one day in hospital, was demanded by her husband, for his "lawful" use, he said.

L.—Aged 11. From great violence done her person, will be a cripple for life. No use of her lower extremities.

M.—Aged about 10. Crawled to hospital on her hands and knees. Has never been able to stand erect since her marriage.

N.—Aged 9. Dislocation of pubic arch, and unable to stand or to put one foot before the other.

The list will be found in the *Legislative Assembly Debates* of 1922, Vol. III, Part I, p. 919, Appendix. See also p. 882 of the *Debates*.

Appendix II

ENFRANCHISEMENT OF WOMEN

In framing the Reform Bill of 1919, the British Parliament decided that the question of enfranchisement for the women of India could properly be determined only by the Indian peoples themselves. Parliament accordingly allowed the old sex disqualification to remain in the Bill; but at the same time so shaped the electoral rules as to leave it in the power of each province's Legislative Council to place women on the provincial electoral register by passing a resolution to this effect.

Pursuant of this power, the Provinces of Madras, Bombay, Bengal, United Provinces, Punjab and Assam have removed their sex disqualifications, granting the vote to women on the same terms as to the male electorate. Further, the Central Legislative Assembly having passed a similar resolution, women may now vote not only for their Provincial Councils but also for the Legislative Assembly. Under the present general qualifications, however, the total number of women entitled to vote throughout India does not exceed 1,000,000, or about 17 per cent of the total electorate.

Sir Alexander Muddiman's Reform Enquiry Committee of 1924, in opening the consideration of a further step—that of women's candidature for elective office—reaffirmed that[1]

the question went deep into the social system and susceptibilities of India, and ... could only with any prudence be settled in accordance with the wishes of the Indians themselves as constitutionally expressed.

It was, however, upon the Muddiman committee's recommendation that the rules of candidature for Provincial Councils were lately amended, enabling the removal of the sex disqualification by vote of Provincial Council. To this invitation Madras and Bombay have already responded.

[1]*Report of the Reforms Enquiry Committee, 1924, p. 57.*

The Muddiman Committee next recommended that the electoral rules of both chambers of the Indian Legislature—the Council of State and the Assembly—be amended by the removal of the sex disqualification, so that constituencies in provinces that have enfranchised their women might at will elect women to both chambers. On September 1, 1926, the Indian Legislature so voted.

Thus far, however, it seems to be the British Provincial Governor rather than the Indian electorate that uses the new privilege. From 1922 to 1926, twenty-two women had become Municipal Councillors or Members of Local Government Boards, of whom only four were elected, the rest being nominated by Government.[2]

The following statement is that of an Englishman deeply conversant with Indian affairs, one who wields much moral influence in India, and who vigorously used that influence to advocate the changes above indicated. It was elicited by my request for the grounds of his position and his view of the present status, and was elsewhere confirmed by ranking Indians.

As for the reason for enfranchising Indian women, I can give you my own reasons, which I put before the Parliamentary Committee which framed the Act. In some places women had long enjoyed the municipal franchise, especially in Bombay. There were a considerable number of women, in Bombay who took a very useful part in our social work. Therefore I pressed for the enfranchisement of women, both to encourage and hearten these where actually so engaged, and to give others inducements to come forward. The *purdah* must be broken as fast as it can ... its influence on the health of Indian women is disastrous. I looked on the franchise as another nail in the *purdah* coffin.

As for the effect of enfranchisement in the Bombay Presidency, as far as I can see, it has been slight; the women in public life are the women who were there in one way or another before enfranchisement took place. In other parts of India I should say the effect was smaller still. Until the social conditions have improved, the franchise can mean nothing to the Indian woman, for she dares not use it.

In observing the position of the women of Bombay, outstanding in India, one heavily contribution factor appears:

[2]*Indian Year Book*, 1926, p. 511.

This city is the great Parsi center. Out of the total number of Parsis in all India—101, 778—nearly 93,000 are domiciled in Bombay Presidency.[3] Descendants of old Persian stock, the Parsis are practically all either merchants or bankers. Eight hundred per 1,000 of their men are literate, as against the 115 literates per 1,000 of male Hindus. The Parsis neither sequester nor suppress their women, but favor their adequate education. Thus 672 per 1,000[4] of the women of the Parsis are literate, as against the 14 per 1,000 female literates of the Hindus.

The presence of such a body, occupying conspicuous position, cannot but influence the whole upper-class population.

[3]*Census of India*, 1921, Vol. 1, p. 118.
[4]*Census of India*, 1921, p. 180.

SELECT CONTEMPORARY RESPONSES TO
MOTHER INDIA IN INDIA

1. Muthulakshmi Reddi's response to Katherine Mayo's *Mother India* from *S. Muthulakshmi Reddi Papers: Speeches and Writings*, volume II, part 2.

2. Communication sent by Women's Indian Association protesting against Katherine Mayo's *Mother India* to The Editor, *Jus Suffragi: The International Woman Suffrage News*. Published in *Jus Suffragi*, vol 22, November 1927, p. 27.

3. Introduction and Conclusion from Chandravati Lakhanpal's *Mother India Ka Jawab*, [The Reply to *Mother India*], Kangri: Gurukul Yantralaya, 1928. Second reprint published by Ganga Pustakmala Karyala, Lucknow.

4. Extract from Kovai A. Ayyamuthu, *Meyo Kutru Moyya Poyya* [Mayo's Charges: True or False?], with a preface by E.V. Ramaswami Naicker, Kanchipuram: Kumaran Printing Press, 1929. The extract has been compiled from translations into English of the original Tamil provided by a Mr. Ramani Iyer and an anonymous translator.

MISS MAYO ANSWERED[1]

From S. Muthulakshmi Reddi Papers: Speeches and Writings,
volume II, part 2.

Any close reader of Miss Mayo's book cannot but conclude that she came to India with a motive, with a set evil purpose to study the evils, not the good of Hindu society, but to hold us up to ridicule and scorn and thus delay the grant of Home-rule or Self-Government. Throughout her book is revealed a contempt for our religion and a wholesale criticism of all our revered national leaders and sweeping condemnation of all that is Hindu. All her venomous attack is directed against the Hindu habits, manners and customs and such a horrid picture cannot but fill one's mind with disgust and righteous indignation.

Regarding her interpretation of the obscene significance of Siva and Vishnu, I may say that even though I am a born Hindu and have been taught to worship the two deities from my early childhood, I could never claim the honour of having been initiated into its significance as Miss Mayo had the uni-

---

[1] I have found no evidence that this text was published. It was in all likelihood the text of a speech given by Reddi at the largest women's protest meeting, organised by the Women's Indian Association, in Madras against *Mother India*. Reddi was very active in the Women's Indian Association. She had been nominated to the Madras Legislative Council and was serving as its Deputy President at the time of the Mayo controversy. She was also a successful medical practitioner and a tireless social reformer for women's causes. See M. Reddy, *Autobiography of Dr. (Mrs.) Muthulakshmi Reddy* (Madras, 1964); and *Dr Muthulakshmi Reddy, the Pathfinder,* (ed.) Aparna Basu (New Delhi: AIWC, 1987).

que privilege of being so instructed by her interested friends here.

Again she says: "In many parts of the country, north or south, the little boy, his mind so prepared, is likely, if physically attractive, to be drafted for the satisfaction of grown men, or to be regularly attached to a temple, in the capacity of a prostitute." [p. 88]. I have been a medical practitioner for the last 15 years and have come in contact with all sections of people, high and low, rich and poor, and I may, I suppose, rightly claim to posses an intimate knowledge of our people's habits and customs. So, I may assert that such immoral and unnatural practices have never been brought to my notice nor do the Hindu parents look upon such abuses as a matter of course if they do exist at all. We have not forgotten the famous Leadbeater case and how the Hindu public was roused into righteous fury and indignation on coming to know of certain unnatural practices alleged to have been practised upon the little boys in Adayar [sic].[2] From my experience of my people I feel I will be fully justified in characterising the above statements of Miss Mayo as gross lies and misrepresentations and as utterly unworthy of an American woman and above all a Christian, if she be at all a true disciple of Christ which she at any rate professes to be.

Again there is a worse tale to tell, that is her calumnious attack upon the morale of the Hindu women. In page 36 [p. 92] she says that "in case, however, of the continued failure of the wife—any wife—to give him a child, the Hindu husband has a last recourse;" etc. etc. Many of my Hindu sisters have come to me for treatment of sterility, never have I heard from any of them, not even from the people of backward areas and from the lowest class of women, such a shocking story; nor

[2]Charles Webster Leadbeater was a prominent associate of Annie Besant at the Theosophical Society in Adyar, Madras. Leadbeater, along with four other priests, was involved in a scandal in the 1920s that had to do with accusations of sodomy with young boys in India. See Gregory Tillet, *The Elder Brother: A Biography of Charles Webster Leadbeater* (London: Routledge, 1982).

even our grand-mothers have nursed us with such demoralising and degrading tales. This is a new piece of information
which I have learnt from Miss Mayo's book about my country
and I wish that we institute an enquiry bureau to detect
whether such customs exist amongst any hill tribe or in any
nook and corner of India.

There is another 'cock and bull story', she says "in some
parts of the country, more particularly in the Presidency of
Madras and Orissa, a custom obtains among the Hindus
whereby the parents, to persuade some favor from Gods may
vow their next born child, if it be a girl, to the gods." [p. 105]
Of course we all know that this is prevalent, if any [sic], certain castes of Hindus such as the Kalavanthulu of the Telugu
or Sengunthars and Isai Vellalars of the Tamil country [are
those] from whom the dasis of the temple are recruited. In this
connection a word about the much despised and much
maligned "Devadasi institution" will not be improper. This
institution[,] according to certain texts in our sacred books,
was started with the purest of motives and the girls so dedicated or given away to temples are said to have been virgins
and devotees as the Roman vestal virgins or the Roman
Catholic nuns of the present day. Now as is the fate of all
human institutions, so this good religious practice based upon
purity and renunciation having degenerated into something
unholy and objectionable both the afflicted communities and
the enlightened Hindu public have been moving earth and
heaven for the last 6 years to eradicate this and I am forced to
infer from the recent proceedings of the Legislative Assembly
dated 13th September when the Hon'ble Mr. Ramadas Pan-
tulu moved a resolution to put an end to the practice of
dedication of minor girls to Hindu temples, it is the unwar-
ranted timidity and dread of the illiterate orthodox public
opinion on the part of the Government that has kept such a
good reform from us even though the adjacent Government of
Mysore has boldly abolished this practice as early as 1909.

Reformers of to-day do not deny there is the system of
early marriage prevalent among the high caste Hindus with
all its attendant evils, but Miss Mayo—to be true to facts—in-

stead of condemning the whole nation might have added that it exists only among a certain section of Hindus and a large section of the Non-Brahmins and untouchables are not affected by it. Again for the evils of early marriage she goes for a list which was drawn up some 33 years back by the women surgeons of this country when a bill for raising the age of consent was brought by one of our Hindu brethren in the Assembly. Again in 1925 when the question for further raising the age of consent came before the Assembly there were speakers both for and against such a measure—those for said (refer Miss Mayo's book pages 43 to 45 [pp. 103 to 105]) there was no text in Hindu religion to sanction early marriage and those against affirmed that religion was in danger. Even at that period, the countless women [sic] associations throughout India held meetings and asked for reform. Miss Mayo who has a ready pen to condemn those orthodox representatives does not find a good conscience and moral courage enough to blame those Christian and cultured European members, her own kith and kin who as the custodians and saviours of our religion have found arguments enough to side with our superstitious, ignorant and orthodox countrymen.

Even yesterday at the Assembly what has happened? When Mr. Sardas [sic] bill to raise the age of marriage was introduced there were still European members who voted against the bill on the plea of caution and on the good excuse of not offending our orthodox religious sentiments when such books like Miss Mayo's—a wholesale condemnation of the Hindu community, men and women—have been circulated even before being reviewed—by reliable Indian authorities.

Regarding her chapter on women and children in spite of her exaggerations and misrepresentations, the evils of early marriage, of enforced widowhood, the evils of caste and untouchability do exist eventhough not to such an enormous extent as she has depicted them to be, but I am surprised to note that she holds our religion to be responsible for all these ills in spite of the repeated pronouncements to the contrary of Mahatma Gandhi and Tagore—our true representatives and able interpreters of our religion. According to her belief she

sees no hope of salvation for India so long as the majority of
the population are Hindus. In page 132 [p. 173] she says "the
head of this institution (Victorial School, Lahore), is an extremely able Indian lady, Miss K.M. Bose, of the third generation of an Indian Christian family" and so on. Miss Mayo has
written certain things about the Hindu girls reading in the
Victoria School, Lahore as told by Miss K.M. Bose, which
statements have subsequently been proved to be inaccurate by
Miss K.M. Bose herself as we read from Rev Popley's letter in
the Social Reformer, Bombay (17th September).[3] Anybody will
note that she has purposely avoided to mention the good
works of Hindu women such as Sarala Devi Choudhrani of
Punjab, Mrs Sarojini Naidu, the late Mrs. Rande [sic] of Bombay who started the Bombay Seva Sadan, Mrs. Chandrasakera
Iyer of Mysore, the Arya Samaj women workers of Punjab and
the widow's home of Poona and Madras and other reputed
Hindu social workers and well conducted women's organisa-
tions. Perhaps she did not find time to consult these true
Hindu minds or she thought that their touch and contact
would spoil her mission and defeat the object of her visit to
this unfortunate country.

I may take this opportunity of impressing upon all people
of Miss Mayo's type that the Hindu religion does not sanction
the practice of all those social ills that are at present preying
upon our society, and it is the centuries of foreign invasions,
oppression and subordination that must account for the
present deplorable condition of India; another reason being
that the modern westernised Hindu is kept completely ignorant of his sacred scriptures like Bhagwat Gita and Kural
[sic] that teach the highest ideals of life, love and service to
humanity, all his time is spent in mastering a foreign tongue
and foreign histories except his own and the modern educational system, while equipping him with every other kind of

[3]Mona Bose's denial first appeared in a letter from Rev. H.A. Popley to
The Indian Witness (Lucknow), Sept. 7, 1927. See Mrinalini Sinha, "Reading
Mother India: Empire, Nation, and the Female Voice", *Journal of Women's
History* 6, no. 2 (Summer 1994): 6–44.

knowledge, denies to him the most essential, that is a moral and spiritual training based upon his religion which is the recognised foundation on which the superstructure of the knowledge of other human science is built in all civilised countries. Again Miss Mayo has gone away with the impression that Hinduism is responsible for the ignorance and the low status of Hindu women—as a reply to which I will only refer her to our deity "Arthanareswarar" (which emphasises equality of man and woman), our goddess Saraswathi and Lakshmi, the presiding deities over learning and wealth and to our familiar prayer

> "O, Mother Divine, Thou art beyond
> the reach of our praises;
> Thou dwellest in every feminine
> form, and all women are Thy living
> representative on earth".

That is the reason why we the Indian women have secured our political rights so smoothly and so easily for which our western sisters have yet to struggle.

I may point out to Miss Mayo that it is the Hindu religion, the Hindu literature and the Hindu atmosphere that has produced the great religious teachers as Sri Krishna, the author of Bhagavat [sic] Gita, Buddha, Chaitanya and Tukkaram, the great reformer Raja Ram Mohun Roy and Pandit Iswara Chandra Vidyasagar, the stern Brahmacharyas like our Sri Ramakrishna Paramahansa and Swami Vivekanand and their disciples, the great philanthropists like Sri Lala Gangaram and the world renowned Ghandi [sic] and Tagore who preach the gospel of unity, peace and love and service to the world. If even a minority of the present day Hindus do not come up to the level of those great men who were and are well versed in their sacred lore, Miss Mayo will find an answer below. The present system of education as it obtains in our English Schools and Colleges having no provision in its curriculum for moral, religious and spiritual teaching based upon one's faith, while it has succeeded in manufacturing so many human machines capable of earning their daily bread, has failed to fulfill the purpose of true education which is the

cultivation of all those rare and divine qualities such as
patriotism and national unity, mutual trust and love and service, compassion, kindness and generosity, qualities which
would only make useful men and women and patriotic
citizens of a country. The curriculum being a crowded one
leaves very little time for a student of the English schools to
study another language like Sanskrit in which unfortunately
the true tenets of Hinduism are embodied. Thus he is made to
learn all other sciences except the science of his soul and thus
he is made to acquire all knowledge except the knowledge of
his country and its great men and women....

... Another most serious charge she levels against the Hindus is "they are a nation of liars". If only Miss Mayo had
taken the trouble to find out the real conception of truth as
illustrated in the lives of the famous king Harishchandra and
his loyal spouse Chandramathi both of who[m] for the sake of
that supreme virtue, sacrificed their all—their religion, their
only child and their wealth and even their personal liberty, at
least Miss Mayo, unsympathetic though she may be, would
have been moved to tears that things have changed very
much for the worse. On the question of mass education she
has tried by hook or by crook to justify the present mass illiteracy in the country, but her arguments and calculations
cannot convince any thinking man or woman on the spot who
are [sic] well versed with present day Indian conditions.

She says that the Hindu drink[s] fluid sewage, bathe in
sewage [that] are so many menageries of hook-worms and
other intestinal parasites, suffer[s] from venereal diseases, in
short their knowledge of health, hygiene and sanitation is almost zero. I being a medical woman take the liberty of impressing upon her that the medical science and knowledge is
ever the monopoly of only a select few in any country and
hence unless those privileged few take the pain of imparting
that precious knowledge to the ignorant mass the latter
should never be blamed, much less laughed at for their non-
observance or neglect of the rules of modern hygiene and
sanitation. Again with 92% illiteracy in the male population
and 98% in the female population; illiterate in the sense that

they cannot read or write in their own vernacular, how could any Indian Municipality, however efficient it may be, find it possible to teach the people in the fundamentals [sic] rules of health, much less in the modern discoveries of medical science especially when most of that knowledge had to be conveyed in a foreign language and make them practice those health laws in their daily lives. True it is that a large percentage of people suffer in this country from venereal diseases in the absence of proper facilities for diagnosing and treatment and in the absence of a true knowledge of the ravaging nature of such disease, but Miss Mayo will be surprised to learn that the charge for a single Wasserman test is 32 Rs. (2½ pounds near-ly in English money) in this 'home of stark want' and there is not yet one special venereal clinic in the whole of my Presidency which has a population of 43 millions and odd and no educational propaganda of any degree has been under-taken by the authorities, while in England it is now 13 years since free diagnosis, free, voluntary and confidential treatment for infected individuals have been instituted and we know also the British public being well educated on the serious na-ture of those disease by lecture, by cinema films and by models etc. We know too that it is the state aid in other countries that has reduced the incidence amongst them, of these most ravaging diseases. If the Indian masses are still kept in ignorance of all the advancement and discoveries in medical science that obtains in the West only Miss Mayo must tell us where to look for the cause.

Again I feel sorry to note that she has created in the Western minds that Hinduism is responsible for the ignorance and backwardness of Hindu women while on the other hand the truth is that the centuries of outside invasions by bar-barians and foreigners and their maladministration have reduced the women of this country into this miserable plight. So, I will advise her to correct herself for the sake of truth by referring to the true authorities. Louis Jaccoliet, the celebrated French author of the 'Bible in India', says, "India of the Vedas entertained a respect for women amounting almost to wor-ship etc."

So, I ask with all humility, those who believe that Hindu religion debars women from a study of the Vedas, to read the pages of the religious history of India wherein are indelibly written the names of all those inspired women and spiritual instructors as Romasha and Lopamudra of the Rigveda, Gargi and Maitryi of the Upanishads who discoursed philosophical topics with the rishi Yagnavalkya, Sakuntala of the famous Hindu drama who argued her own case with her husband Dushyanta, the Jhansi Ranee, all Hindu queens who have distinguished themselves even on the battlefields, not to speak of our able female administrators Tarabai, Ahalyabai, the Malwa queens and the queen Aburkour of a recent date. Ancient Hindu legislators had said that both sexes were equal and that women had equal rights with men for freedom, for the acquirement of knowledge, freedom and spirituality. No early marriage, no purdah and no burning of widows have ever been sanctioned by pure and true Hinduism and these evil practices and denial of all rights to women have been introduced into the Hindu society during the turbulent period of the Mahammadan [sic] and Moghul invasions to protect women from being disgraced and dishonoured by those ruthless invaders. So, if true Indian history with the aspiring examples and valiant deeds of India's great men and women and a study of the Hindu religion, a religion embodying the highest ideals of life, had found a place in the modern school curriculum of the English schools then the Hindus would have long ago purged their society of all these pernicious practices that have hindered the national growth.[4]

[4]Although here Reddi appears as an unabashed apologist for a certain highly problematic cultural-nationalist version of the Indian past, there were also times when she excoriated male nationalists for invoking the ancient past as the yardstick for measuring women's reforms in her day. For a discussion of the implications of this kind of cultural-nationalist recreation of the 'Indian' past, however, see Uma Chakravarti, "Whatever Happened to the Vedic Dasi? Orientalism, Nationalism and a Script for the Past", in *Recasting Women: Esays in Indian Colonial History* (eds.) Kumkum Sangari and Sudesh Vaid (New Delhi: Kali for Women 1989), pp. 27–87.

In conclusion, I feel that everyone of us, Hindu, in particular, should study Miss Mayo's "Mother India" closely and "see ourselves as others see us" for the reason that she only represents the opinions and views of thousands of her kind behind her: because the book contains some exaggerations, half-truths and misrepresentations, we in our anxiety to defend ourselves should not be into the same error as hers, by flattering ourselves that we are all up to the mark, but on the other hand we must redouble our efforts to hasten the pace of social reform that the progressive Indians have recognized as absolutely necessary to the attainment of a healthy and robust manhood and womanhood of the country....

... A word about caste will not be out of [place. When the] caste system are [sic] explained to our people, a few amongst us get up and justify the existence of caste in this country with all its horrors and rigidity on the plea that it also exists in one form or other in other European countries. From my experience of the European society during my stay and my travels in those countries, I have only observed differences based upon wealth and learning, differences created by different status and conditions of life and no unapproachability, no untouchability exists there among the Europeans, nor did I see any separate dining halls or luncheons for the different classes in any hotel, schools or colleges. True it is that the Lord's daughter may not marry a labourer's son, but once the latter gets wealth and learning enough to bring him up to the social status of the former, all those differences disappear. Is that what we call caste here?

Again a few may say that what suits the West may not suit the East, but my answer whether East of West, if a certain remedy is found effective for a certain disease, the progressive nations of the world must adopt it and be benefited by it from whichever quarter it might have originated, if it wants to out live in the world's struggle for existence as after all human nature is the same everywhere in spite the extraneous differences in colour, dress and food which will certainly vary according to climate and other environment.

So we, whether Brahmins, Non-Brahmins or untouchables, can no longer remain either exclusively by ourselves or will be allowed to remain as such any length of time in this world's struggle for existence. In spite of ourselves we know that the West has come in contact with the East bringing in its train all its cherished ideals and practices which have [made] them our conquerors and our masters. So, [unless] we also rise to the occasion and assimilate some of those ideals to gain unity and strength amongst ourselves we, Brahmins, Non-Brahmins and untouchables stand the risk of complete extinction. So let us follow the inspiring example of that great Indian, the reformer and father of Modern India, our Raja Ram Mohan Roy, to achieve unity amongst ourselves and thus win real swaraj [self-rule] to our country.

CORRESPONDENCE

From *Jus Suffragi: The International Woman Suffrage News,*
vol 22, November 1927, p. 27.

Women's Indian Association[1]
Adyar, Madras
29.9.27

To the Editor, *Jus Suffragi*[2]

Dear Madam,

In view of the wide publicity that Miss Mayo's book is receiving we women in India would thank you to try and ensure equally wide publicity for the reports which will be coming to you of the many meetings, newspaper articles, etc., that are denying the statements made by her book in the form of generalisations from sad particulars.

Kindly secure publicity for the accompanying in the Press of your country so that the slanderous charge of being a 'world menace' may be refuted at once.

Yours sincerely,
M.E. Cousins, Hon. Sec.

[1]Women's Indian Association was the oldest of the three all-India women's associations in 1927. It had been founded in 1917 by two women from the Theosophical Society in Adyar, Dorothy Jinarajadasa and Margaret Cousins.

[2]The *Jus Suffragi* was the official paper of the International Alliance of Women for Suffrage and Equal Citizenship. Earlier known as the International Women's Suffrage Alliance, it was a self-consciously international feminist organisation that counted the Women's Indian Association among its affiliates.

Indian Womanhood Protests Against
Miss Mayo's Book

The Women's Indian Association has held a large, representative and influential meeting of men and women in Madras, the Headquarters of the Association, on the 28th Sept., to vindicate the character and life of Indian womanhood as against the statements in Miss Mayo's book "Mother India".

The following resolutions were passed unanimously:

1. "That this meeting denies that Indian womanhood as a whole is in a state of slavery, superstition, ignorance and degeneration as Miss Mayo falsely concludes from individual instances and from statistics unproportioned to other balancing figures: it points out that the men of India have given their Indian sisters political equality and enfranchisement on equal terms with themselves, and in advance of the status of British women; it also maintains that illiteracy does not connote ignorance in India where the women have an ancient culture derived orally from their religious literature and through their indigenous arts and crafts, and these have given the womanhood of India intelligence of a high order and virtues of religious character."

2. "(a) That notwithstanding the misrepresentations and false generalisations of Miss Mayo's book there are admittedly social evils in our country which need reform and for which we have been keenly working, and this meeting calls upon the Legislative Assembly and the Legislative Councils to enact such measures as will prohibit child-marriage, premature parentage, child-widowhood, dedication of girls to temples, and commercialised vice.

    (b) It further calls on the Government of India to follow the precedent it laid down in the Indian woman suffrage legislation and to direct that its official members shall exercise their vote freely in these social reform questions."

The meeting was presided over by Dr. Mrs. Muthulakshmi Reddy[3], Deputy-President of the Madras Legislative Council, and amongst the speakers were women Magistrates, Members of Educational Boards, a Woman University Senator, and men supporters.

The Women's Indian Association is the largest Woman's organisation in India and is pledged to these social reforms. It was the only organisation one of whose objects was the political enfranchisement of the Indian women, now an accomplished fact.

Strong indignation exists among its members at the exploitation of Indian women that has been made by Miss Mayo in the interests of Western domination of India.

[3]This spelling of her name was used in conjunction with Reddi.

"MOTHER INDIA KA JAWAB"[1]

Extract from Chandravati Lakhanpal, *Mother India Ka Jawab* [*The Reply to Mother India*] (Kangri: Gurukul-Yantralaya, 1928).[2]

Two Words

This is the century of the dominance of the white races. The black races are considered akin to the inhabitants of a zoo. In January 1929, a German Company exhibited Gujrati and Tamil boys like exotic animals at one of the big zoos in Berlin. In June of the same year, 150 Indian villagers were exhibited at a zoo in Paris with the aim of demonstrating the sorry state of this unfortunate country. Negative attitudes towards India and other countries of Asia are being spread all over Europe and America. Miss Mayo's *Mother India* has been written precisely with this mission in mind. This book has not been written to be read in India—it has been written for Europe, for America, and for those white nations that consider themselves, and have been considered, as civilized. Miss Mayo has made a loud proclamation to the civilized world (?)—"Look at India! Here, in the name of the Gods, goats are sacrificed,

[1] I have translated the following from the original in Hindi

[2] Chandravati Lakhanpal's book was reprinted several times and received rave reviews in the national Indian press. Mayo's contacts, however, reported to her that the book was merely a *tu quoque* response by an unimportant Indian, and hence not deserving her consideration. Lakhanpal was involved in nationalist and women's causes in the United Provinces in India. Her subsequent book, *Striyon Ki Stithi* [The Situation of Women] (Lucknow: Shukla Printing Press, 1934) won the first prize at the Delhi Hindi Sahitya Sammelan. Lakhanpal was also later active in the Gandhi-led Civil Disobedience Movement in the 1930s.

women are abused, cows are subject to cruelty, and the ostensibly-pure sites of pilgrimage are filled with filth." Miss Mayo has carried this message to each and every corner of Europe and America. Miss Mayo's mind is saturated with the principle of the natural superiority of the white races. She has not concerned herself with matters of truth or falsehood in making India out to be like a zoo. In this present book I have revealed Miss Mayo's various falsehoods, and at the end, in the form of an appendix, I have also exposed the horrors of the underworld of Europe and America. The point that arises, however, is whether this is really an appropriate reply to *Mother India*? There is no doubt that problems associated with drink, sex, larceny, and violence are daily on the rise in both Europe and America; yet at the same time I want to make clear that pointing these things out cannot serve as the real reply to *Mother India*. Many of Miss Mayo's statements are false, not only are they false but they are also downright dirty and degrading; but no one perusing through the pages of her book can deny that many of Mayo's statements are also true— it breaks one's heart to write that many of the statements are, indeed, absolutely true! I therefore want this book to reach the hand of each and every individual in India, and I want it known to all that Mayo in her effort to disgrace India has shrunk neither from any falsehood nor from any truth about the condition of India! Readers, let these words echo in your ears as you turn the pages of this book and may you resolve to take off the blinkers from your eyes and expel the filth from your society. This alone can be the proper reply to *Mother India*!....

— Chandravati

Conclusion

… Readers! You have in Miss Mayo's words read about the condition of India! By now you are also aware that there are many countries whose condition may be considered in certain respects to be worse than that of India. Yet before completing this book and bidding you farewell I want to repeat the words with which I began this book. We may acknowledge that Europe and America are becoming increasingly mired in the world of sin, we may acknowledge too that these same nations have for their own selfish interests victimized weaker nations in the name of protecting them, and, finally, we may also acknowledge that the kinds of abuses that exist in these nations would strike terror in the heart of the devil himself; but by saying these things can we really expect to shut the mouth of Miss Mayo? Is it not true that in India in the name of God defenceless creatures are sacrificed, in the name of worshipping women women themselves are treated as dirt, and in the name of protecting cows they are ill-treated? If this indeed is true—and who can deny that it is—and if these ills have not been removed from our society, then, whether the world is good or bad, we for our part cannot simply offer books as our reply to Miss Mayo! Do the Hindus accept Miss Mayo's challenge? If they do, then I can see before my eyes the dawn of a New India!

MEYO KUTRU MOYYA POYYA[1]

Extract from Kovai A. Ayyamuthu, *Meyo Kutru Moyya Poyya [Mayo's Charges: True or False?* [with a Preface by E.V. Ramaswami Naicker] (Kanchipuram: Kumaran Printing Press, 1929).[2]

The Critic is After All our Friend

Many of my compatriots have been outraged by the book *Mother India* written and published by the American lady Katherine Mayo. They have contended that India has been much maligned and slandered in the book. Yet no one has tried to prove that the content of the book is total lies. Some people have asked whether such failings are not to be found in other countries. Some others have satisfied themselves with the argument that it is only natural that a human society has its flaws. Some others have described the book as full of perverted exaggerations. The quantity of rice, cereal, and vegetables that we consume daily may appear to be small in our eyes, but if someone were to enter the amount of our daily intake into a diary we would be stunned at the end of the year

[1] I have compiled the following from two separate translations of the original Tamil provided by Mr. Ramani Iyer of Madras and by an anonymous translator in New Delhi

[2] This book was first serialised in the columns of the *Kudi Arasu*, the weekly Tamil paper started by E.V. Ramaswami Naicker in 1925 to represent the views of his Self-Respect Movement. In the Foreword, E.V. Ramaswami Naicker, better known as Periyar, identifies Kovai A. Ayyamuthu as a comrade from the Non-Cooperation Movement and the Vaikom *satyagraha*. Ayyamuthu was also engaged in propagating the ideals of the Self Respect Movement and in working for the social reform of Tamil society.

to learn of the total quantity of food that has entered into our stomach! Likewise there should really be no surprise at the list of our follies that Miss Mayo has collected and compiled so painstakingly just because we ourselves do not take full measure of these follies that occur in our daily life. Therefore we should not be surprised that many people have reacted to Miss Mayo's book as if it were sacrilege. These self-proclaimed guardians of religion have indulged in calling her book smut. There are, of course, also those impartial social reformers who recognize that our society has many more ills than have been even acknowledged in Miss Mayo's book.

My affectionate and admirable colleague Dr. P. Varadarajulu[3] has written that Miss Mayo came to India as a spy of the government in the guise of a tourist with the sole purpose of indicting Indians and demonstrating that such a base and debauched people were not eligible for self-rule. However, he expresses his anguish at the deficiences found among Indians and urges that these undesirable evil practices be stopped. He accepts that unpardonable evils exist in Indian society as a whole and emphatically advocates the need of eradicating them once and for all. He goes on to state however that the lady miscreant had a deliberately mischievous intent in writing her book which was to give the flaws of Indian society a political colouring and to deny Indians the right to their freedom. My friend asserts that social and communal conflicts exist in all countries and occur among all people.

I do without any hesitation agree with the view that Miss Mayo's book is written with an overbearing attitude and with the intent of strengthening white dominion over the world. I am sure she has written this book to insult Indians and portray India in a bad light in front of the rest of the world. Undoubtedly, her intentions were to strengthen the iron hold of the British over India. I too vehemently condemn Miss

[3]The reference here is to the Foreword written by Dr. Varadarajulu Naidu for a Tamil translation of Mother India, Inthiya Mata (Madras: K.S. Muttaya and Co., 1928). Dr. Varadarajulu Naidu, a non-Brahman member of the Congress, had spearheaded a campaign against Brahman dominance in the Congress in the recent Gurukulum controversy of 1925.

Mayo's ill motives, her sinister intentions, her incendiary remarks, and her impertinence. However whatever her motivations, I have tried to demonstrate in my previous essays that what she has to say is true enough. I hope my friends will agree that if an individual were to accuse me vengefully in front of an assembly of persons for being a drunk, that my first duty would be to remove that evil in me rather than to waste my time quarrelling over the degree of my addiction or the objective of the individual making the charge against me. Moreover, I would be bound to thank my critic who insulted me in that way because it made me give up my habitual drinking so that no one in the future could insult me that way again.

The Difference Between Our Country and Other Countries

The second point that Mr. Naidu makes is that social evils exist in all countries and among all people. When corrupt practices exist everywhere and among all the people then how do people of other countries enjoy their freedom, liberty, and sovereignty? Why must India alone remain a slave to foreign rule for centuries? Let our friend find a suitable explanation to this query. There is a fundamental difference between corruption in other countries and in our country. For almost 90% of our activities are based on religion and casteism. We veil every activity of ours in the name of religion, from eating to excreting, from dawn to dusk, and from birth to death. Our religious fervour fortifies our stupidity and our superstition. This is not the case in the West: even the ignorance of their rural folk disappears with good education. Despite their corruption, the people in the West work together with a sense of commitment to their nation with the feeling that they belong to one nationality and they have equal share in their prosperity and despair. Their aims and objectives are directed towards industrial and financial improvement and hence their differences arise from differences based on their professions and possessions. The differences among them therefore are subject to change with changes in profession and degree of prosperity. We have all heard the story of the boy who having been neglected by his parents sold newspapers on the streets and later grew up to be the Prime Minister of his country, feted by the rulers of other nations. We also know the story of a person who was born in the family of a common labourer and who became a religious leader and was honoured and obeyed by crowned kings.

Things are different in our country. Even if a person like Dr Subbarayan[4] were to become Chief Minister, Governor, or Viceroy, he will be looked upon as a *shudra*, a person of low birth. In the eyes of our believers in the *varnashramadharma*,[5] lower caste people, whether parishioners or porters, will always appear only as lowly persons. Even Shri Narayan Guru Swamiji, who was a renowned sage from Travancore with great education, character, devotion and wisdom, was treated as an untouchable by our Namboodri Brahmins and was not even allowed to walk through their streets where dogs and pigs could freely roam about. Let my dear friend realise at least hereafter that it is this fundamental difference which has made slaves of us and rulers of our masters....

[4]Dr. P. Subbarayan, a non-Brahman, was associated with the Non-Brahman Justice Party in the Madras Presidency. He, however, won elections to the Madras Legislative Council in 1926 as an independent candidate and was the Chief Minister in the Independent Ministry formed after the elections.

[5]Orthodox Brahmans had launched a *"varnashramadharma"* movement in the Madras Presidency. In 1915 they had formed the Varnashrama Sabha and published a journal called the *Varnashrama Dharma* to propagate their views on Hinduism. See Eugene F. Irschick, *Politics and Social Conflict in South India: The Non-Brahman Movement and Tamil Separatism, 1916–1929* (Berkeley: University of California Press, 1969).

This is Also What Miss Mayo Has Said

...Miss Mayo has after all only said this much. You boiled over instead of realizing this. Since you are entangled in the web of Brahmanism, you waste your time and money on rituals, temples, priests, festivals and prostitutes. You sacrifice animals in the name of God. You sacrifice your chastity and morality for the sake of begetting a son. You drink excreta and call it holy water. You condemn the lady who has tried to expose the accumulated rubbish in our society as a 'rubbish woman'. You don't feel ashamed in occupying yourselves with empty words. You get your little girls married at a tender age and deny them education and enslave them. You have exploited the condition of widows and subjected them to your lust, you have aborted their pregnancies and killed their children, and you have harrassed and neglected pregnant women. You have humbled yourself at the feet of the Brahman of the sacred thread. You have dedicated your wife, daughters, wealth, and all other comforts of your life to the Brahmans in accordance with the prescriptions of Manu. You have exploited the 'Panchamas,' the lowly persons of the fifth caste, treacherously; you have refused them education and denied them good food, good dress, and good shelter. You have countless other follies and corruptions that are like ornaments to your society. This is the house that you have built for yourself. Only when you abandon these practices will the "fruits of your past actions" leave you. Only on that day will you become the real fighters for freedom. The Self-Respect Movement has come into being to endow you with the necessary courage for this struggle. If you adopt the principles of the Self Respect Movement and act according to your own rationality, accept what needs to be accepted and reject what should be rejected, become a virtuous people following the ideals of discipline, courage, honesty and overflowing with kindness, wear the ornament of unity by bringing together the Pariah and the Brahman without any attention to the distinctions of caste, and stand erect with dignity: only then will a lady like Miss Mayo be unable to revile you. It is then that alien domination and the rule of others will disappear from India.

Our Thanks

We express our gratitude to Miss Katherine Mayo who by exposing our stupid follies bluntly has opened our eyes to the realities and helped us discard our deformities. By pointing out our faults, she has helped us stand up as humans and fight for our freedom from alien rule.